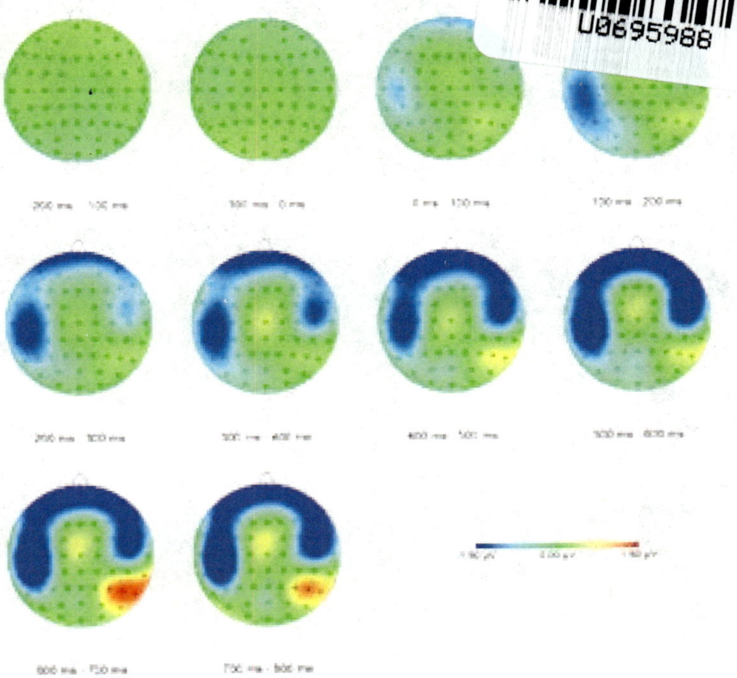

Figure 5　Mean wave differences for fast speed SV processing

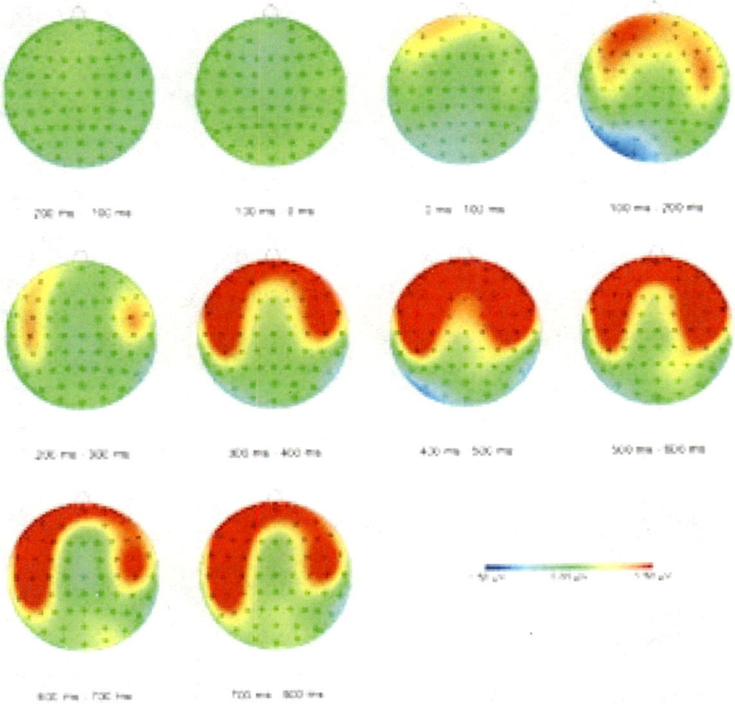

Figure 6　Mean wave differences for fast speed AO processing

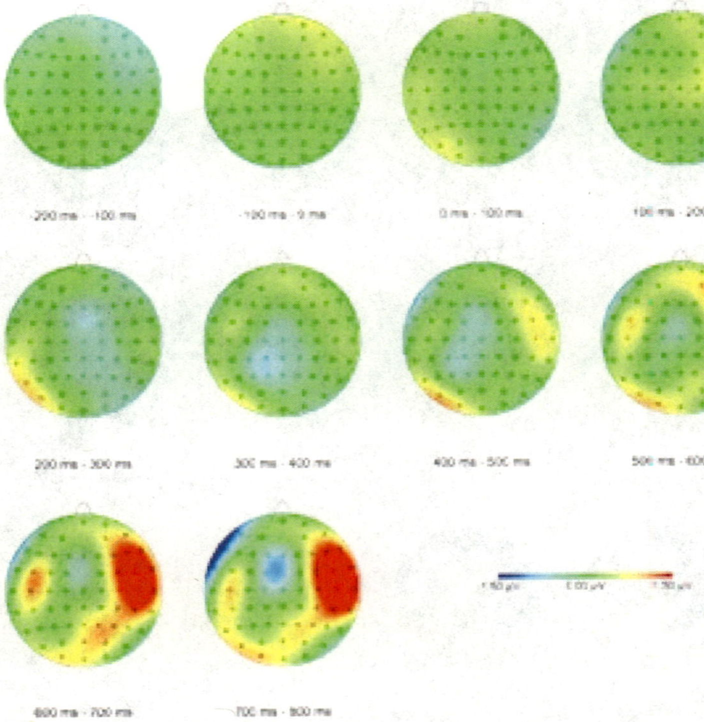

Figure 7 Mean wave differences for slow speed SV processing

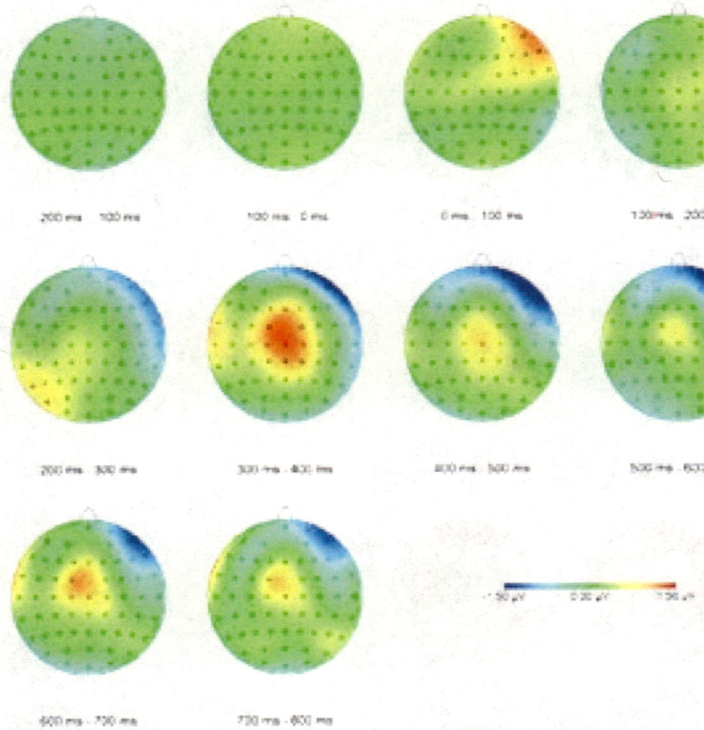

Figure 8 Mean wave differences for slow speed AO processing

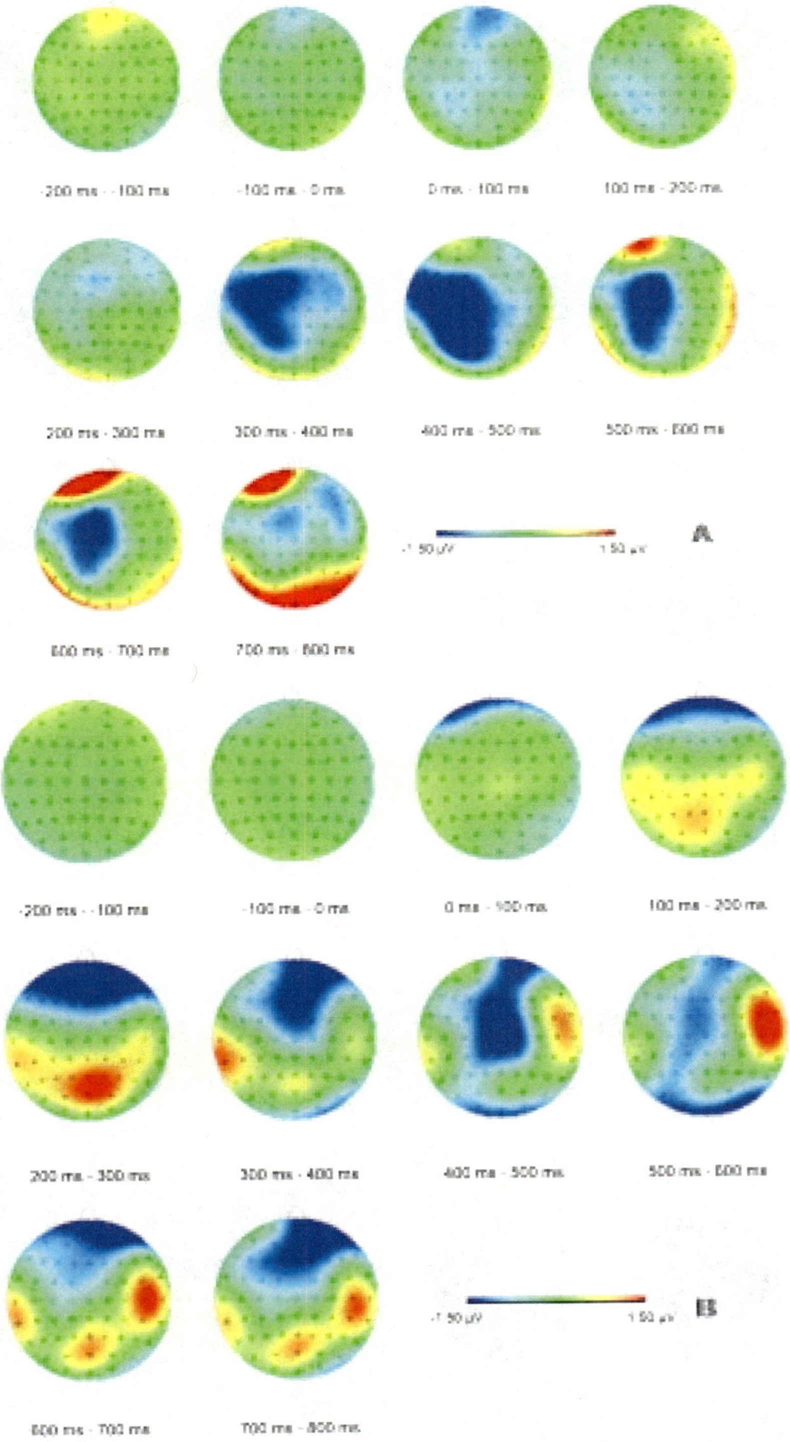

Figure 23 N400 effect (measuring by N400 amplitude in inconsistent context minus consistent context) in processing dominant (A) and subordinate meanings (B) by skilled readers

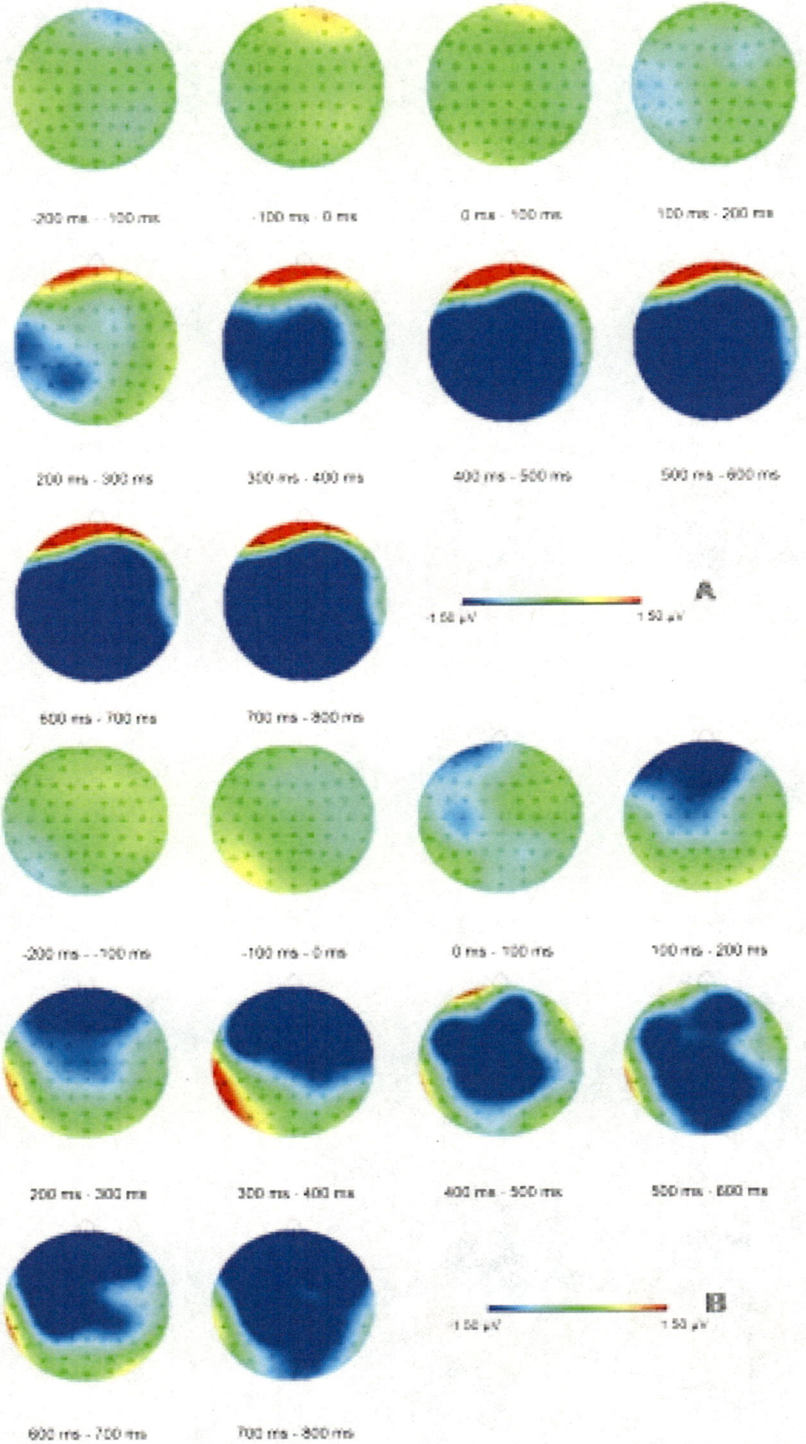

Figure 24 N400 effect（measuring by N400 amplitude in inconsistent context minus consistent context）in processing dominant (A) and subordinate meanings (B) by less-skilled readers

国家社科基金一般项目：
汉语母语者英语习得年龄的效应规律及其认知神经机制研究 (16BYY077) 的资助

汉英双语者的阅读研究：影响因素、困难预测和教学干预

Chinese-English Bilingual Reading: Factors, Difficulty Prediction and Intervention

薛　锦 ◎著

中国出版集团公司
世界图书出版公司
广州·上海·西安·北京

图书在版编目（CIP）数据

汉英双语者的阅读研究：影响因素、困难预测和教学干预：英文 / 薛锦著．—广州：世界图书出版广东有限公司，2016.11（2025.1重印）
ISBN 978-7-5192-2203-1

Ⅰ．①汉… Ⅱ．①薛… Ⅲ．①英语－阅读教学－教学研究－英文 Ⅳ．① H319.37

中国版本图书馆 CIP 数据核字（2016）第 288332 号

书　　名　汉英双语者的阅读研究：影响因素、困难预测和教学干预
　　　　　HANYING SHUANGYUZHE DE YUEDU YANJIU: YINGXIANG YINSU KUNNAN YUCE HE JIAOXUE GANYU
著　　者　薛　锦
策划编辑　宋　焱
责任编辑　冯彦庄
装帧设计　黑眼圈工作室
出版发行　世界图书出版广东有限公司
地　　址　广州市新港西路大江冲 25 号
邮　　编　510300
电　　话　020-84460408
网　　址　http:// www.gdst.com.cn
邮　　箱　sjxscb@163.com
经　　销　新华书店
印　　刷　悦读天下（山东）印务有限公司
开　　本　710mm × 1000mm　1/16
印　　张　16
字　　数　299 千
版　　次　2017 年 1 月第 1 版　　2025 年 1 月第 3 次印刷
国际书号　ISBN 978-7-5192-2203-1
定　　价　78.00 元

Contents

List of Figures

List of Tables

导 读

我国英语的学习从小学贯穿到大学。根据我国教育部推出的《义务教育英语课程标准》和《大学英语课程教学要求》，阅读是英语学习者应掌握的一种基本技能，阅读能力也成为衡量英语水平的一个重要指标。汉语母语背景下，将有相当比例的英语阅读困难者产生。阅读困难对学习者的学业成绩和日常生活交流均会产生一定影响。大学英语阅读困难将同时影响语言技能和专业知识的获得。可以说，汉英双语的跨语言性质更易导致汉语母语者英语阅读困难的多样性。因而，在英语教学中，根据阅读困难的成因进行针对性训练就显得尤为重要。

本书首先梳理前人对双语阅读和发展的相关文献；在此基础上，整合前期研究成果和国际上阅读困难的筛查工具，筛选出具有鉴别力的汉英两种语言的阅读及阅读相关的认知和元认知加工技能的测查工具；对各测查进行预实验，最终生成实证研究使用的阅读、认知、元认知技能测查工具，对我国大学生的汉语母语者的英语阅读发展和阅读加工进行系列的实验研究，考察汉语母语者阅读及阅读困难的影响因素、表现形式、困难根源以及相应的教学干预的有效性。

一、研究内容及研究思路

（一）研究问题

字词阅读、阅读流畅性和阅读理解是阅读的三个重要成分。汉语阅读与许多认知技能，比如，语音意识、语素意识、正字法意识、工作记忆及快速命名等存在很强的相关（Anderson, Ku, Li, Chen, Wu. & Shu, 2004; Ho, Chan, Lee, Tsang & Luan, 2004; Li, Anderson, Nagy & Zhang, 2002; McBride-Chang, Shu, Zhou, Wat & Wagner, 2003; McBride-Chang et al., 2005; Shu, Chen, Anderson, Wu & Xuan, 2003; Shu & Anderson , 1999; Shu, McBride-Chang, Wu & Liu , 2006）。这些因素对阅读的贡献作用在拼音语言的研究中也得到了证实（如，Adams, 1990; Arnbak & Elbro, 2000; Bradley & Bryant, 1983; Brittain, 1970; Carlisle & Fleming, 2003; Carlisle & Nomanbhoy, 1993; Carlisle, 1995,

2000; Casalis & Louis-Alexandre, 2000; Cassar & Treiman, 1997; Cunningham, Perry & Stanovich, 2001; Ehri, 1997; Ehri, 2005; Goswami & Bryant, 1990 ; Mahony, Singson & Mann, 2000; Mattingly, 1984）。在阅读（含三个成分：字词阅读、阅读流畅性和理解）的预测上，除了上述认知层面的因素（如工作记忆）（如，Xue, Shu, Li, Li. & Tian, 2013）外，还有语言学层面的（如词汇、语法）（如，Cain, 2007; Carlisle, 1995）和元认知层面的因素（如杨小虎，张文鹏，2002；张庆宗，刘晓燕，2009）对阅读起重要作用。同时，阅读障碍者在上述因素上存在缺陷（如，刘文理，刘翔平，张婧乔，2006；Shu, McBride-Chang, Wu, 2006）。然而，汉语母语背景下，英语阅读及阅读障碍的研究尚存三个方面的不足：大多数研究局限于理论探讨，因此缺乏有力的实证的研究证据；英语学习者阅读困难的研究大多针对小学阶段儿童，而成人阅读的认知机制将在某种程度上有别于儿童；更重要的是，针对汉语母语成人的英语阅读的大多数研究都仅探讨元认知加工层面的问题，并在此基础上探讨元认知技能对阅读的贡献，从而忽略了低层认知技能对阅读机制的重要作用，而对第二语言阅读困难的研究仅限于理论解释或者语言层面的词汇或语法问题。因此，本书首先探讨：汉英双语阅读技能之间存在的关系；认知因素和元认知因素的英语学习者阅读发展和阅读加工中的贡献或影响作用；汉英双语者在字词通达、句法加工和语义整合在线加工的神经机制存在跨语言的普遍性。

阅读障碍亚类型发生率在不同语言系统中也存在差异。粒度理论（Ziegler & Goswami, 2005）和粒度和透明度假设（Wydell & Butterworth, 1999）从理论的高度解释语言特性对阅读障碍亚类型发生率造成的影响。汉语和英语分属不用的语系。汉语本身的特点，汉字阅读依靠的形和音节之间的匹配，并不像拼音语言英语那样从形到音的直接应对。由于母语汉语和第二语言英语在类型距离相对较远。但是，汉语母语背景下英语阅读困难的研究尚处于探索阶段。因此，本书还探索汉语母语者在英语阅读中困难的表现形式。汉英双语者如果呈现英语阅读困难，那他们的母语汉语的阅读情况如何？二语英语认知、元认知上是否也存在缺陷？汉语母语者的第二语言英语阅读困难是否存在神经基础？

在语言学领域，第二语言阅读的研究大多数研究局限于理论探讨（如姚喜明，梅晓宇，2003）。英语阅读的认知诊断研究相对较少，此类研究发现，词汇量少、阅读速度慢、句法分析能力差等因素导致英语阅读理解困难（如 Cain，2007；刘丹丹，2002；徐锦芬等，2010；杨小虎，张文鹏，2002；张庆宗，刘晓燕，2009）。因此，本书继续探讨如何结合语言变量和认知变量来有效识别汉语母语者的英语阅读困难。

（二）研究思路

本书主要解决理论问题如表 1 所示，研究分五大部分，共 17 个实验和研究。在汉语母语背景下，英语学习大多是通过课堂教学。而课堂教学的质量，特别是国内英语语言输入的环境存在很大的变异，因此为了有效控制由阅读经验缺乏造成阅读困难这个干扰变量，研究中筛选的被试均为国内大学的英语专业学生。

第一部分的内容（第1—3章），使用文献法和元分析的方法，查阅双语阅读习得和加工相关文献，确定预测双语读写能力的相关因素。

（1）第1章是对“双语发展和读写能力的影响因素”的书评，论文题为“A review on ‘Bilingual Development and Literacy Learning: East Asian and International Perspectives’”（双语发展和读写学习：东亚和国际视角），发表于*Language Problems and Language Planning*, 37（3）: 298-300（SCI 索引）。

（2）第2章是“An analysis on effects of language experience on bilingual neural representation”（双语经验对大脑表征的影响的分析），这是针对双语分属不同语种的双语者的阅读加工的研究结果进行分析，重点考察双语阅读加工机大脑表征的差异。

（3）第3章使用文献法，总结并梳理前人文献，论文题为“A review and reflection on the study of bilingual reading difficulties”（双语者阅读困难研究：回顾与思考），为后续汉语母语背景下英语阅读和阅读困难的研究做理论铺垫。

Table 1　Theoretical and research questions in this book

研究	理论问题	具体问题
一	双语阅读文献综述	双语和读写能力发展特点 双语经验对大脑表征的影响 双语者阅读困难的鉴别方式
二	英语学习者阅读困难评估工具的编制和修订	阅读相关的认知因素的测查工具 元认知技能的调查量表
三	汉英双语阅读加工和习得的影响因素	汉英双语字词通达机制 英语阅读理解和词汇语素之间的关系 第二语言英语的不同类型的句法加工的神经机制 第二语言句法加工脑电模式差异的根源 句子理解中不同虚拟世界信息的辨别：脑电研究 汉英双语语言特异性对大脑表征和神经机制的影响 汉语母语者英语阅读困难的表现形式
四	二语英语阅读困难特点、表现形式和困难的根源	英语阅读困难原因探析 工作记忆缺陷和汉英双语阅读的关系 阅读能力差异对字词加工的大脑神经机制的影响 二语英语阅读困难者和普通读者句子阅读中字词语义整合机制的差异
五	二语英语阅读困难者的有效鉴别和教学干预	汉语母语者的英语阅读困难者进行有效鉴别 阅读元认知的教学干预效果 教学干预和汉英双语语素意识的发展的关系

第二部分的内容包括两个小部分。

首先，确定汉英双语阅读、认知加工技能和元认知测查工具。整合前期研究成果和国际上阅读困难的筛查工具。先对北京第二外国语学院英语专业二年级学生进行调查取样 58 人，并测查了他们的汉英双语阅读加工相关技能（如词汇量、语法、阅读理解、解码、语音）。这批数据用于分析各测验的信效度，以确定最终测验的难易度和信效度，筛选出具有鉴别力的汉英两种语言的阅读及阅读相关的认知加工技能的测查工具。最终确定信效度良好的工具如下：

（1）汉语 / 英语阅读理解：英语阅读理解任务使用标准化的阅读任务 Gates MacGinitie Reading Comprehension (Form 4, Level F) ；汉语阅读为英语标准化测试翻译本。

（2）汉字 / 英语单词阅读：汉字阅读为自编材料；英语单词阅读，字词阅读使用 Woodcock Reading Mastery Test-Revised (WRMT-R: Woodcock, 1987) 分测验。

（3）汉语 / 英语句子阅读流畅性：自编，以 EPRIME 软件呈现。

（4）解码（Word Attack）：使用 WRMT-R: Woodcock，1987 的分测验。

（5）语音意识：使用 Comprehensive Test of Phonological Processing (CTOPP) Elision Subtest (Wagner, Torgesen & Rashotte, 1999)。

（6）工作记忆：节选 Working Memory (Daneman & Carpenter, 1980)。

（7）语素意识：自编材料，主要考察英语派生词产生。

（8）词汇知识：用 Gates-Macgintie Vocabulary Knowledge Test, Level E Form 4。

（9）句法意识：自编材料。

（10）阅读元认知意识：选自 Sheorey & Mokhtari（2001）。

（11）汉英双语阅读环境调查问卷：自编。

其次，使用上述研究工具进行实验研究，考查双语者阅读加工和习得的影响因素。

第三部分的研究(第4—9章)的内容包括如下: 其一，是考察语言特征、语言技能、认知、元认知等因素对英语阅读中的解码、阅读流畅性和阅读理解的影响。研究中使用问卷调查和行为测试（集体和个别测试），测查了汉语母语成人的英语解码、阅读流畅性、认知和元认知技能。其二，使用汉英双语者语阅读加工的脑电（Event-related potentials, ERP）研究，考察汉语母语成人在汉英双语字词阅读、阅读理解、句法加工、语义整合等过程中的影响因素和大脑神经反应模式。具体内容如下：

（1）第 4 章考察汉英双语字词通达机制，论文题为“Implicit sublexical access to the first language: An ERP study on Chinese-English bilinguals”，发表于 *The Fifth Annual Meeting of the Society for the Neurobiology of Language*, November 6-8, 2013 San Diego, California（第五届语言神经生物年会）上以 POSTER 海报形式报告结果。

（2）第 5 章探讨英语阅读理解和词汇和语素之间的关系，论文题为“英语阅读中的意义构建：构词法和理解的关系”，发表于《外语教学》，2013，32，145-146。

（3）第 6 章考察汉语母语成人在第二语言英语的不同类型的句法加工的神经机制，论文题为“An ERP study on Chinese natives' second language syntactic grammaticalization”（汉语母语者第二语言句法语法化的脑电研究），发表于 *Neuroscience Letters*, 2013, 534: 258-263（SCI 索引）。

（4）第 7 章继续考察第二语言句法加工脑电模式差异的根源，论文题为“The locus of on bilinguals' L2 syntactic grammaticalization: transfer or competition”（双语者第二语言句法语法化过程中语言相似性效应的根源：迁移还是竞争），在第三届全国语言认知神经与二语习得高层论坛（2013 年 7 月 14—16 日）上宣读研究结果。

（5）第 8 章考察汉语母语者的字词层面加工的大脑神经表征。论文题为“The role of age of acquisition on Chinese native learners' English word processing: An ERP Study”（汉语母语者英语单词加工中的习得年龄效应：一项脑电研究）。

（6）第 9 章考察汉英双语语言特异性对大脑表征和神经机制的影响。论文题为“Chinese-English bilinguals processing temporal-spatial metaphor”（汉英双语者时间—空间隐喻加工），发表于 *Cognitive Processing*, 2014, 15 (3): 269-281（SSCI 索引）。

第四部分的研究（第10—14章）探索汉语母语背景下英语学习者阅读困难特点、表现形式和困难的根源。研究中结合横断研究和追踪研究，使用低于年级平均分 1SD 作为标准，筛选英语阅读理解困难者，并分析①汉英双语阅读困难的表现形式和发生率；②英语学习者阅读中理解、解码和阅读速度缺陷情况；③英语阅读困难者认知缺陷和元认知缺陷情况，以及缺陷对二语英语阅读的影响。同时，使用脑电技术，通过实验设计，考查阅读能力差异的两组读者在字词加工、阅读理解的语义整合过程中表现出的大脑神经机制的差异。

（1）第 10 章使用低于年级平均分 1SD 作为标准，筛选英语解码困难、阅读理解困难、速度缺陷三种不同类型，论文题为“汉语母语者英语阅读困难的表现形式”。

（2）第 11 章同样使用低于年级平均分 1SD 作为标准，筛选英语阅读理解困难者，探析英语阅读困难原因。论文题为“英语学习者阅读理解困难的认知缺陷”，在全国第二届心理语言学国际论坛（2013 年 11 月 22—24 日）上宣读此论文。

（3）第 12 章继续考察工作记忆缺陷和汉英双语者的两种语言阅读的三个层面解码、流畅性和阅读理解之间的关系。论文题为“Study on the relationship between Chinese-English bilingual reading and working memory deficits”（工作记忆缺陷和汉英双语阅读关系的研究）。这个章节在第十五届中国当代语言学国际研讨会（哈尔滨，黑龙江大学，2014 年 7 月 18 日 21 日）上做了口头报告。

（4）第 13 章使用 ERP 技术，分析阅读能力差异对字词加工的大脑神经机制的影响，论文题为“A revisit on L1 automatic activation during L2 reading: An ERP study on Chinese-English bilinguals”（再论二语阅读中的一语的自动激活）。

（5）第 14 章考察二语英语阅读困难者和普通读者句子阅读中字词语义整合机制的差异，论文题为“An ERP Study on the semantic unification mechanism of Chinese native learners of English during L2 English reading comprehension”（汉语母语的英语学习者在二语英语阅读理解中的语义整合机制的脑电研究），在第三届全国语言认知神经与二语习得高层论坛（2013 年 7 月 14—16 日）上宣读。

第五部分（第 15—17 章）试图回答两个问题：①不同因素对阅读困难预测的准确性和有效性；②不同的教学干预怎样有效提高普通英语读者和阅读困难者的英语阅读成绩。研究中使用解码、认知和元认知三个关键的阅读加工过程对英语阅读困难进行预测。同时，以影响阅读困难的重要语言和认知因素为着眼点，根据认知和元认知缺陷情况制定教学干预策略，使用追踪研究，对阅读困难者进行一年的教学干预，并比较干预前后，阅读和相关语言和认知加工技能的变化。

（1）第 15 章是在整合上述研究结果的基础上，以影响阅读困难的重要语言和认知因素为着眼点，尝试对汉语母语者的英语阅读困难者进行有效鉴别和预测。论文题为“语码和语言变量对二语英语阅读理解困难鉴别的敏感性和准确率”。

（2）第 16 章是通过对照自然发展状态下和教学干预状态下的阅读元认知和阅读理解的变化。研究论文题为“Reading metacognitive intervention: A preliminary study on EFL learners”（阅读元认知的教学干预：英语作为外语的学习者的初步研究），第三届全国语言认知神经与二语习得高层论坛（2013 年 7 月 14—16 日）上宣读该论文。

（3）第 17 章考察教学干预和汉英双语语素意识的发展的关系。论文“The relationship between bilingual morphological awareness and reading for Chinese EFL adult learners”（成人双语语素意识和阅读的关系），第十五届中国当代语言学国际研讨会（哈尔滨，黑龙江大学，2014 年 7 月 18—21 日）上口头报告过该论文。

二、本书的主要观点

（1）汉语母语者的第二语言英语的阅读受母语的迁移作用的影响，但这种迁移是动态变化的；随着第二语言水平的提高，双语之间阅读及相关技能之间的迁移的深度和广度不断提高。除此之外，第二语言英语语言内，认知和元认知技能对阅读的相对重要性来说，元认知对二语阅读的直接作用比较小。不仅如此，汉英两种语言在形—音对应关系、语义概念、语法规则上存在其特异性，这也导致汉英双语者在线加工这些特异的语言规则或概念时，大脑反应模式存在差异。

（2）汉语母语成人的英语阅读困难主要表现出速度缺陷和理解困难。而第二语言英语阅读困难是由诸多因素造成的，包括：词汇量缺乏、语法分析能力差、阅读元认知水平低、认知加工技能（如语音加工技能、工作记忆等）缺陷和语素意识缺陷。

（3）尽管汉英双语阅读和阅读相关的认知技能之间存在迁移或相关性，但在汉语母语者的英语阅读困难的诊断上，需要考虑汉英双语之间的差异以及差异带来的大脑神经机制的差异。因此，在第二语言英语阅读困难的鉴别上，应从英语的解码、认知和元认知三个层次对阅读困难进行鉴别。

（4）在第二语言英语阅读困难的鉴别和预测上，语言变量（词汇、语法和语素）和语码变量（工作记忆、解码、语音意识、快速命名）对阅读水平组的预测效果存在差异。相对于语码变量而言，语言变量能更有效地鉴别阅读困难。而且，把语言和语码变量结合，还能提高鉴别的准确率。不仅如此，第二语言的诊断还需要考虑母语阅读技能。

（5）在教学干预上，首先需要确定导致阅读理解困难的根本原因。如果二语英语阅读理解困难源自母语阅读加工困难，那阅读困难的教学干预需要对双语相应的阅读成分进行训练。如果阅读理解困难是由于二语字词识别困难和阅读流畅性缺陷，从而消耗更多的认知资源，导致阅读理解困难，那教学干预的重点应该放在快速字词搜索能力、流畅性训练和扩大词汇量上。如果学生存在纯粹的理解困难，那这种理解困难可能源自个体的阅读策略、知识背景、推理能力、文本难度等因素。

（6）从教学干预的效果看，第二语言英语阅读策略训练能有效地提高学生的整体阅读理解水平和阅读速度，阅读元认知知识、策略和监控的训练是帮助提高阅读理解。为了提高学生的阅读成绩，教师应该提高学生元认知水平，帮助学习者获得元认知知识（如阅读任务特点、读者本身特点和水平）和元认知监控技能（如帮助学习者确定学习目标和计划）。英语构词法的教学干预也是可行的和有效的。然而，语素意识和元认知教学干预对不同类型的英语学习者的效果存在差异。

本书的特色之一是将语言学和心理学的实证研究相结合，具有跨学科的特点。本书的特色之二是在国际前沿理论的指导下，结合汉语特点，对跨语言阅读困难的机制进行研究，具有原创性。本书的特色之三是研究方法先进，能将行为实验和大脑神经反应模式相结合。本书的特色之四是静态分析与动态分析有机结合起来，既有对阅读困难特点充分的描写又有合理的解释，还有对阅读困难的预测。

研究成果系统揭示了汉语母语者第二语言英语阅读的影响因素、阅读困难的表现形式、阅读困难的预测因素，成果的应用价值体现在：①在某种程度上丰富和发展汉英双语者阅读习得和加工方面的理论；②为教师从解码、认知加工和元认知加工三个维度来建立汉语母语者英语阅读学习的评价系统提供理论依据；③初步构建一个关于汉语母语者英语阅读困难的认知诊断框架，为英语学习者阅读困难评估提供理论依据；④便于教师制订适当的教学策略、采取相应的教学干预措施，以提高二语阅读困难者的阅读水平；⑤汉英双语阅读发展的科学数据将为筛查二语英语阅读困难的标准化测验做铺垫。

参考文献

刘丹丹 . (2002). 中国英语学习者的阅读策略研究 . 外语界 , 6:13-18.

刘文理 , 刘翔平 , 张婧乔 . (2006). 汉语发展性阅读障碍亚类型的初步探讨 . *心理学报* , 2006, 38(5) : 681-693.

徐锦芬 , 李红 , 李斑斑 . (2010). 大学生英语阅读能力自我评价的实证研究 . *解放军外国语学院学报* , (5): 46-50.

杨小虎 , 张文鹏 . (2002). 元认知与中国大学生英语阅读理解相关研究 . *外语教学与研究* , 3: 213-218.

姚喜明 , 梅晓宇 . (2003). 我国阅读理论研究的发展 . *山东外语教学* , 6 : 15-18.

张庆宗 , 刘晓燕 . (2009). 英语阅读自我效能感、阅读策略和阅读成绩关系的实证研究 . *教育研究与实验* , (1): 92-96.

Adams, M. J. (1990). *Beginning to read: Thinking and learning about print.* Cambridge, MA: MIT Press.

Anderson, R. C., Ku, Y.-M., Li, W., Chen, X., Wu, X. & Shu, H. (2004). *Learning to see the patterns in Chinese characters.* Champaign, IL: Center for the Study of Reading.

Arnbak, E. & Elbro, C. (2000). The effects of morphological awareness training on the reading and spelling skills of young dyslexics. *Scandinavian Journal of Educational Research*, 44: 229-251.

Bradley, L. & Bryant, P. E. (1983). Categorizing sounds and learning to read—a causal connection. *Nature*, 301: 419-521.

Brittain, M. M. (1970). Inflectional performance and early reading achievement. *Reading Research Quarterly*, 6: 419-421.

Cain, K. (2007). Syntactic awareness and reading ability: Is there any evidence for a special relationship? *Applied Psycholinguistics*, 28(4): 679-694.

Carlisle, J. F. & Fleming, J. (2003). Lexical processing of morphologically complex words in the elementary years. *Scientific Studies of Reading, 7,* 239-253.

Carlisle, J. F. & Nomanbhoy, D. (1993). Phonological and morphological development. *Applied*

Psycholinguistics, 14: 177-195.

Carlisle, J. F. (1995). Morphological awareness and early reading achievement. In L. B. Feldman (Ed.), *Morphological aspects of language processing* (pp. 189-209). Hillsdale, NJ: Erlbaum.

Carlisle, J. F. (2000). Awareness of the structure and meaning of morphologically complex words: Impact on reading. *Reading and Writing: An Interdisciplinary Journal*, 12: 169-190.

Casalis, S. & Louis-Alexandre, M. F. (2000). Morphological analysis, phonological analysis and learning to read French: A longitudinal study. *Reading and Writing: An Interdisciplinary Journal*, 12: 303-335.

Cassar, M. & Treiman, R. (1997). The beginnings of orthographic knowledge: Children's knowledge of double letters in words. *Journal of Educational Psychology*, 89: 631-644.

Cunningham, A., Perry, K. & Stanovich, K. E. (2001). Converging evidence for the concept of orthographic processing. *Reading & Writing: An Interdisciplinary Journal*, 14: 549-568.

Ehri, L. C. (1997). Learning to read and learning to spell are one and the same, almost. In C. A. Perfetti, L. Rieben & M. Fayol (Eds.), *Learning to spell: Research, theory, and practice across languages* (pp. 237-269). Mahwah, NJ: Erlbaum.

Ehri, L. C. (2005). Learning to read words: Theory, findings, and issues. *Scientific Studies of Reading*, 9:167-188.

Goswami, U. & Bryant, P. E. (1990).*Phonological skills and learning to read.* Hillsdale, NJ: Lawrence Erlbaum.

Ho, C. S., Chan, D. W., Lee, S.-H., et al. (2004). Cognitive profiling and preliminary subtyping in Chinese developmental dyslexia. *Cognition*, 91: 43-75.

Li, W., Anderson, R. C., Nagy, W. & Zhang, H. (2002). Facets of metalinguistic awareness that contribute to Chinese literacy. In W. Li, J. S. Gaffney & J. L. Packard (Eds.), *Chinese language acquisition: Theoretical and pedagogical issues* (pp. 87-106). Norwell, MA: Kluwer Academic Publishers.

Mahony, D., Singson, M. & Mann, V. (2000). Reading ability and sensitivity to morphological relations. *Reading and Writing: An Interdisciplinary Journal*, 12:191-218.

Mattingly, I. G. (1984). Reading, linguistic awareness, and language acquisition. In J. Downing & R. Valtin (Eds.), *Language awareness and learning to read* (pp. 9-26). New York: Springer-Verlag.

McBride-Chang, C., Cho, J.-R., Liu, H., Wagner, R. K., Shu, H., Zhou, A., Cheuk, C. S-M., Muse, A. (2005). Changing models across cultures: Associations of phonological awareness and morphological structure awareness with vocabulary and word recognition in second graders from Beijing, Hong Kong, Korea, and the United States. *Journal of Experimental Child Psychology*,

92: 140-160.

McBride-Chang, C., Shu, H., Zhou, A., Wat, C. P. & Wagner, R. K. (2003). Morphological awareness uniquely predicts young children's Chinese character recognition. *Journal of Educational Psychology*, 95: 743-751.

Shu, H. & Anderson, R. C. (1999). *Learning to read Chinese: The development of metalinguistic awareness*. In J. Wang, A. Inhoff, H.-C. Chen (Eds.), *Reading Chinese script: A cognitive analysis* (pp. 1-18). Mahwah, NJ: Lawrence Erlbaum.

Shu, H., Chen, X., Anderson, R. C., Wu, N. & Xuan, Y. (2003). Properties of school Chinese: Implications for learning to read. *Child Development*, 74:27-47.

Shu, H., McBride-Chang, C., Wu, S. & Liu, H. (2006). Understanding Chinese developmental dyslexia: Morphological awareness as a core cognitive construct. *Journal of Educational Psychology*, 98: 122-133.

Wydell, T.N. & Butterworth, B. (1999). A case study of an English-Japanese bilingual with monolingual dyslexia. *Cognition*, 70: 273-305.

Xue, J. Shu, H., Li, W., Li. H. Tian. (2013). The stability of literacy-related cognitive contributions to Chinese character naming and reading fluency. *Journal of Psycholinguistic Research*, 42(5): 433-450.

Ziegler, J.C. & Goswami, U. (2005). Reading acquisition, developmental dyslexia, and skilled reading across languages: a psycholinguistic grain size theory. *Psychological Bulletin*, 131(1): 3-29.

Part 1 Literature Review on Bilingual Reading

内容简介

这一部分为文献综述，使用文献法和元分析的方法，查阅双语阅读习得和加工相关文献，确定预测双语读写能力的相关因素。包括三个研究：分别就双语和读写能力发展特点、双语经验对大脑表征的影响和双语者阅读困难的鉴别方式进行描述和评论。

（1）第 1 章的论文题为“A review on ‘Bilingual Development and Literacy Learning: East Asian and International Perspectives’”（“双语发展和读写学习：东亚和国际视角”述评）。该论文对《双语发展和读写学习：东亚和国际视角》进行述评。本书从神经语言学、心理语言学和社会语言学的视角，讨论双语读写能力发展的研究热点、研究趋势以及研究成果。该论文主要评论四个问题：①双语不平衡的问题，提出语言习得机制并不是在第二语言习得中退化，导致双语不平衡的原因在于双语资源通达机制存在差异。②语言模块理论（或语言技能分解）的研究视角。极端情境下的语言习得（如特异性语言损伤、聋哑、失语症等）研究发现语言模块之间的双分离现象。模块理论也反映了双语者的认知的特异性和多样性，以及语言亚系统间的交互作用。③汉语读写技能的独特特征和拼音语言存在差异。汉语母语背景也为第二语言学习和研究提供独特的视角。④如何根据第二语言读写学习中产生正面（positive evidence）和负面证据（negative evidence），制定合适的教学策略，来进行语言教学和干预。

（2）第 2 章是“An analysis on effects of language experience on bilingual neural representation”（双语经验对大脑表征的影响的分析），这是针对双语分属不同语种的双语者的阅读加工的文章的研究结果进行分析总结，重点考察双语阅读加工及大脑表征的差异。关于第一语言和第二语言如何在大脑中表征的，这还是一个未决的问题。导致前人研究结果存在差异的一个原因是两种语言系统之间的差异。语言的形—音对应的粒度和透明度决定了一些词汇加工技能是否从母语迁移到第二语言词汇加工中。为了阐释语言系统之间的差异如何决定了双语词汇加工的神经机制，本研究对30篇关于一语和二语词汇加工的核磁（fMRI）研究结果进行分析，把双语按形音匹配的粒度和透明度分成三组三双语家族类型（组1：一语不透明粒度大，二语不透明粒度小；组2：一语透明粒度小，二语不透明粒度小；组3：一语不透明粒度小，二语透明粒度小/不透明粒度大）。研究结果发现：①一语和二语的词汇加工存在共同的脑区，例如，负责语义加工的额中脑区；②词汇加工中存在语言家族的差异导致大脑激活模式的差异，形—音之间匹配的粒度和透明度影响了参与双语加工的脑区是否存在差异；③第一语言词汇加工的脑区和第二语言加工的脑区有很大的重合，在某种程度上，一语词汇加工的模式决定了在二语词汇加工中这些脑区是否要被激活。

（3）第3章是“A review and reflection on the study of bilingual reading difficulties”（双语者阅读困难研究：回顾与思考），使用文献法，总结并梳理前人文献，为后续汉语母语背景下英语阅读和阅读困难的研究做理论铺垫。该文提出母语阅读困难的鉴定方法从智力—阅读成绩差异诊断模式转变到阅读的低成就和核心技能结合的诊断模式。母语阅读困难表现出字词解码缺陷、阅读流畅性差和阅读理解困难，其认知根源受语言特征的影响有所差异。而二语阅读困难主要使用教师评定、以母语阅读成绩预测和以双语一致的认知技能预测这三种筛选方法。受母语特征的影响，二语阅读困难在行为和脑电上表现出双语缺陷一致性和双语阅读困难双分离两种模式，而中枢加工假说和文字依赖假设为这两种模式提供理论解释。尽管研究已发现，汉语母语背景下英语阅读困难者呈现出语音技能缺陷，脑功能出现左脑激活不足等特点，汉英双语者阅读困难的认知诊断还需更多的证据。

Chapter 1 A review: *Bilingual development and literacy learning: East Asian and international perspectives*[1]

Norbert Francis, Professor of Education at Northern Arizona University, surveys the advances in recent investigations on bilingualism. Key issues in bilingual competence and second language literacy are addressed: asymmetries in bilingual acquisition, age of acquisition effects, language attrition, and the concept of modularity in how it is applied to literacy learning. "International perspectives" in the book title implies new avenues in research on problems of bilingualism shared by speakers of all languages.

Chapter 1 is an introduction to the main themes. Chapter 8 reviews a selection of recent studies on bilingualism and thus further elaborates on the above mentioned key issues from the perspectives of neurolinguistics, psycholinguistics and sociolinguistics. Chapter 9 summarizes the themes of the book. The remaining chapters follow two lines of current work in the field.

The first line (Chapters 2-4) is concerned with mechanisms of second language learning and biliteracy. Chapter 2 (Balanced and imbalanced bilingualism) addresses the issue of asymmetrical bilingualism. Francis proposes that the Language Acquisition Device is not degraded in second language (L2) learning, and that the locus of imbalanced bilingualism lies in the differential access to linguistic resources, including competence itself and component mechanisms of language processing. The research problem of modularity is carried over into Chapter 3 (Bilingual development in exceptional circumstances). It is a

[1] This paper "A review: Norbert Francis. Bilingual Development and Literacy Learning: East Asian and International Perspectives. Hong Kong: City University of Hong Kong Press. 2013. xvi+257pp." was published in Language Problems and Language Planning, 2013, 37(3): 298-300.

framework of mental architecture emphasizing components and modules. Evidence from deaf bilingualism, aphasia and specific language impairment reveals dissociations between primary language (L1) and L2 as well as interconnections in language subsystems. Chapter 4 (Bilingual literacy and comparative research on writing systems) mainly illustrates how the Chinese writing system demonstrates universal features, as well as how it differs from alphabetic writing. The role of phonology in Chinese literacy provides evidence for understanding modularity, especially the distinction between phonological competence and meta-level awareness of phonological constituents (Francis, 2010).

The second line of investigation (Chapters 5-7) involves more practical issues: specific problems of instruction and effective approaches in second language teaching. In Chapter 5 (Self-correction-negative evidence in second language literacy learning), the argument is presented for the important role of negative evidence and self-correction in bilingual writing. Two research questions are particularly interesting for future research: ① what aspects of negative evidence could "be necessary for higher levels of attainment in one or more domains of L2 learning"? (91); ② how focus on form strategies might differ between Chinese and alphabetic scripts. Chapter 6 (Corrective feedback in language learning) further expounds on the differences between positive and negative evidence, and their differential effects on L1 and L2 learning. These distinctions evoke a number of pedagogical considerations regarding: types of feedback (corrective and non-corrective), levels of correction (word, sentence, or discourse level), and reliability of corrective feedback (in relation to closed-ended and open-ended items). In Chapter 7 (The foundation of immersion education-integration of language and content), the componential nature of language ability as well as concepts of positive and negative evidence are brought back into the discussion of the different instructional models of immersion. Generally, Francis attaches great importance to negative evidence, self-correction, metalinguistic awareness, and the efficacy of direct instruction in L2 immersion.

Of fundamental importance is the application of modularity theory to bilingual literacy. "What characterizes this kind of componential mental architecture is internal heterogeneity and specialization." (Francis, 2008: 102) On the one hand, this idea provides a lens on diversity in bilingualism. Modularity implies both internal cognitive diversity and interactivity among language subsystems. Bilinguals possess an intermixed lexical and morphosyntactic organization (Golestani, Alario, Meriaux, Le Bihan, Dehaene & Pallie (2006). That not all cognitive domains are equally encapsulated partially explains the individual differences in bilinguals' ultimate attainment in L2. On the other hand, differential modularity has important implications for diagnosis and intervention in the area of language delay or Specific Language Impairment (SLI).

On a related note, in bilingual development generally, the two kinds of cross-language inhibition, involving both "competence modules and processing components," (34) could result in performance deviation or a new modified competence. In learning and teaching, cross-language access inhibition in imbalanced bilinguals could be compensated by cognitive general learning mechanisms, metalinguistic awareness training, deliberate attention and practice with feedback. According to recent imaging studies, "the plasticity in brain development shows that cortical activations increase initially at the onset of acquisition, followed by the maintenance of the activations, and then a fall in activations during consolidation of linguistic competence" (Sakai, 2005). Thus, we should be cautious when interpreting activation changes during L2 acquisition and consolidation.

In conclusion, *Bilingual development and literacy learning* abounds in debates on how relevant second language acquisition theory and new concepts from cognitive science might be applied to practical problems in education. Along with the presentation of these controversies, a series of proposals are offered for further comparative research on cross-language writing systems. The theoretical and practical observations in the book should be of interest to readers of *Language Problems and Language Planning*.

Chapter 2 An analysis on effects of language experience on bilingual neural representation[1]

Abstract: Whether the first language (L1) and second language (L2) are represented in overlapping brain areas is unclear. One factor causing the controversial results is the differences between language systems. Language difference in granularity and/or transparency of the grapheme-to-phoneme determines the transfer of appropriate lexical processing skills in L2 lexical processing. To clarify how these language differences determine the neural substrates for bilingual lexical processing, we conducted a meta-analysis on 30 fMRI studies investigating L1 and L2 word processing. The language family was defined by granularity and transparency of grapheme and phoneme mapping system. Based on the analysis, we found that L1 and L2 generally involve similar neural substrates, though lexical processing in different language families elicits different brain activation patterns. These results suggest that ① L1 and L2 share common neural substrates, and ② the L1 experience determines where this common neural substrate should be.

Key words: bilingual lexical processing brain activation pattern

2.1 Introduction

A large body of studies has been devoted to identifying the neural correlates of bilingual processing. One line of research is to examine whether the first language (L1) and second language (L2) are represented in overlapping or separate brain areas. The majority of studies along this line have demonstrated there is a large part of shared neuronal systems

---

[1] The 30 papers in this study were selected by Dr. YANG Jie, ARC center of Excellence in Cognition and its Disorders, Department of Cognitive Sciences, Macquarie University, Sydney, Australia Hereby, the author thanks Dr. YANG for her contribution.

(Chee et al., 1999; Klein, Milner, Zatorre, Meyer & Evans, 1995; Crinion et al. 2006). Some authors have reported common areas of activation for both languages (Chee et al., 1999; Klein, Milner, Zatorre, Meyer & Evans, 1995; Marian, Spivey & Hirsch, 2003). For instance, Xue et al.'s (2004) found a high degree of overlapping brain activation in the bilateral DLPFC, precentral cortex, pars opercularis cortex, pars triangularis cortex, and parietal lobule during L1 Chinese and L2 English tasks. The authors interpreted this to mean that L1 and L2 verbal working memory processing share the same neural substrates. This line of research seems to support the language-universal processing system.

However, recent evidence also indicates differences in cortical organization for L1 and L2, especially for "late bilinguals" (Kim et al., 1997; Weber-Fox & Neville, 1996). For those who begin to learn L2 in early adulthood, language-specific processing and representation systems are involved (Holm & Dodd, 1996; Hu & Catts, 1993; Siok & Fletcher, 2001). Differences in cortical organization were found for L1 and L2 in late bilinguals (Kim et al., 1997; Wartenburger et al., 2003). Common brain substrates are involved during processing when L2 is acquired when the level of proficiency is high (Chee et al., 1999; Kim, Relkin, Lee & Hirsch, 1997; Perani & Abutalebi, 2005; Klein, Milner, Zatorre, Meyer & Evans, 1995). Findings regarding shared areas of activation in L1 and L2 have been inconclusive for late and/or less proficient bilinguals.

The controversial results are partly contributed to age of acquisition and language fluency of the two languages involved in the processing (e.g., Weber-Fox & Neville, 1996). In recent years, an important segregation of cortical representations phonological information for bilinguals whose two languages differ in the orthography-phonology mapping rules, for instance, Chinese and native English speakers (Tan et al., 2003). The processing of L1 Chinese phonology (where logographic characters are pronounced monosyllabically) carries over to L2 English processing. The Chinese subjects were applying the strategy of processing Chinese to processing English words. They did not automatically use the letter-to-sound conversion rules to pronounce English words. Nam et al. (1999) examined the role of orthographic and phonological information for Korean-English bilinguals and native speakers of English using a primed-lexical decision task. They found that Korean-English bilinguals do not actively use phonology-related information at the prelexical and lexical levels, and rely mainly on orthographic information when they are recognizing English words. Similar results were found by Kim et al., (2011) that distinct brain areas are associated with Korean (L1) and English (L2) processing, and more diverse and right hemisphere areas are activated during L2 processing compared to L1 processing among low to moderately proficient late bilinguals. L2 processing relative to L1 processing were the left precuneus (BA 7), right superior parietal lobule (BA 7), left middle occipital gyrus (BA 19), and left cerebellum, suggesting that participants might rely more on visual cues and visual processing for word recoding and visual analysis during L2 processing than during L1 processing.The above findings (e.g., Kim et al., 2011; Nam et al., 1999; Tan et al., 2003) seem to implicate that L1 and L2 differ in granularity and/or transparency of the grapheme-to-phoneme mapping such that they do not share neuronal representations during language processing.

The results from empirical studies are intriguing when different tasks in the various studies tap into different components of language processing. Further, a specific experimental study is usually limited to exploring a small number of languages. Therefore, a broad aim of the present study is to examine how these language differences in transparency and granuality of O-P mapping determine the neural substrates for bilingual lexical processing by using a meta-analysis study. One advantage of a meta-analysis study is to examine a number of studies in the field at the same time in order to draw a more conclusive conclusion. One hypothesis in the present study is that L1 and L2 different in granularity and/or transparency do not share neuronal representations. Alternatively, native language experience may tune the neuronal representations of L2 processing.

2.2 Methods

Thirty fMRI studies investigating L1 and L2 lexical processing in healthy adults were selected from PubMed database and ScienceDirect using key terms "second language", "L2", "bilingual", "lexical processing", "word processing", and "fMRI". L1 and L2 involved in each study were coded as opaque, transparent, coarse, or fine based on their granularity and transparency of the grapheme-to-phoneme (Wydell and Butterworth, 1999).

We searched papers from the PubMed database (http://www.ncbi.nlm.nih.gov/pubmed/) using three key words together. The first key word indicated neuroimaging techniques, including "fMRI" and "PET". The second key word indicated studies about bilingual mechanism, such as "second language", "L2", or "bilingual". The third key word indicated studies about word processing, such as "lexical processing" or "word processing".

Twenty-nine papers were revealed. The inclusion criteria for the current meta-analysis are listed as follows:

Table 2 Sample papers selected for the present analysis

Sources	L1	L2	Method	Stimuli	task
Abutalebi et al., 2007	Italy	German	fMRI	word	silent reading
Bick et al., 2011	Hebrew	English	fMRI	word	lexical decision
Chee et al., 2000	Chinese	English	fMRI	word/ picture	semantic judgment
Chee et al., 2001	English	Mandarin	fMRI	word/ picture	semantic judgment
Chee et al., 2003	English	Chinese	fMRI	word	word reading
De Bleser et al., 2004	Dutch	French	PET	picture	naming
Ding et al., 2003	Chinese	English	fMRI	words	orthographic/semantic task
Guo et al., 2011	Chinese	English	fMRI	picture	word production
Halsband et al., 2002	Finnish	English	PET	word	word learning
Halsband, 2006	Finnish	English	PET	word	word learning
Hernandez et al., 2000	Spanish	English	fMRI	picture	naming
Illes et al., 1999	Spanish	English	fMRI	word	semantic /uppercase or lowercase type
Kim et al., 2011	Korean	English	fMRI	word	working memory task
Klein et al., 2006	English	French	PET	word/non-word	word repetition
Lehtonen et al., 2009	Swedish	Finnish	fMRI	word	lexical decision
Leonard et al., 2011	Spanish	English	MEG/ MRI	word	semantic judgment
Liu et al., 2010	Chinese	English	fMRI	picture	word production
Mahdavi et al., 2010	Persian	English	fMRI	word	word production
Meschyan& Hernandez, 2006	Spanish	English	fMRI	word	word reading
Nosarti et al., 2010	Italian/ English	English/ Italian	fMRI	word	word reading
Pillai et al., 2003	Spanish	English	fMRI	word	semantic association
Raboyeau et a., 2004	French	English	PET	picture	word learning
Raboyeau et al., 2010	French	Spanish	fMRI	word	word learning
Tham et al., 2005	Chinese	English	fMRI	word	sound likeness judge
Videsott et al., 2010	Ladin	Italian/ English	fMRI	word	word production

First, studies that used neuroimaging technique that has high spatial resolution and collected data from healthy adult bilinguals were selected. We excluded studies that employed EEG techniques. Studies that recruited children or monolinguals were also excluded. Six of the 29 papers met this criterion.

Second, studies that studied a language from non-dyslexia language family (opaque and coarse, transparent and fine) and a language from the dyslexia language family (transparent and coarse, opaque and fine) were selected. Nine of the 23 papers met this criterion.

Third, studies that included a word processing task (e.g., word comprehension, word naming, lexical decision) in L1 *and* L2 and reported results from bilingual subjects in *both* languages were selected. Studies that investigate phrase, sentence or narrative processing and studies in which bilingual subjects only perform a word processing task in L1 or L2 were excluded. All of the 9 remaining papers met this criterion.

We performed an additional search in ScienceDirect (http://www.sciencedirect.com/) with the same key words and found that 21 extra papers met the criteria. These papers were also included. Table 2 lists sample papers included in the study.

2.3 Discussion

2.3.1 A contrast between L1: opaque and coarse, L2: opaque and fine

In Group 1(L1: opaque and coarse; L2: opaque and fine), L1 lexical processing indicated significant in the left middle frontal gyrus (MFG, BA 9), bilateral precentralgyrus (BA 4), bilateral medial frontal gyrus (BA 32), and bilateral fusiform gyrus (FG, BA 19). L2 lexical processing indicated effects in the left inferior frontal gyrus (IFG, BA 45), left precentralgyrus (BA 4/6/9), left medial frontal gyrus (BA 32), left superior frontal gyrus (SFG, BA 6) and bilateral FG (BA 19/37).

2.3.2 A contrast between L1: transparent and fine, L2: opaque and fine

In Group 2 (L1: transparent and fine, L2: opaque and fine), L1 lexical processing elicited activation in left MFG (BA 6), left precentralgyrus (BA 6), right medial frontal gyrus (BA 25), right SFG (BA 10/9), right supramarginalgyrus (SMG, BA 40) and right inferior temporal gyrus (ITG, BA 20). L2 lexical processing indicated effects in the left MFG (BA 6), left precentralgyrus (BA 6), right medial frontal gyrus (BA 25), left middle temporal gyrus (MTG, BA 39), bilateral SFG (BA 10/9), right SMG (BA 40), and right ITG (BA 20).

2.3.3 A contrast between L1: opaque and fine; L2: transparent and fine/opaque and coarse

In Group 3 (L1: opaque and fine; L2: transparent and fine/opaque and coarse), L1 lexical processing showed effects in the left MFG (BA 9), left IFG (BA 9/13), left medial frontal gyrus (8), and left precentralgyrus (BA 6). L2 lexical processing elicited effects in the left MFG (BA 9), left IFG (BA 9), and left precentralgyrus (BA 6/9). Again, no difference was found between L1 and L2.

One important result revealed from the above findings is that some brain substrates were found to be involved in bilingual word processing regardless of the language groups. For instance, MFG (BA 6) and precentralgyrus (BA 9) etc. were involved in all the three language groups during language processing. The shared frontal lobe system was reported for semantic analysis of two languages similar in granularity (Xue et al., 2004). We interpreted this to mean that L1 and L2 verbal working memory processing share the same neural substrates.

The second important result is a high degree of overlapping brain activation in BA4, BA32 and BA19 during L1 and L2 tasks for the first language group (i.e., L1: opaque and coarse; L2: opaque and fine). Likely, the overlapping brain activation was also found in the second language group (L1: transparent and fine, L2: opaque and fine) as in BA6, BA 25, BA 10/9, BA40, BA20. And for the third language group (L1: opaque and fine; L2: transparent and fine/opaque and coarse), L1 and L2 word processing activated similar brain in BA 9 and BA 6. The above findings indicate that brain areas activated in L1 processing transfer to the L2 processing. It is likely native language experience has some effects on the neuronal representations of L2 processing. Native language experience seems to tune the cortex during second language processing. Thus, the source of variation on representations in brain areas among bilingual processing has stemmed from the language experience. On this account, the present results replicate previous findings that native language experience has some effect on the cortex representation during second language processing (Tan et al., 2003).

However, the comparison between language groups showed some difference between L1 and L2 processing. Granularity and transparency in terms of the orthography and phonology mapping have some effect on bilingual processing difference. The results indicate differences between bilingual language systems explain some variation among bilingual processing. The distance between L1 and L2 will show some influence on neural substrate devoted to the bilingual processing.

Taken together, L1 and L2 common neural substrate is likely to be attributed to the similarity of the substrates involved in processing the two languages for the bilinguals. Language similarity in orthography, phonology, and syntax determines the transfer of appropriate processing skills, and in return determines the shared neural representation during bilingual processing. A dissociation of neural substrates is more likely involved in processing L1 and L2 when the grapheme-phoneme mapping systems in the two languages which differ greatly in terms of granularity and transparency.

2.4 Conclusion

The meta-analysis indicates that L1 and L2 generally involve similar neural substrates and thus support the language-universal processing system. However, lexical processing in different language systems elicits different brain activation patterns, suggesting that the granularity and/or transparency of a language can determine the neural substrate for word processing. The distance between L1 and L2 will show some influence on neural substrate devoted to the bilingual processing. The finding implies that native language experience can shape the neural substrates of L2 processing.

Chapter 3 A review and reflection on the study of bilingual reading difficulties

Abstract: This paper reviews the identification method of the mother tongue reading difficulty, proposing the identification methods change from the intelligence-reading achievement discrepancy diagnosis model to the combination low reading achievement and the core cognitive skills related to reading. Mother tongue reading difficulties are usually reflected in the performance of the word decoding defects, poor reading fluency and reading comprehension difficulties. Their cognitive roots are affected by the impact of language characteristics. In the bilingual reading difficulties, the three screening methods are mainly used: the evaluation by teachers, the prediction from the mother tongue reading performance and the prediction from the cognitive skills of bilingual teaching. Influenced by the language features of the mother tongue, the second language reading difficulties from both behavior and EEG evidence showed bilingual defects consistency and dissociate modes. Although studies have found that, under the background of Chinese mother tongue, the second language English reading difficulties presented deficiencies in phonological processing skills, brain malfunction in the left brain activation and so on, cognitive diagnosis on Chinese-English bilinguals' reading difficulty still need more evidence.

Key words: bilingual mother tongue two languages reading difficulties identification

3.1 Identification of reading difficulties in mother tongue

Early diagnosis of dyslexia in native language usually uses the intelligence-reading achievement discrepancy diagnosis model. Over the past 20 years, the influence of cognitive psychology, componential view of reading is oriented (Koda, 2004). This kind of research not only surveys the different components of reading skills, but also probes into the relationship between different kinds of cognitive skills such as perception, cognitive skills, linguistic factors and reading in different reading groups. The study found that success in reading was determined by three key processes: visual information processing (i.e. decoding), cognitive processing, and meta-cognitive processing (activating the text information and associated pre-stored knowledge) (Koda, 2004). In the context of this view, reading difficulty is screened by the gap between low achievement and core skills (刘云英 & 陶沙, 2007).

From the perspective of cognitive psychology, the most typical characteristic of reading difficulty is reflected in word reading deficiency. This kind of word reading difficulties will hinder the reading speed and bring about the defects of reading comprehension in a certain degree. As can be seen from the above table, there is difference in defining the difficulty of reading across languages. Regardless of the diagnosis of the standardized tests, the relatively consistent criteria are normal intelligence and reading scores at least one standard deviation or two grade lower than the average scores.

Researchers from the behavior, cognition, neural and genetic level study have identified manifestations and causes for dyslexia (e.g., Ho & Lai, 1999; Ho et al., 2004; 何胜昔，尹文刚，杨志伟，2006; 买合甫来提・坎吉，刘翔平 & 王燕，2010 孟祥芝，舒华，1999; Shu et al., 2006; 赵微，荆伟，方俊明，2012). There are three forms of reading disability: decoding difficulties, comprehension difficulty and reading speed defects (Geva & Limbos, 2001). One consistent view is that decoding difficulty is the core deficit. Thus, screening dyslexia is usually based on defects in word decoding (Lyon, Shaywitz & Shaywitz, 2003) and some reading related cognitive skills (e.g., Ho & Lai, 1999; Limbos & Geva, 2001; Shu et al., 2006).

Table 3 Screening methods for reading difficulties

(Adapted from Xue, Shu & Wu, 2009)

Sources	Languages	Screening Criteria	Age
Bailey et al., 2004	English	Word identification (Woodcock,1987) < 25 percentages IQ >= 85 (PPVT)	Grade 4-5
Borsting et al., 1996	English	IQ（WAIS-verbal）higher than 85	
Ho, et al., 2004	Chinese	Raven higher than 85 Hong Kong Dyslexia Screening Tests (HKT-SpLD) Literacy combined score and at least one cognitive skill 1SD below average	99.5 months, Grade 2.4
Ho et al., 2007	Chinese	HKT-SpLD Literacy combined score 1SD below average; Raven >= 85	Mean age = 9.0 years
Lorusso et al., 2004	Italian	WAIS-R >= 85 Reading accuracy and speed 1SD above those by chronological age group Reading and spelling 2sd lower than the grade mean	10.52 years, Grade 5.32
Manis, et al., 1996	English	Word identification lower than 30 percentages 140>IQ>85	9-15 years
Manis et al., 1997	English	WRMT(word identification < 25 percentages IQ (WISC-III) > 86	Grade 4-10
McDougall, et al., 2005	English	WRMT-R 1SD lower than mean; IQ (WICS) >90	Grade 2- 5
Shu et al., 2005	Chinese	IQ (Raven) > 50 percentages, Chinese character identification 1 grade lower	9 years 10 months-12 years two months
McPherson et al.,1998	English	Normal IQ, reading（WRMT）two grade lower	Between 13-18 years

Notes: PPVT: Peabody Picture Vocabulary Test; WAIS: Wechsler Adult Intelligence Scale; WRMT: Woodcock Reading Mastery Test; WISC-III: Wechsler Intelligence Scale for Children third edition.

Deficits in phonological awareness, morphological awareness, working memory and other cognitive skills are the cognitive sources for dyslexia (Ho et al., 2004; Leij & Morfidi,

2006; Shu et al., 2006; Vellutino et al., 2004). Due to the differences in language systems, the cognitive mechanism of reading processing is different (Goswami et al., 2002, 2005; Siegel, 2003). The phonological deficit is the core for dyslexia in alphabetic languages (mainly including phonological awareness, phonological memory and phonological processing) (Leij & Morfid, 2006; Goswami, 2005). In contrast, deficits in morphological awareness and rapid naming are the key to Chinese reading difficulties Chinese mother tongue reading difficulties (Ho et al., 2002, 2004; Ho & Lai, 1999; 刘文理 & 刘翔平 , 2006; Shu et al., 2006; Shu et al., 2006). Accordingly, the corresponding teaching intervention mainly focuses on cognitive processing skills, such as phonological processing skills training, word recognition training, and orthographic training (王文静 , 2010).

In theory, Ziegler & Goswami (2005) put forward the theory of transparency to explain the differences in the incidence of dyslexia and reading performance in different languages. According to the theory, it cost around 3 to 4 years for the children to develop decoding skills (Goswami, 2002; Ziegler & Goswami, 2005). It also resulted in difference in the screening time in different languages. Besides, the characteristic of reading difficulty in Finnish is manifested in low decoding speed (Lyytinen et al., 2006). Whereas, in English dyslexia, deficits in phonological processing skills defects lead to the low accuracy in decoding.

In traditional research, developmental dyslexia is known as the specific reading impairment. It is manifested in the defects on word reading, reading fluency, decoding and spelling (Lyon, Shaywitz & Shaywitz, 2003). Usually, defining dyslexia should exclude mental retardation, sense of perceptual deficits, educational opportunity loss and other factors. Reading difficulties not only make the students have difficulties in language learning. Sometimes reading difficulties even affect the learning of other domains, such as arithmetic, understanding, learning motivation and self-concept. Reading disabilities may have the following characteristics (Chan et al., 2002; Sawyer et al., 1999; 刘文理 , 刘翔平 & 张婧乔 , 2006; 杨志伟 , 龚耀先 & 李雪荣 , 1998; 周晓林 & 孟祥芝 , 2001):

In the aspect of reading, the dyslexia children are worse in literacy ability than the same age children, and the gap may be more than one grade. Reading speed is relatively slow. It is difficult for them to identify some easy words. They will mispronounce and confuse pronunciation similar words. In writing, they will write typos, and strokes or letters of font structure are not symmetrical. There are also bad effects on other aspects of learning. For instance, in mathematics, they do not understand the digital values. Recitation of the multiplication table is also difficult for them.

In terms of cognitive ability, children with reading disability show poor memory, phonological awareness, naming speed, and so on. In memory, they are not able to effectively transfer information from short time memory to long time memory. For the performance in daily life, they are often not able to t keep in mind the information or more complex schedule and so on; they also lost personal items or forget to do homework, etc. In terms of phonological awareness, the phonological representation in the brain is relatively poor. Thus they are weak in phoneme segmentation and combination, initials/finals and tones identification. In terms of naming speed, they are slow to retrieve some familiar images or symbols.

3.2 Identification of bilingual reading difficulties

The study on native language has some implications for the related aspects in the second language study. The rate of reading difficulties in different languages was about 10% (孟祥芝 & 舒华 , 1999). However, second language learning reading ability is influenced by L1 features, second language acquisition level, social cultural background, bilingual development speed imbalance and other factors, resulting in potential difficulties in screening difficult readers in a second language (Schiff-Myers, 1992; Paradis, Genesee & Crago, 2010). At present, there are three main methods for the identification of second language reading difficulties.

First, behavior evaluation. Interviews with teachers or rating by teachers according to the reading difficulties scale is used to identify the second language learners reading problems (Limbo & Geva, 2001). This is due to the fact that the second language learners do not have the standardized test, and second language teachers have enough time and opportunities in contact with readers. This is a method of time and cost saving method. However, teachers often rated according to the second language learners' oral expression ability and vocabulary to be assessed (Geva, 1998; limbo & Geva, 2001) . These measures have different demanding on language skills (such as communicative principle). For instance, there is only marginally significant correlation between word reading and vocabulary (Limbo & Geva, 2001). In view of the relationship between oral vocabulary and traditional reading difficulties, the method also suffers some degree of lack of accuracy in screening.

Second, performance in native language diagnosis test provides some prediction for the second language reading difficulties. There is evidence that native language cognitive processing skills (for example, the phonological processing skills) can effectively predict the L2 decoding ability or decoding difficulties (Knell et al., 2007), and the correlation between bilingual phonological processing skills and decoding level is significant (Chiappe, Siegel & Wade-Woolley, 2002; Wang, Perfetti & Liu, 2005). In particular, in the case of bilinguals of two alphabetic languages (e.g., English language learners learn French), phonological awareness in one language often predicts the decoding level of another language (e.g., Jared et al., 2011). Diagnostic tests in their native language are used to predict the second language reading difficulties. However, it should be pointed out that there are differences in the effects of native language features on the second language reading. For example, for Chinese or Korean natives learning English as a second language, the second language learners rely more on orthographic features to read English, and Korean speakers are to greater extent dependent on the phonological features of English (Wang, Koda & Perfetti, 2003) voice. This makes the method limited in the predictive power.

Third, using the common factors between native language and the second language to identify the reading difficulties in a second language. Because in bilingual study, a lot of research results show that the native language and the second language reading share some characteristics (e.g., Knell et al., 2007; Wolf & Bowers, 1999). For example, when there is difficulty in one language for the bilingual, the other language should also show deficits in phonological awareness and rapid naming (Hong & Ho, 2005; Wolf & Bowers, 1999). However, the situation is more complicated when the bilinguals' two languages belong to different language families. For instance, for Chinese-English bilinguals, the most effective predictor variables will vary in bilingual reading (Cheng, Wang & Chen, 2006).

3.3 Manifestation and theoretical interpretation for bilingual reading difficulties

Although the study of bilingual reading is relatively scarce, it has been found that the second language reading difficulties are affected by the mother tongue characteristics. This effect can be summarized as two modes. The first model is that the mother tongue transfer caused the bilingual reading difficulties to show similar characteristics. For example, Leij & Morfidi (2006) found that there was a decoding difficulty in both languages for Dutch-

English bilinguals. Ho & Fong (2005) examined the Chinese reading difficulties in English reading and related skills, and obtained similar results. The results of these studies have also been supported by neuroimaging findings. In an EEG study on Hebrew English bilinguals (Oren and Breznitz, 2005), this study analyzed the N1 (characterizing the attentional processing), P2 (characterizing of feature recognition and classification), P3 (referring to updating memory representation and selection) and behavioral data (accuracy and reaction time). The study found that the two languages have difficulty in reading, showing the automatic processing deficits. The long latency, low amplitude and late latency of the brain waves in the natives were more obvious in the second language. The study found that the processing mode in mother tongue will be moved to the second language in a certain extent.

Another model is that there is a dissociation between mother tongue and the second language reading difficulties. For example, a case study of the English and Japanese bilingual found that reading difficulties only existed in English reading (Wydell & Butterworth, 1999; Lundberg, 2000). Everatt et al. (2002) study also reported that bilingual children had difficulty in word reading in the deep orthography (English), but the other language is not defective. Not only that, a Hebrew-English bilingual EEG study found not only the bilingual processing model had some certain similarity, but also found reading difficulty in Hebrew did not necessarily represent in another language (Oren & breznitz, 2005). According to this, the characteristics of the two languages also have influence on the performance of reading difficulties.

Theoretically, two different theories arise, i.e., the Central Processing Hypothesis and the Script Dependent Hypothesis (Breznitz, Oren & Shaul, 2004; 赵微，荆伟 & 方俊明，2012) The former proposes common features in reading two languages and reading skills acquisition is not dependent on characteristics of the language, but rather depended on the short-term verbal memory, working memory, phonological processing skills such as potential reading cognitive skills. Reading ability in different languages develops with the development of cognitive processing skills. In contrast, the latter claims that reading in different languages demands different cognitive skills. Thus, it is reasonable to have a dissociation between the two languages for the bilinguals.

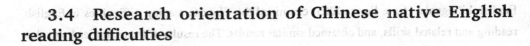

3.4 Research orientation of Chinese native English reading difficulties

Research on bilingual reading difficulties is still at the starting point. Domestic studies are limited to theoretical discussions (e.g., 姚喜明 & 梅晓宇, 2003). Related research found that small vocabulary size, slow reading speed, poor syntactic analysis ability and other factors lead to English reading comprehension difficulties (赖朝晖, 2006). Most of the teaching interventions for reading difficulties are meta-cognitive training for adults (李俊 & 倪杭英, 2007; 刘丹丹, 2002; 孟悦, 2004; 张庆宗 & 刘晓燕, 2009). Some studies from the componential viewpoint focus on Chinese speaking children (Chow, Burgess & McBride-Chang, 2005; Chung & Ho, 2010; Knell et al., 2007; 李荣宝 et al., 2011; Ho & Fong, 2005; 彭鹏 & 陶沙, 2009). In the limited number of studies on second language, English cognitive diagnosis on reading difficulty is based on teacher evaluation (陶沙, 2009), reading screening (郭楠 et al., 2009; 林新事, 2008) or the disease diagnostic criteria by the World Health Organization (董燕, 段建平 & 邵波, 2004).

Part 2 Influencing Factors for Chinese-English Bilingual Reading

内容简介

这部分是基础研究，共包括六个研究，研究结果为后续的阅读困难的诊断和鉴别提供科学依据。主要内容包括两方面：其一，是行为研究；其二，是脑电（Event-related potentials, ERP）研究。具体包括六个研究，分别考察汉英双语字词通达机制、英语阅读理解和词汇语素之间的关系、第二语言英语的不同类型的句法加工的神经机制、第二语言句法加工脑电模式差异的根源、句子理解中不同虚拟世界信息的辨别:脑电研究、汉英双语语言特异性对大脑表征和神经机制的影响。

（1）研究 1（第 4 章）论文题为“Implicit sublexical access to the first language: An ERP study on Chinese-English bilinguals”（一语亚词汇信息的内隐通达：一项关于汉英双语者的脑电研究），考察汉英双语字词通达机制。双语者如何通达词汇信息是一个热门话题。本研究旨在考察双语者在第二语言的阅读理解中，一语汉语的亚词汇信息如何通达的。研究中，要求一语为汉语、二语为英语的熟练双语者对所呈现的一对词进行语义相关性判断，同时收集他们的行为和脑电数据。对于被试来说，他们并不知晓汉语词对中，词形存在一样的部件，例如，蓝—监；在英语词对中，语义并不相关，但如果把英语翻译成汉语时，词对中的汉语对译词也存在一样的部件，如 bell（铃）—now（今）。研究结果发现，部件重复启动对汉语和英语的词汇判断的脑电波存在影响。研究结果说明在二语英语阅读中，母语汉语被自动地、内隐地激活，这种激活存在于部件中。

（2）研究 2（第 5 章）论文题为“Meaning Construction in English Reading: The Relationship between Morphology and Comprehension”（英语阅读中的意义构建：构词法和理解的关系），探讨英语阅读理解和词汇和语素之间的关系。本研究对英语专业学生进行英语构词法的教学干预，并测查了他们的英语构词法和阅读水平。在此基础上，使用方差分析考察构词法教学干预的有效性，使用皮尔逊相关分析探讨构词法和五种阅读技能（归纳主题、因果关系、细节搜索、推理和词汇猜测）之间的关系。研究结果证实构词法训练的有效性，也发现构词法和阅读理解的不同技能呈现相关性。本文就此提出了一些教学建议。

（3）研究3（第6章）论文题为“An ERP study on Chinese natives' second language syntactic grammaticalization”（汉语母语者第二语言句法语法化的脑电研究），考察汉语母语成人在第二语言英语的不同类型的句法加工的神经机制）。本研究旨在探讨汉语母语者英语学习中如何对英语的句法规则进行语法化。研究中收集汉语母语者在英语句法判断中的事件相关脑电数据。研究中以句法相似性为因素，操纵了一语汉语和二语英语的相似性程度：①双语差异；②双语相似；③二语独有。研究结果发现，二语句法加工的P600效应（语法化的脑电指标）出现在“双语相似”和“双语独有”这两个条件中，但双语差异的语法上，并没有呈现P600效应。研究说明一语和二语相似性和二语熟练度呈现比较复杂的交互作用。

（4）研究4（第7章）论文题为“The locus of language similarity effects on bilinguals' L2 syntactic grammaticalization: transfer or competition”（双语者第二语言句法语法化过程中语言相似性效应的根源：迁移还是竞争），继续考察第二语言句法加工脑电模式差异的根源。一语和二语之间的相似性决定了双语间迁移的可能性，也因此决定了是否促进第二语言句法层面的习得。英语句法加工的脑电研究发现，句法违反常引起P600效应，而在汉语句法加工的脑电研究中，对于错误句法，常出现N400效应。本研究旨在探索在线句法加工语言相似性效应的根源。研究中收集了汉语母语者英语学习者（中高程度英语水平）的脑电数据。本研究包括两个实验（快速加工、慢速加工），要求被试对二语英语句法正确性进行判断。实验刺激操纵了一语一二语相似性程度：独特的还是冲突的。研究发现，在快速加工时，并且在加工冲突的语言特征时，脑电加工更倾向于产生一语汉语加工模式（N400效应）。研究说明，语言相似性确实影响P600效应是否产生。研究也说明，在线加工中，一语和二语原有的加工模式是潜在的，一语和二语之间加工模式的竞争一直延续到二语学习的后期高级阶段。

（5）研究5（第8章）论文题为“The role of age of acquisition on Chinese native learners' English word processing: An ERP Study”（汉语母语者英语单词加工中的习得年龄效应：一项脑电研究）。本研究的目的是考察汉语母语的英语学习者是如何区分早期和晚期习得的英语单词。研究中要求28名中国本土成人英语学习者进行语义相关判断任务，并收集了他们的行为和脑电数据。准确度和反应时间的分析表明，早期学习的单词在处理精度和速度上有优势。ERP结果显示早期习得的单词更容易加工、效率也更快；更大的习得年龄效应上看，比起可预测性高的单词，低可预测

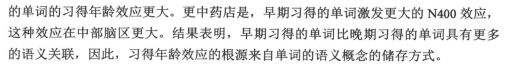

的单词的习得年龄效应更大。更中药店是，早期习得的单词激发更大的 N400 效应，这种效应在中部脑区更大。结果表明，早期习得的单词比晚期习得的单词具有更多的语义关联，因此，习得年龄效应的根源来自单词的语义概念的储存方式。

（6）研究 6（第 9 章）论文题为“Chinese-English bilinguals processing temporal-spatial metaphor”（汉英双语者时间—空间隐喻加工），考察汉英双语语言特异性对大脑表征和神经机制的影响。时间概念映射到空间范畴是具身认知理论（Cognitive Embodied Theory）的重要议题之一。而时空之间隐喻隐射理论有两个版本：强版和弱版（Kemmerer, 2005）的观点。强版的观点提出人们加工时间顺序时候，空间位置的关系框架会被激活，这导致时—空之间的跨模块一一隐射关系。而弱版的隐喻映射理论认为，时—空之间的隐喻隐射关系并不是必需的；时间意义的表征和加工可以不依赖于空间意义，虽然两者之间的隐喻隐射关系是可选择的一种加工策略。因此，时间顺序的加工并不是完全依赖于应用时—空之间的隐喻关系。在汉语中空间位置（如，大树前）和时间顺序（如，三月前）有一个相同的术语“前”。相比之下，英语母语者使用不同的介词来描述时空和空间关系，例如，用“before”来表示时间顺序，而用“in front of”来表示空间位置。这种语言间词汇编码方式的差异可能导致时间和空间的映射关系产生差异。本研究收集脑电数据。研究中测查汉英双语者加工一语汉语（实验 1）和二语英语（实验 2）的时间顺序和空间位置时的脑电反应模式。研究发现，虽然词汇编码在两种语言间存在差异，早期的感觉运动模拟在一语汉语和二语英语的时间加工中都产生作用。研究结果支持了涉身认知理论，表明概念知识是表征在感觉—运动系统中（Gallese & Lakaff，认知神经心理学，22: 45-479）。此外，汉英两种语言中，人们对时间顺序和空间位置的理解的神经表征在汉英两种语言系统中是不同的。时间—空间之间的关系是非对称的。空间图式框架可以被应用到时间顺序加工中，但反过来却行不通。这些研究结果支持弱版的隐喻隐射理论。

Chapter 4 Implicit sublexical access to spelling forms of the first language: An ERP study on Chinese-English bilinguals

Abstract: How bilinguals access lexical items in the two languages is a subject of hot debate. The present study was aimed at examining whether sublexical forms of the first language Chinese was activated during second language English reading comprehension. Fluent Chinese (L1) -English (L2) bilinguals were required to decide whether words presented in pairs were related in meaning or not. Behavioural and electrophysiological data were collected. Implicit to the participants, for Chinese word pairs, half of the word pairs shared a character component (or a radical), for instance, 蓝 (blue)- 监 (monitor); for English word pairs, half are not related in meaning but shared a radical component when translated into Chinese, for instance, bell (铃)-now (今). It was found that the hidden factor (radical repetition) modulated the brain potential for both Chinese and English word pairs. The findings established L2 English words were automatically and unconsciously translated into L1 Chinese at sublexical spelling level.

Key words: bilingual sublexical lexical access ERP

4.1 Introduction

How bilinguals access lexical items in the two languages is a subject of hot debate. This line of research assumes that a word's representation is divided in a lexical and a conceptual (or semantic) level (e.g., Kroll et al., 2010). Some studies indicate bilinguals' lexical representations of the two languages are independent (e.g., Altenberg & Cairns, 1983). Whereas, the dominant view assumes bilinguals rarely deactivate the other language totally (e.g., Guo et al., 2012; Schwartz & Kroll, 2006; Sunderman & Kroll, 2006).

Despite, the levels of lexical access to the other language vary in different studies (Dijkstra & van Heuven, 2002). It remains an open question whether reading in L2 should be associated with implicit activation of L1 translations at sublexical levels, especially when the L1 and L2 belong to two different scripts, for instance, Chinese vs. English. In contrast to the alphabetic scripts, Chinese does not have the grapheme-phoneme correspondence rules of alphabetic languages. Chinese characters are developed in six principles including pictographic, ideographic, logical aggregates, semantic-phonetic compound, transference, and loan. These characters are typically composed of one or more than one radical components.

Further, although most studies on Chinese-English bilinguals showed the strong lexico-semantic links between L1 and L2 can exist (Kroll et al., 2010) even for relatively high proficiency speakers (Guo et al., 2012), findings in Wu & Thierry (2010) entail a modality driven effect on lexical access to L1 during L2 comprehension. In their study, processing L2 activates the sound of L1 translations, instead of the spelling.

The present study examined whether processing L2 activates L1 spelling. To avoid priming effect attenuation due to masking or artificial dual-language activation, the present study collected both behavioral and ERP (Event-related potential) data. ERPs can capture neural activities throughout a time period, and they are quite sensitive in revealing second language processing that may not emerge in behavioural studies (e.g., ratings and reaction times) (e.g., Tokowicz & MacWhinney, 2005). The N400, a negative deflection, occurs approximately 400ms after stimulus onset (Friederici, 2002). This late ERP component is associated with the completion of cognitive processing and it has been reported as an index of difficulty in semantic integration (Hagoort, 2008; Kutas & Hillyard, 1984).

4.2 Methods

4.2.1 Participants

A total number of 28 Native speakers of Chinese volunteered for the experiment. They majored in English and had an experience of English immersion class for more than two years in a university in China. They acquired English after mean age of 8.35 (SD = 2.7) (late beginning to intermediate bilinguals). According to the self evaluation on the 10-point scale, their language proficiency is M = 7.70, SD = 1.21 for Chinese, and M = 6.36, SD = 0.95 for

English. They were compensated by money for their participation.

4.2.2 Materials

The key stimuli included Chinese word pairs and English word pairs, all of the pairs are semantic unrelated (see Table 4).

Table 4 Examples of stimuli used in the semantic-related tasks

Chinese word pairs						English word pairs					
Chinese Explicit			Chinse Unrelated			English Implicit			English Unrelated		
monitor	-	blue	circle	-	blue	first	-	elect	seize	-	elect
jian	-	lan	huan	-	lan	xian	-	xuan	zhua	-	xuan
监	-	蓝	环	-	蓝	先	-	选	抓	-	选

Notes: Each cell contains one example of a word pair used in the semantic-relatedness task, its simplified Chinese translation, the corresponding Chinese Pin Yin (alphabetic transposition of the phonological form).

The fillers were semantic related word pairs. For Chinese word pairs, half of the word pairs shared a character component (or a radical), for instance, 蓝 (lan, blue)- 监 (jian, monitor); Chinese-English bilinguals perceived spelling repetitions explicitly. For English word pairs, half were not related in meaning but shared a radical component when translated into Chinese, for instance, bell (铃)-now (今). Participants were unaware that some of the unrelated English words concealed radical component repetition via translation in Chinese. Thus, the participants perceived spelling repetitions implicitly. Spelling repetition in Chinese word pairs would reveal the explicit priming effect in semantic relatedness task. This would provide guideline for lexical access in L2 semantic-related task. For English word pairs, any effect of spelling repetition in Chinese would then reveal implicit access to the native language during second language processing. To control the confounding factors of meaning and sound in lexical access, the Chinese word pairs shared a radical component, but they differed in both meaning and sound. Similar considerations were taken for English word pairs. Chinese translations for the English word pairs did not share meaning or sound.

To avoid possible eye movements during the reading experiment, no English word had more than 5 letters and all Chinese translations featured less than two Chinese characters. To verify the Chinese translations used in the experiment, 15 Chinese students from Beijing International Studies University performed a translation task. These participants were randomly drawn from the same population as the bilingual participants tested in the study to minimize the differences attributable to levels of proficiency and everyday use of English.

The "first translation" method (Tokowicz & Kroll, 2007) was used, in which participants provide the first translation that comes to their mind and cannot change their responses. Participants generated over 99% consistency in the translation.

The word-pairs across experimental conditions were controlled for the level of semantic relatedness as rated by 15 native Chinese learners of English. For Chinese word pairs, ratings for semantic relatedness was significant different between related and unrelated, $t\ (1, 29) = 18.19, p < 0.001$, but not different between spelling repetition (explicit) and unrelated word pairs, $t\ (1, 29) = 1.43, p = 0.16$. For English word pairs, ratings for semantic relatedness was significant different between related and unrelated, $t\ (1, 29) = 16.59, p < 0.001$, but not different between spelling repetition (explicit) and unrelated word pairs, $t\ (1, 29) = 0.038, p = 0.97$.

4.2.3 Tasks

Participants viewed 120 Chinese word pairs and 120 English word pairs in two separate blocks (see Table 4). For each block, 60 pairs of targets were semantic unrelated word pairs for "no" response and 60 fillers semantic related word pairs for "yes" response, and they were presented in a pseudorandomized order. Participants were required to decide whether words presented in pairs were related in meaning or not. Explicit to the participants, for Chinese word pairs, half of the word pairs shared a character component. However, participants were unaware that some of the unrelated English words concealed radical component repetition via translation in Chinese.

After a prestimulus interval of 300ms, the first word was flashed for 500ms at fixation followed by the second word after an interstimulus interval of 300ms. After the offset of the final word, a blank screen appeared for 300ms, followed by a question mark "?" that served as a prompt for 1 500ms. When the prompt appeared, participants were supposed to respond by pressing either "1" or "2".

4.2.4 Data acquisition

Continuous EEG was recorded from 64 active electrodes (ActiCap, Brain Products GmbH, Munich) at standard international 10-20 system, referenced to bilateral mastoids and grounded to forehead. To control for vertical eye movements, a vertical electro-oculogram (VEOG) was recorded from Ag/AgCl electrodes placed closely above and below the left eye. Horizontal eye movements were measured by a horizontal electro-oculogram

(HEOG) recorded from Ag/AgCl electrodes that placed at the outer canthus of each eye. All impedances were kept below 5 kΩ during the experiment. EEG signals were bandpass filtered between 0.01 and 100Hz, and amplified and digitized at a rate of 500Hz using a BrainAmp amplifier (Brain Products GmbH, Munich). All EEG data were collected using Brain Vision Recorder software from Brain Products.

4.2.5 Data analyses

The analyses were conducted on data from 28 participants. The EEG data were processed offline using Brain Vision Analyzer 2. They were re-referenced to the mean of the left and right mastoid, and filtered with a 0.2Hz high-pass filter to remove drifts and a 30Hz filter to eliminate line noise. The eight electrodes centered on Cz where the N400 component is typically maximal (FC1, FC2, C1, C2, Cz, CP1, CP2, CPz) were selected for analysis. Effects of anomalies were assessed by measuring the mean amplitude (average of non-rejected epochs from 0 to 800ms after the onset of the key words, calculated relative to a baseline from −200 to 0ms) of ERPs for each participant. We performed two sets of repeated-measures ANOVAs with within-subject factor of spelling repetition. For all analyses, original degrees of freedom were reported. A Greenhouse-Geisser correction for sphericity was applied to p-values when more than two levels of a factor were present (Greenhouse & Geisser, 1959). Any main effects not reported below were all non-significant (all $ps > 0.05$).

4.3 Results

4.3.1 Behavioral performance

The accuracy rates in the acceptability judgment were computed as the percentage of yes-responses in the four conditions by the participants. One participant had missing behavioral data in Chinese experiment. The acceptability ratios of sentences in Chinese unrelated condition and Chinese explicit condition were $M = 0.84$, $SD = 0.14$ and $M = 0.48$, $SD = 0.18$, respectively. Results from ANOVA on the within-subject factor of conditions showed that the acceptability ratio of Chinese unrelated condition differed from that of explicit condition [$F(1, 26) = 88.75$, $p < 0.001$].

The acceptability ratios of sentences in English unrelated condition and English implicit condition were $M = 0.81$, $SD = 0.20$ and $M = 0.83$, $SD = 0.15$, respectively. Results from within-subject ANOVA showed that the acceptability ratio of English unrelated condition did not differ from that of implicit condition [$F(1, 27) = 0.36$, $p = 0.56$].

4.3.2 Electrophysiological data

Grand-averaged ERPs time-locked to the onset of the critical words were showed at electrode sites Cz (for Chinese unrelated and Chinese explicit, Fig. 1A; for English unrelated and English implicit, Fig. 1B), and the waves represent the mean signal evoked. Visual inspection also showed a positive going wave around the first 300ms after stimulus onset. A clear negative-going component with a peak around 400ms post word onset (N400) was found in the central sites for both Chinese and English conditions. Significant ERP differences were observed on Chinese explicit ("监" /jian/, monitor) vs. Chinese unrelated ("环" /huan/, circle). An attenuated differences were observed on English implicit ("先" /xian/, first) vs. English unrelated ("抓" /zhua/, seize). These effects were compared between the two conditions through a statistical analysis on the mean amplitudes in the time window of 300-500ms.

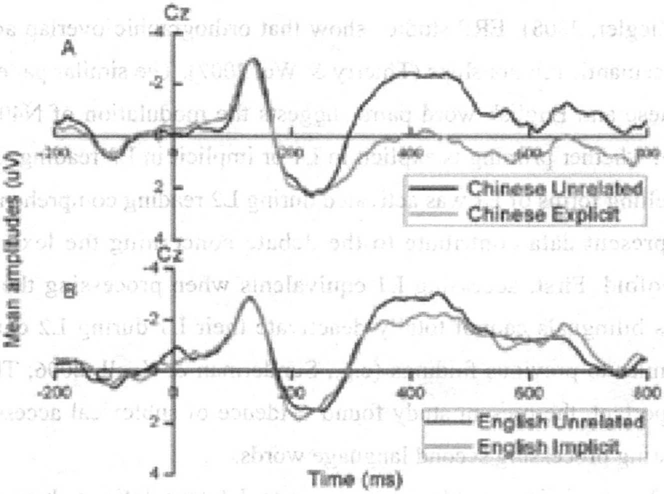

Figure 1 Grand-average ERPs for Chinese word pairs (A) and English word pairs (B)

Chinese explicit effects

For Chinese word-pairs (Fig. 1A), explicit Chinese component repetition reduced ERP mean amplitude significantly between 360 and 460ms [F (1, 27) = 30.34, p <0.001)] which is the N400 component typical window (Kutas & Hillyard, 1980, 1984).

English implicit effects

In the English word relatedness experiment, a main effect of hidden Chinese character repetition was found [F (1, 27) = 9.05, p < 0.005] (Fig. 2), reproducing the pattern of variations found in Chinese word pairs. For the Chinese-English bilinguals who read English translations with covert Chinese component repetition, the same pattern of priming was found as was seen in Chinese word pairs, although the magnitude of the priming effect was smaller in English word pairs.

4.4 Discussion

The participants showed a priming effect of explicit radical repetition in L1. The pattern was identical to results in L2 English implicit radical repetition. For L2 English word targets with concealing spelling repetition via translation in L1 Chinese, response times were significantly slower and the N400 effect was attenuated. Previous studies also report a correlate of orthographic consistency within the N400 window (Pattamadilok et al., 2009; Perre & Ziegler, 2008). ERP studies show that orthographic overlap activates N400 effect similar to semantic relationships (Thierry & Wu, 2007). The similar pattern of spelling priming in Chinese and English word pairs suggests the modulation of N400 reflects the same mechanism whether priming is explicit in L1 or implicit in L2 reading. Therefore, we can conclude spelling forms of L1 was activated during L2 reading comprehension.

Thus, the present data contribute to the debate concerning the lexical access for bilinguals in twofold. First, accessing L1 equivalents when processing the L2 word for meaning implies bilinguals cannot totally deactivate their L1 during L2 comprehension. The result is similar to previous findings (e.g., Sunderman & Kroll, 2006; Thierry & Wu, 2007). More important, the present study found evidence of sublexical access to L1 forms automatically during processing second language words.

Second, the unconscious sublexical access to L1 translations during L2 reading comprehension is contrasting with findings in Wu & Thierry (2010). In their study, they found unconscious access to sound form, but not spelling, of native language translations. Different from the present study, Wu & Thierry's (2010) participants studied in L2 English speaking country and had higher L2 proficiency. The difference in language experience is expected to modulate accessibility of processing components. On the one hand, the relatively reduced L1 input might cause the linking more vulnerable between L2 English semantic representations and L1 Chinese characters. It is well established that lexical-semantics interface is more susceptible to L1 attrition (Montrul, 2005). On the other, access to phonological representations should be easier than graphical representations. Previous evidence shows phonological encoding in word recognition is obtained better when target word processing is after the homophonic prime than after the graphemic control prime (Dijkstra & van Heuven, 2005). Thus, we tentatively propose that the bilingual semantic network, or at least the access to L1 word forms, is likely to be modified during the course of L1 attrition.

To conclude, explicit priming effect in semantic relatedness task were found for L1 radical repetition as well as in L2 words with radical component repetition concealed in Chinese translations. The findings indicate that native-language activation operates in everyday second-language use at sublexical level. Nevertheless, further research is necessary to examine neurophysiological correlates of the changes due to higher L2 language proficiency and concurrent L1 attrition.

Chapter 5 Meaning construction in English reading: The relationship between morphology and comprehension[1]

Abstract: In the present study, an English morphology intervention study was conducted on English majors, who were administered English morphology and reading tests. ANOVA was used to explore the validity of morphology intervention and the correlation analysis was used to test the relationship between morphology and the five reading skills (main idea, cause and effect, detail, inference and vocabulary). The results confirmed the validity of the morphology intervention and also revealed the positive correlations between morphology and the different reading skills.

Key words: EFL reading morphology intervention

5.1 Background

In the second language English reading, lexical analysis plays an important role. Word morphology is also known as word-formation studies (孟俊一 , 2006; Kieffer & Lesaux, 2007). Morpheme in English is often divided into bound morpheme and a free morpheme (unbound morpheme). Bound morphemes cannot stand alone, for instance, pre- and -ity, and as for suffix bound morphemes include derivatives (such as-ity) and inflections of words (such as -ing). The free morpheme often refers to the root, which becomes a word. With the relevant knowledge of word-formation, readers can often base on the context to understand new words encountered in reading (Nagy, Berninger & Abbott, 2006). Knowledge of word-

---

[1] Data in this paper was published in *Foreign Language Education* (Special Issue) [《外语教学》(专刊), 2013, 32,145-146].

formation helps lexical analysis.

Studies on English speakers found that children acquire first inflectional morphemes, and in the upper grades, they gradually acquire derivative (Tyler & Nagy, 1989). Although the acquisition of individual differences, but this sequence is relatively stable (Bear, Invernezzi, Templeton & Johnston, 2000). Meanwhile, there is correlation between word-building knowledge and reading comprehension (Nagy, Berninger & Abbott, 2006). It can be said that in reading comprehension, word-formation strategies are helpful in reading comprehension and can be taught. However, numerous studies have investigated the relation between English word formation and vocabulary acquisition (e.g., 段士平, 2008), there is little empirical research on how English word formation contributes to reading comprehension, although a handful of studies focus on the theoretical perspective (e.g., 张景, 2012). This study used empirical methods to explore the relationship between word formation and reading comprehension. There were two research questions: first, how does the English word-formation help improve reading comprehension during the teaching intervention? Second, how are the English word-formation and reading comprehension skills related?

5.2 Research methods

5.2.1 Participants

Four classes of English majors in college Grade 2.

5.2.2 Procedures

In order to investigate the effectiveness of word-formation training, this paper adopted a between-subject experimental design. Participants were asked to complete a reading proficiency test (pre-test) and then randomly assigned to the control or the experiment classes. Two classes received teaching intervention. The students were trained in English word-formation. Whereas, the other two classes were non-intervention classes, which were taught in a conventional teaching. Namely, they did not participate in word-formation training. Based on previous research (胡伟, 2012; Kieffer & Lesaux, 2007; 李学建, 1984), teaching intervention includes teaching English word-formation knowledge (e.g., synthesis, transformation, derivation, compounding and so on) and demonstrating examples, and doing related exercises. The intervention in the classroom only gave a brief introduction to the above contents; students were asked to complete relevant exercised after class. After 1 month of training, students participated in another word-formation and reading tests (post-test).

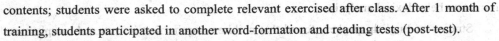

To study the relationship between word formation and different reading skills, reading tests include five types of questions (Hargrove & Poteet, 1984): causality, questions of details, inferences, main idea questions and vocabulary questions.

5.2.3 Measures

(1) Reading proficiency test. Reading proficiency test was a standardized multiple-choice reading (pre-test) (reading comprehension section of Year 2008 English Majors Grade 4 exam. There were 20 points in total with one item one point. Reading (post-test) was selected from reading comprehension section of Year 2000 and 2003 TOEFL tests. There was 1 point for each question with 40 points in total. Reliability was Cronbach Alpha coefficient of 0.71.

(2) English word-formation. Self-designed materials were used. Students were asked to fill in the blank of 10 sentences according to the meaning of the sentence with a suitable form of a given word. There were 10 questions with each question 1 point. For example, "He has gained his _____ in the match. (popular)". Cronbach alpha was 0.72.

5.2.4 Data collection

English word-formation training and testing were performed in regular English classes. All analysis used SPSS 11.0 (Statistical Package for Social Sciences), and the mean, standard deviation, and mathematical statistics were reported.

5.3 Results and analysis

In pretest reading test, there was a total of 109 participants. For the experiment classes, N=53, M = 15.92, SD = 1.95. For the non-intervention classes, N = 56, M = 15.14, SD = 2.62. ANOVA showed there was no significant difference in pretest between the intervention and non-intervention classes, F (1, 108) =3.13, $p > 0.05$. Two groups of participants are comparable in the reading level. Thus, any impact on reading achievement levels cannot be attributed to the original reading.

Table 5 The results of comparison between groups in post-test

Measures (total scores)	Groups	*N*	*M*	*SD*	Max	Min	*F*	*p*
Morphology (10)	Non-intervention	55	6.67	2.60	10.00	0.00	9.48	0.00
	Intervention	55	8.00	1.87	10.00	3.00		
Reading (40)	Non-intervention	55	28.87	4.45	36.00	16.00	4.81	0.03
	Intervention	54	30.61	3.80	38.00	23.00		
Causality (4)	Non-intervention	55	2.96	0.79	4.00	1.00	0.91	0.34
	Intervention	55	3.11	0.81	4.00	1.00		
Detail (4)	Non-intervention	55	2.76	0.77	4.00	1.00	7.63	0.01
	Intervention	55	3.18	0.82	4.00	1.00		
Inference (14)	Non-intervention	55	10.09	2.05	13.00	3.00	0.84	0.36
	Intervention	55	10.40	1.44	13.00	7.00		
Theme (4)	Non-intervention	55	3.24	0.90	4.00	1.00	0.22	0.64
	Intervention	55	3.31	0.72	4.00	1.00		
Vocabulary (14)	Non-intervention	55	9.82	1.92	13.00	4.00	4.35	0.04
	Intervention	55	10.56	1.83	14.00	5.00		

To study the effectiveness of the teaching intervention, scores in word-formation and reading in posttest were compared between interference and non-intervention classes. Results show that intervention classes performed significantly between non-intervention classes. The results proved the effectiveness of word-formation training. Differences on the five types of reading ability were found in detail and vocabulary, but not in causality and detail questions.

Further analysis found that there was significant correlation between detail, reference, theme and vocabulary. Besides, morphology was related to the five reading skills, with the correlation coefficient between the 0.27-0.44, $p < 0.01$. This not only confirmed the importance of training on reading comprehension, but also pointed to the potential of morphology intervention in helping improve reading comprehension skills. However, it should be noted that the correlation between vocabulary and morphology was only moderate ($r = 0.30$). And this means that word formation in some way is different from the vocabulary acquisition.

Table 6 The correlation between morphology and reading

	Morphology	Causality	Detail	Inference	Theme
Causality	0.08				
Detail	0.49*	0.09			
Inference	0.43*	0.15	0.46*		
Theme	0.33*	0.18	0.33*	0.38*	
Vocabulary	0.30*	0.18	0.27*	0.44*	0.29*

Note: *$p < 0.01$.

5.4 Conclusions and recommendations

In short, under the Chinese background, teaching intervention on English word-formation is feasible, and intervention on English reading comprehension and word-formation is effective. The results of this study also shows word formation and vocabulary are two related but they are two different reading related skills or knowledge. These research results have implications for reading instruction. In the China context, English word-formation training is necessary. It will not only facilitate vocabulary acquisition, but also it can improve their reading skills. However, teaching of word formation is not simply memorizing of the word formation rules. On one hand, vocabulary teaching should be combined with word formation. Vocabulary teaching needs to emphasize those words with same roots, prefixes and suffixes (Carlo et al., 2004; Graves, 2006). On the other hand, teachers should teach students to use explicit cognitive strategies to learn word-formation. The cognitive strategy consists of four parts: the students should know how to guess word meaning under context (Kieffer & Lesaux, 2007).

Chapter 6 An ERP study on Chinese natives' second language syntactic grammaticalization[1]

Abstract: The present study is concerned with how the Chinese learners of English grammaticalize different English syntactic rules. The ERPs (Event Related Potentials) data were collected when participants performed English grammatical judgment. The experimental sentences varied in the degree of the similarity between the first language Chinese (L1) and the second language English (L2): ① different in the L1 and the L2; ② similar in the L1 and the L2; and ③ unique to the L2. The P600 effect was found in L2 for structures that are similar in the L1 and the L2 and that are unique in L2, but there was no P600 effect of sentence type for the mismatch structures. The results indicate L1-L2 similarity and L2 proficiency interact in a complex way.

Key words: bilinguals language similarity grammaticalization ERP

6.1 Introduction

Traditionally, age of exposure and language proficiency are regarded as the two most important factors explaining the distinct processing patterns between the native language (L1) and the second language (L2) (Kotz, 2009). Recent studies indicate L1-L2 similarity determines the possibility of transfer and thus facilitates the learning at the grammatical aspects of an L2, including on-line computation of morphosyntactic information (Rossi et al., 2006; Sabourin, 2003). But there are fewer consensuses for features that are present in the L2 but absent in the L1. Some argue the novel L2 rules are not acquirable after puberty

[1] This paper "An ERP study on Chinese natives' second language syntactic grammaticalization" was published in *Neuroscience Letters*, 2013, 534: 258-263.

(Franceschina, 2005). Others claim that these features could be acquired, although more slowly. The present study concerns how the Chinese learners of English grammaticalize different L2 English syntactic rules.

Grammaticalization is "the instantiation of rule-based knowledge into the learner's real-time language processing system" (Mclaughlin et al., 2010). The grammaticalization processes should be accompanied by concomitant changes in learners' neural systems. The sensitivity of ERPs (event-related potentials) to syntactic processes makes them appealing for examining the stages of grammaticalization. In the context of an L2 grammaticalization, two ERP components are observed robust: ① The P600, a positive-going deflection elicited during 500 to 700ms period, is attributed to processes of syntactic integration, reanalysis, and repair (Hahne, 2001). The P600 effect has been used with great success to study the degree to which individuals are sensitive to syntactic anomalies, and hence is regarded as an indicator for the grammaticalization process (Tokowicz & MacWhinney, 2005). In an L2, the P600 effect has been reported to be delayed, reduced, or altogether absent in the beginning learners (Hahne & Friederici, 2001). ② The N400, the negativity often elicited in middle-posterior sites approximately 400ms after stimulus onset, is attributed to the integration of semantic and morphosyntactic information. The N400 observed in L2 syntactic anomalies are interpreted as weaker or slower morphosyntactic processes in beginning stages of grammaticalizationor increased semantic integration (wrap-up) demands in L2 (Osterhout & Nicol, 1999). Longitudinal studies revealed that learners' brain response varied systematically along the N400/P600 continuum. Generally, P600 is thought to replace N400 in reasonably fluent bilingual years following the onset of L2 learning. On the other, those who showed faster learning of the syntactic rule would be quicker to progress from the N400 to the P600 stage.

An intriguing neuroimaging outcome from Chinese/English bilingual studies are the different patterns of developmental change between Chinese learners of English as a foreign language and English learners of Chinese as a foreign language in sentence processing transfer (Li et al., 2004; Liu & Perfetti, 2003; Siok et al., 2004; Su, 2001). The asymmetrical hypothesis proposes that, "alphabetic readers have a neural network that accommodates the demands of Chinese by recruiting neural structures less needed for alphabetic reading. Chinese readers have a neural network that partly assimilates English into the Chinese system, especially in the visual stages of word identification" (Perfetti et al., 2007). Accordingly, no matter whether the language rules are shared or conflicting or unique in the two languages, Chinese natives are expected to transfer L1 neurological patterns during processing L2 English.

It is well established that the N400 (not P600) is elicited in L1 Chinese morphosyntactic violation for structures that mismatch in English (Chen et al., 2007; Dowens et al., 2011). The robust N400 effect in L1 Chinese is conflicting with the divergent findings in an L2. There is no consensus, especially for properties that exist in an L2 but are absent in Chinese. Some reported an N400 effect in L2 English morphosyntactic violation (Guo et al., 2009), while some found a P600 effect in Chinese learners of Spanish when processing gender and number (the two Spanish structures are absent in L1 Chinese). The former argues for the transfer effect, while the latter indicates an accommodation effect. Thus, the effect of the asymmetrical hypothesis on Chinese natives' L2 grammaticalization is far from clear.

Focusing on the comparison between L1 Chinese and L2 English, the present study examined three structures: first, different structures (subject verb agreement, SV) for which the L2 pattern directly conflicts with or competes against the L1 pattern; second, similar structures (subject-number-verb agreement, SN) for which the L1 pattern supports and matches the L2 pattern; and third, unique structures (auxiliary omission, AO) that differ between the two languages without any direct competition or mismatch. Samples for these three structure types were shown in Table 7.

Table 7 Examples of the three experimental conditions

Condition (similarity)	Type	Example
SV (different)	Acceptable	*The cats eat the food that Mary gives them.*
	Unacceptable	*The cat eat the food that Mary gives them.*
SN (similar)	Acceptable	*Several rules were difficult to understand.*
	Unacceptable	*One rule were difficult to understand.*
AO (unique)	Acceptable	*These grapevines grow well in sandy regions.*
	Unacceptable	*These grapevines growing well in sandy regions.*

Note: The underlined parts are the critical words.

Subject-verb agreement (SV)

Chinese and English are different in the situation of subject-verb agreement. English verbs must always agree with the number of the subject. Chinese verbs do not have grammatical morphology for marking number, gender, and case. The same verb is used for different tenses and for both plural and singular nominal subject. Learning to apply the subject-verb agreement system is a challenge for Chinese native learners of English.

Subject-number-verb agreement (SN)

In the case of some collective verbs such as "讨论"(discuss), Chinese and English are similar. Because the collective verb provides information regarding the number of subject, Chinese natives learn to activate the expectations that the subject noun should be in plural forms. In this perspective, the subject-verb agreement rule in Chinese is identical to that in English.

Auxiliary omission (AO)

Generally speaking, the using of auxiliary is unique in English. English forms the progressive tenses by placing the auxiliary before the participle. For most Chinese sentences, they make no grammatical use of the auxiliary verbs. Chinese native learners of English should learn the grammatical rule explicitly.

Numerous studies proved the P600 effect in syntactic violations for SV, SN and AO structures in English natives (Mclaughlin et al., 2010; Osterhout & Mobley, 1995; Osterhout & Nicol, 1995). In order to maximize the comparison between English natives and L2 English, we adapted the materials from the above mentioned studies and examined only L2 English processing patterns by following Tokowicz & MacWhinney's (2005) study. From the perspective of the language similarity effect and transfer hypothesis, we predict a significant P600 for SN or AO but not for SV. Alternatively, according to the asymmetrical hypothesis, we predict an N400 effect (with or without P600) will be elicited across the three structures.

6.2 Method

6.2.1 Participants

The present study included nineteen English majors (seven men, average age 22.5 years, range 20 to 26 years) from Beijing International Studies University of China. All reported Chinese as L1 and English as L2. They were exposed to L2 English after age 9.5 and had history of English learning for an average of 14 years. They had English Immersion classes for more than 2 years (range from 2 to 5 years) and all passed the national test for English majors, Level 4. According to a 10-point self-rating scale, the means for their English reading, writing, speaking and speech comprehension were respectively 7.75, 7.06, 6.56, and 6.94. All participants had normal or corrected to normal vision and got compensation for their participation.

6.2.2 Procedure

By following the similar procedure used in Tokowicz and MacWhinney's (2005), the sentences were presented in a random order determined by the computer program E-Prime, which also recorded the accuracy and reaction times and sent critical word onset information to the ERP acquisition software. The block of English sentences was counterbalanced. Participants read sentences on a computer screen; half the sentences were well formed and half were not. The participants responded by pressing buttons on a computer keyboard; they pressed a button marked "1" with their left hand to indicate if they thought the sentence was acceptable and a button marked "2" with their right hand if they thought the sentence was unacceptable. During a trial prior to each sentence, a fixation cross appeared at the center of the computer screen. Participants were asked to blink when the fixation was on the screen. Sentences were presented words by words, at the center of the computer screen. Each stimulus remained on the screen for 300ms with a blank screen appearing for 350ms between words. After the offset of the final word of the sentence, a blank screen appeared for 200ms, followed by a question mark "?" that served as a prompt. When the prompt appeared, participants were supposed to respond by pressing either "1" or "2".

6.2.3 Stimuli

The English syntactic stimuli include three experimental structures. The subject-verb agreement sentences and the auxiliary omissions were adapted from Osterhout & Nicol (1999). The subject-number-verb agreement sentences were adapted from previous research. A total of 180 English sentences were presented; all were experimental items, with 60 items for each experimental condition. Half of the sentences were in their acceptable form and half in unacceptable form. There were 10 instances of each structure type. The sentences were randomly assigned to two versions of the stimuli, with right hand and left hand response types counterbalanced. The critical word in each sentence was at the violation point. As shown in the following table, in unacceptable sentences, the critical word was defined as the word at which a violation was noticeable, for instance, the word "*eat*" in "*The cat eat the food that Mary gives them*". In acceptable sentences, the critical word was in the same position as the critical word in the corresponding unacceptable sentence, e.g., the word "*eat*" in "*The cats eat the food that Mary gives them*".

6.2.4 Data acquisition

Continuous EEG was recorded from 64 active electrodes (ActiCap, Brain Products GmbH, Munich) at standard international 10-20 system, referenced to bilateral mastoids and grounded to forehead. To control for vertical eye movements, a vertical electro-oculogram (VEOG) was recorded from Ag/AgCl electrodes placed closely above and below the left eye. Horizontal eye movements were measured by a horizontal electro-oculogram (HEOG) recorded from Ag/AgCl electrodes that placed at the outer canthus of each eye. All impedances were kept below 20 kΩ during the experiment. EEG signals were bandpass filtered between 0.01 and 100Hz, and amplified and digitized at a rate of 500Hz using a BrainAmp amplifier (Brain Products GmbH, Munich). All EEG data were collected using Brain Vision Recorder software from Brain Products.

6.2.5 Data analyses

The analyses were conducted on data from the 15 participants, excluding three subjects who have the overall behavioral accuracy below chance level and the other one due to equipment failure. Our analysis of the ERP data included both correct and incorrect trials because past studies indicate that the ERPs produced by beginning L2 learners show sensitivity to grammaticality. The EEG data were processed offline using Brain Vision Analyzer 2. They were re-referenced to the mean of the left and right mastoid, and filtered with a 0.2Hz high-pass filter to remove drifts and a 30Hz filter to eliminate line noise. Electrode sites from midline site (3 levels - corresponding to Fz, Cz, Pz), medial site (with 2 levels of hemisphere - left and right- and 5 anterior-posterior levels -F1/F2, FC1/FC2, C1/C2, CP1/CP2, P1/P2), and from lateral sites (with 2 levels of Hemisphere - left and right- and 5 anterior-posterior levels- F3/F4, FC3/FC4, C3/C4, CP3/CP4, P3/P4) were selected for analysis.

Effects of anomalies were assessed by measuring the mean amplitude (average of non-rejected epochs from 0 to 1 000ms after the onset of the key words, calculated relative to a baseline from −200 to 0ms) of ERPs for each participant. Since the materials across the three conditions are not comparable and sentence type is of great interest in the present study, we performed three sets of repeated-measures ANOVAs with within-subject factor of sentence type. For all analyses, original degrees of freedom were reported. A Greenhouse-Geisser correction for sphericity was applied to p-values when more than two levels of a factor were present (Greenhouse & Geisser, 1959). Any main effects not reported below were all non-significant (all *ps* > 0.05).

6.3 Results

6.3.1 Behavioral results

Accuracy for each condition was calculated for each participant. These data were analyzed with ANOVA using sentence type and similarity condition as factors. Overall, the acceptability ratio of sentences in different structures (SV), similar (SN), and unique (AO) were 0.69, 0.91, and 0.77, respectively. Individuals did not respond equally well to acceptable and unacceptable structures, t (14) = 2.47, $p < 0.05$. Individuals responded more accurately to the acceptable than the unacceptable structures in the three structures. Specifically, the means for acceptable and unacceptable sentence are 0.82 vs. 0.56 for SV, 0.94 vs. 0.88 for SN and 0.82 vs. 0.72 for AO. Results from ANOVAs showed that incorrect sentences were more acceptable than correct sentences for SV, F (1, 14) = 2.99, $p = 0.065$, indicating the subjects are not liable to reject the incorrect sentences; however, there was no difference between acceptable and unacceptable for SN, F (1, 14) = 0.078, $p = 0.78$ and for AO, F (1, 14) = 2.01, $p = 0.18$.

6.3.2 ERP Results

On average, only a few segments were affected by artifacts, and there were 86.7% artifact-free segments in SV sentences, 90% in SN and 86% in AO. The grand averages across participants for each condition were then calculated. The grand-average waveforms for acceptable and unacceptable sentences for the three similarity conditions were shown in Fig. 2- Fig. 4, respectively.

The mean latency and amplitudes around peak of the ERP components are shown in the following table. To evaluate those predictions, we ran two sets of ANOVAs, the first corresponding to the early N400 time window (330 - 430ms poststimulus) and the second corresponding to a P600 time window (528 - 628ms poststimulus).

Table 8 Mean latencies and peak amplitudes across conditions

Sentence Type		N400				P600			
		Latency		Amplitude		Latency		Amplitude	
		M	*SD*	*M*	*SD*	*M*	*SD*	*M*	*SD*
SV	Acceptable	384.80	14.76	-2.15	1.53	560.93	16.88	3.13	1.18
	Unacceptable	388.00	15.95	-2.35	1.65	611.07	18.12	3.13	1.49
SN	Acceptable	372.00	14.76	-1.20	1.14	558.27	16.88	3.24	2.01
	Unacceptable	374.80	15.95	-0.88	1.37	569.73	18.12	4.64	2.79
AO	Acceptable	386.13	14.76	-2.26	2.06	593.60	16.88	3.10	1.69
	Unacceptable	375.33	15.95	-2.10	1.99	576.53	18.12	3.85	2.21

6.3.2.1 Anomaly effect in the different structure (SV)

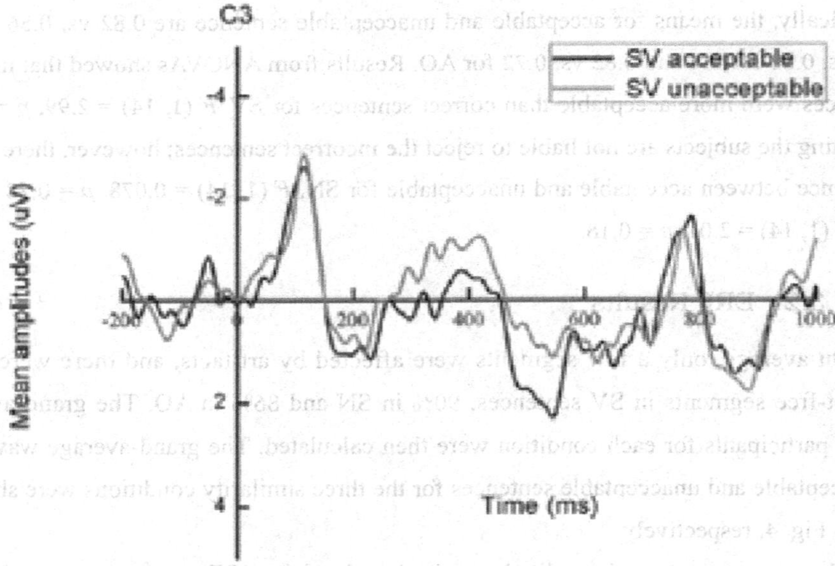

Figure 2 Grande average waveforms for SV

In the N400 time window, ANOVA showed that unacceptable sentences elicited larger negative effect than the acceptable sentences in C3 [F (1, 14) = 4.23, p = 0.059], indicating the N400 effect revealed in the violation in SV. In the P600 time window, the positive-going waves in the unacceptable sentences were not larger than the acceptable sentences. The results indicate that grammaticalization responses to SN are not found.

6.3.2.2 Anomaly effect in the similar structure (SN)

In the N400 time window, ANOVA showed there was no effect of sentence type. In the P600 time window, unacceptable structures elicited more positive going ERP responses than the acceptable structures in Pz, F3, C1, C3, CP1, CP3, P1, P3 (all $ps < 0.05$). The widely-distributed significant main effect indicates that learners are sensitive to syntactic violations, which is revealed in the P600 effect.

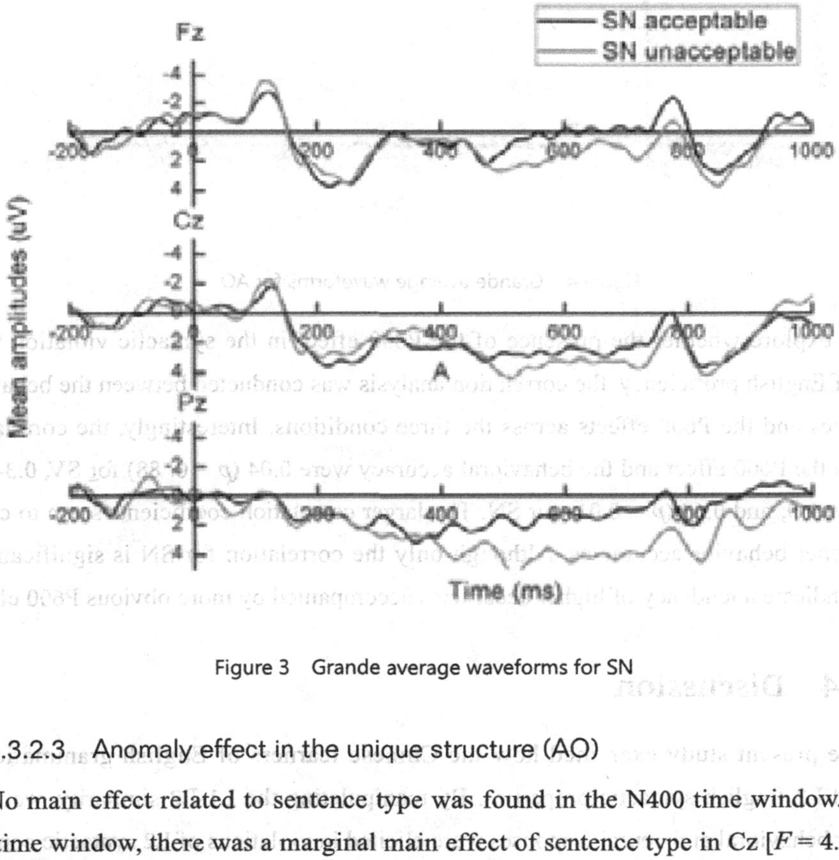

Figure 3 Grande average waveforms for SN

6.3.2.3 Anomaly effect in the unique structure (AO)

No main effect related to sentence type was found in the N400 time window. In the P600 time window, there was a marginal main effect of sentence type in Cz [$F = 4.71$], Pz [$F = 6.88$], C1 [$F = 7.28$], CP1 [$F = 7.07$], P1 [$F = 10.72$], P3 [$F = 9.19$], P2 [$F = 7.25$], all $ps < 0.05$.

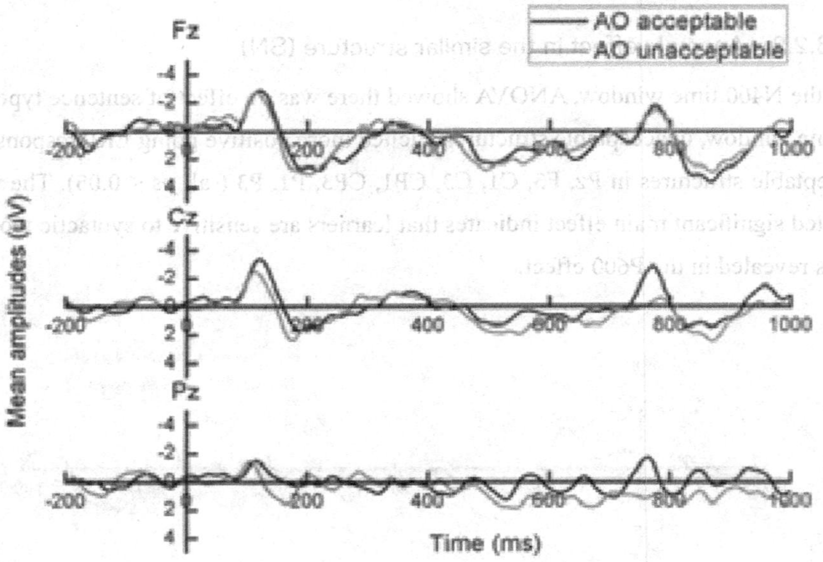

Figure 4 Grande average waveforms for AO

To explore whether the presence of the P600 effect in the syntactic violation was a result of English proficiency, the correlation analysis was conducted between the behavioral accuracies and the P600 effects across the three conditions. Interestingly, the correlations between the P600 effect and the behavioral accuracy were 0.04 (p = 0. 88) for SV, 0.34 (p = 0.22) for AO, and 0.63 (p = 0.01) for SN. The larger correlation coefficients seem to couple with higher behavior accuracies. Although only the correlation for SN is significant, the results indicate a tendency of higher accuracies accompanied by more obvious P600 effect.

6.4 Discussion

The present study examined how the Chinese learners of English grammaticalize different L2 English syntactic properties. By manipulating the L1-L2 similarity, we found stronger behavioral and neural responses were elicited in violations of L2 syntactic contrasts that were expressed in the L1 than those that mismatch between the L1 and L2. Overall, the results show that the distribution of the effect varies as a function of sentence structure. L1-L2 similarity plays an important role in the speed of L2 grammaticalization.

The asymmetrical hypothesis posited that Chinese natives have the neural networks that are likely to assimilate English into Chinese system. Accordingly, the violations in the three syntactic rules are supposed to elicit an N400 effect, which was found robust in L1 Chinese subject-verb agreement violations (Dowens et al., 2011). However, the present findings indicate the N400 effect only for the SV structure. The results dispute the assimilation effect. Coupling the behavioral data with syntactic violation effects on the neural system across the three grammatical structures, we tentatively propose that Chinese natives are likely to accommodate the neural systems on the demands during L2 syntactic grammaticalizing.

When comparing across different studies on Chinese-English bilinguals (Chen et al., 2007; Guo et al., 2009), we found language proficiency is a possible factor for the accommodation processes. There was a tendency of shifting from N400 in non-English majors and to P600 in L2 majors (English majors in the current study and Spanish majors in Dowens et al. (2011). Non-L2 majors vs. L2 majors may result in whether the P600 was evoked. The contrasting view attaches great importance of to language experience. Theoretically, the neurocognitive model posits that learners rely first on declarative knowledge, revealing the N400 during processing L2 grammar, and then on the procedural knowledge, thus eliciting the P600 (Ullman, 2001).

Further, the accuracy rates for SV (0.69), AO (0.77) and SN (0.91) are increasing. This pattern corresponds with the shift from the no P600 effect to the P600 effect. L2 grammatical rule acquisition level, indexed by the accuracy in the behavior data, devotes to the shift from semantic processing (the N400) to syntactic processing (the P600) during L2 grammaticalization. Semantic versus syntactic difference is related to how fast L2 learners can grammaticalize the non-native patterns. The results indicate that the P600 could be an ERP marker that might help language learners identify what they learn. Even though learners might not show the sensitivity to a novel structure in behavioral judgment, the P600 might assist the learners in harnessing the sensitivity.

6.5 Conclusion

L2 proficiency and L1-L2 similarity interact in complex ways in shaping patterns of neural responses in L2 grammaticalization. Nevertheless, a novel structure in the L2 is acquirable, which could be observed from the neural processing patterns and the accuracy data. Despite, in order to determine whether the different processing patterns across the three structures are qualitative or quantitative, a longitudinal study is necessary. Besides, a larger number of L2 learners should be evaluated their language proficiency to identify possible individual differences.

Chapter 7 The locus of bilinguals' syntactic grammaticalization: A process of transfer or competition?

Abstract: Similarity between the native language (L1) and the second language (L2) determines the possibility of transfer and thus facilitates the learning at the grammatical aspects of an L2. The present study is aimed at exploring the locus of language similarity effects on online syntactic processing. The ERP (Event-related potentials) data from Chinese native learners of English with moderate to advanced English proficiency were collected when they performed L2 English grammatical judgment. Two experiments were run with the same stimuli but with different processing speeds. The stimuli varied in the degree of L1-L2 contrast: unique or conflicting. It was found that when processing resources are limited in fast processing speed and in conflicting features, the stronger L1 Chinese patterns will return. The findings indicate L1 and L2 remain potentially active during online processing and the competition between L1 and L2 is likely to persist even in later stages of language learning.

Key words: language similarity ERP grammaticalization competition transfer

7.1 Introduction

When adults attempt to learn a second language (L2), they start with an already-established grammar system, replete with well-articulated concepts and labels for those concepts. They are influenced by typical properties in their first language (L1). Recent studies indicate the similarity between L1 and L2 determines the possibility of transfer and thus implicates both the L2 acquisition rate and on-line processing patterns (Osterhout & Nicol, 1999; McLaulin et al., 2010).

According to the transfer hypothesis, adults are able to transfer large segments of their L1 over new L2 (e.g., Verhoeven, 2007; Wang, Perfetti & Liu, 2005). Positive transfer occurs when the features across two languages are similar; while cross language mismatches will impede the process of learning. Contrastively, the competition hypothesis views transfer as arising from the fact that the L1 and L2 remain potentially active during online processing (e.g., Frenck-Mestre, 2006; Kroll, Bogulski & McClain, 2012; Kroll & Tokowicz, 2006; Marian & Spivey, 2003). Although the transfer hypothesis and the competition hypothesis propose similar assumptions for the L2 grammaticalization processes, the two theories have different consequences (Tokowicz & MacWhinney, 2005). Transfer from the L1 to the L2 would cause an initial problem. The problem should be resolved as L2 information is learned. In comparison, online competition between languages is a more pervasive problem. Although L2 learners will eventually revise the L1-like structures to more closely match those appropriate to the L2 with the increasing of L2 fluency, the problem is likely to persist even in later stages of language learning.

Syntactic aspects are particularly difficult to master during later acquisition (e.g., McLaughlin et al., 2004). The major concern of the present study was whether the L2 grammaticalization was a process of transfer from L1 or a competition between L1 and L2 for Chinese native learners of English. Within linguistic theory (Radford, 1988), grammatical properties are encoded in the morphology of grammatical categories, which are associated with grammatical features such as number, case, gender, person. These features vary between Chinese and English. English has subject-verb agreement in terms of verbal person and number. But Chinese verbs have no inflectional markings to indicate the gender, number, case, and tense. Despite the few neurophysiological studies on cross language transfer (e.g., Dowens et al., 2011; Mclauglin, et al. 2010; Oren & Breznitz, 2005), more neurosphysiological evidence on syntactic interference in bilinguals is still necessary for Chinese-English bilinguals.

The ERP (Event-related potential) technique has the advantages to temporally unfold neural events associated with different subprocesses of language processes. It provides a direct measure of real time brain activity at the millisecond level. The sensitivity of ERPs makes them appealing for examining the grammaticalizaiton stages. Two ERP components are important in L2 grammaticalization (Mclauglin, et al., 2010; Osterhout & Nicol, 1999). The P600 effect has lately been reported to index grammatical complexity or an encounter with less preferred syntactic structures. It is an indicator of syntactic grammaticalization.

The N400 is attributed to lexical integration and integration process necessary to form a meaningful representation of the sentence. The N400 observed in an L2 syntactic anomalies are interpreted as weaker or slower morphosyntactic processes in beginning stages of grammaticalization or increased semantic integration (wrap-up) demands in L2 (Weber & Lavric, 2008). The N400 effect found in Chinese native learners of an L2 was usually attributed to low language proficiency and the influence from the first language (Chen et al., 2007; Dowens et al., 2011). Less research was devoted to whether the L2 syntactic properties exist in L1.

Thus, the goal of the present study was pursued by measuring the ERP responses to two different L2 syntactic features. The two structures were adapted from Xue et al. (2013): first, different structures (subject-verb agreement, SV) for which the L2 syntactic features conflict with L1 and thus on-line processing demands representations of both L1 and L2; second, unique structures (auxiliary omission, AO) that differ between the two languages and no competition from L1 is evoked during L2 syntactic processing. To tap into the possibility of transfer effect, the task was manipulated by using two different speeds for presenting the stimuli (fast vs. slow processing speed). Generally, it could be predicted from perspective of the transfer hypothesis that the processing speed does not elicit different on-line processing patterns. In contrast, from perspective of the competitive hypothesis, the N400 effect will return with the more taxed cognitive resources in the fast processing speed.

7.2 Method

7.2.1 Participants

The present study included thirty-five English majors (seven men, average age 20.20 years, range 19 to 22 years) from Beijing International Studies University of China. All reported Chinese as L1 and English as L2. They had a history of English learning for an average of 8.07 years. They had English Immersion classes for more than 1 year (range from 1 to 2 years). According to a 10-point self-rating scale, the means for their English reading, writing, speaking and speech comprehension were respectively 7.53, 7.00, 6.87, and 6.87. All participants had normal or corrected to normal vision and got compensation for their participation.

7.2.2 Procedure

The sentences were presented in a random order determined by the computer program E-Prime, which also recorded the accuracy and reaction times and sent critical word onset information to the ERP acquisition software. By following the similar procedure used in Tokowicz and MacWhinney's (2005). Sentences were presented words by words, at the center of the computer screen. Participants read sentences on the computer screen. During a trial prior to each sentence, a fixation cross appeared at the center of the computer screen. Participants were asked to blink when the fixation was on the screen. After the offset of the final word of the sentence, a blank screen appeared for 200ms, followed by a question mark "?" that served as a prompt. When the prompt appeared, participants were supposed to respond by pressing either "1" or "2" on the computer keyboard; they pressed a button marked "1" with their left hand to indicate if they thought the sentence was acceptable and a button marked "2" with their right hand if they thought the sentence was unacceptable. Participants were randomly allocated to either fast or slow stimulus-presenting speed versions. For fast speed version, each stimulus word remained on the screen for 300ms with a blank screen appearing for 350ms between words. For slow speed, each stimulus remained on the screen for 500ms with a blank screen appearing for 350ms between words.

7.2.3 Stimuli

The English syntactic stimuli include two experimental structures (see Table 9). These stimuli appeared in Xue et al. (2013). The key stimuli included 120 English sentences, with 60 items for each experimental condition. Half of the sentences were in their acceptable form and half in unacceptable form. There were 10 instances of each structure type. The sentences were randomly assigned to either of two versions, with right hand and left hand response types counterbalanced. The critical word in each sentence was at the violation point. As shown in Table 9, in unacceptable sentences, the critical word was defined as the word at which a violation was noticeable, for instance, the word "*eat*" in "*The cat eat the food that Mary gives them*". In acceptable sentences, the critical word was in the same position as the critical word in the corresponding unacceptable sentence, e.g., the word "*eat*" in "*The cats eat the food that Mary gives them*".

Table 9 Examples of the two experimental conditions

Condition	Type	Example
SV	Acceptable	*The cats eat the food that Mary gives them.*
	Unacceptable	*The cat eat the food that Mary gives them.*
AO	Acceptable	*These grapevines grow well in sandy regions.*
	Unacceptable	*These grapevines growing well in sandy regions.*

Note: The underlined parts are the critical words.

7.2.4 Data acquisition

Continuous EEG was recorded from 64 active electrodes (ActiCap, Brain Products GmbH, Munich) at standard international 10-20 system, referenced to bilateral mastoids and grounded to forehead. To control for vertical eye movements, a vertical electro-oculogram (VEOG) was recorded from Ag/AgCl electrodes placed closely above and below the left eye. Horizontal eye movements were measured by a horizontal electro-oculogram (HEOG) recorded from Ag/AgCl electrodes that placed at the outer canthus of each eye. All impedances were kept below 20 kΩ during the experiment. EEG signals were bandpass filtered between 0.01 and 100Hz, and amplified and digitized at a rate of 500Hz using a BrainAmp amplifier (Brain Products GmbH, Munich). All EEG data were collected using Brain Vision Recorder software from Brain Products.

7.2.5 Data analyses

Excluding five subjects whose accuracies in grammatical judgment were lower than 50%, there were remaining 30 subjects, respectively, 15 participating in the fast speed experiment and another 15 participating in the slow speed experiment. The analyses were conducted on data from these participants. Past studies indicate that the ERPs produced by beginning L2 learners show sensitivity to grammaticality (Tokowicz & MacWhinney, 2005). Actually, the incorrect trials are evidence for the process of language acquisition. Thus, our analysis of the ERP data included both correct and incorrect trials. The EEG data were processed offline using Brain Vision Analyzer 2. They were re-referenced to the mean of the left and right mastoid, and filtered with a 0.1Hz high-pass filter to remove drifts and a 30Hz filter to eliminate line noise. 46 Electrode sites (AF3, AF4, C1, C2, C3, C4, C5, C6, CP1, CP2, CP3, CP4, CP5, CP6, CPz, CZ, F1, F2, F3, F4, F5, F6, FC1, FC2, FC3, FC4,

FC5, FC6, Fp2, Fpz, Fz, O1, O2, Oz, P1, P2, P3, P4, P5, P6, PO3, PO4, PO7, PO8, Poz, PZ) were selected for analysis.

Effects of anomalies were assessed by measuring the mean amplitude (average of non-rejected epochs from 0 to 800ms after the onset of the key words, calculated relative to a baseline from −200 to 0 ms) of ERPs for each participant. Since the materials across the two conditions are not comparable and sentence type is of great interest in the present study, we performed two sets of repeated-measures ANOVAs with within-subject factor of sentence type. For all analyses, original degrees of freedom were reported. A Greenhouse-Geisser correction for sphericity was applied to p-values when more than two levels of a factor were present (Greenhouse & Geisser, 1959). Unless indicated, any main effects not reported below were all non-significant (all $ps > 0.05$).

7.3 Results

7.3.1 Behavioral results

Accuracy for each condition was calculated for each participant. For the slow speed, the acceptability ratio of sentences in different (SV) and unique (AO) structures were 68% and 73%, respectively. The means for acceptable and unacceptable sentence are 0.73 vs. 0.62 for SV and 0.75 vs. 0.70 for AO. For the fast speed, overall, the acceptability ratio of sentences in different (SV) and unique (AO) structures were 61% and 62%. Specifically, the means for acceptable and unacceptable sentence are 0.72 vs. 0.50 for SV, and 0.73 vs. 0.51 for AO. The accuracies between the fast and slow speeds are not significantly different for SV [$F(1, 28) = 2.63$, $p = 0.12$], but the accuracy for AO in the slow speed ($M = 0.73$, $SD = 0.13$) is higher than the fast speed ($M = 0.62$, $SD = 0.13$), $F(1, 28) = 5.08$, $p = 0.03$.

7.3.2 ERP Results

7.3.2.1 Fast speed

Table 10 Mean latencies and peak amplitudes of ERP components for the fast speed

	condition	acceptability	Latency	Fz	Cz	Pz
N400	SV	acceptable	406.53	−0.8	−2.04	−0.63
		unacceptable	390.4	−1.62	−1.35	−1.16
	AO	acceptable	386.53	−0.52	−1.48	−0.85
		unacceptable	379.6	0.55	−0.92	−0.73
P600	SV	acceptable	593.47	2.47	1.94	2.69
		unacceptable	600.27	1.85	2.18	1.56
	AO	acceptable	583.6	2.77	2.43	1.11
		unacceptable	575.2	3.57	2.84	2.06

On average, only a few segments were affected by artifacts, and there were 83.89% artifact-free segments in SV sentences and 80.22% in AO. The grand averages across participants for each condition were then calculated. The mean latency and amplitudes around peak of the ERP components across conditions are shown in Table 10. The grand-average waveforms differences between unacceptable and unacceptable sentences for the two similarity conditions were shown in the following figures respectively. We ran two sets of ANOVAs on mean neural activities in about 100ms around peak, the first corresponding to the early N400 time window (330-430ms poststimulus) and the second corresponding to a P600 time window (528-628ms poststimulus).

Anomaly effect in the different structure (SV)

Analysis of mean activity in the area relative to 330 to 430ms poststimulus showed no N400 effect. Analysis of mean activity in the area relative to time 530.00ms - 630.00ms showed that the unacceptable sentence evoked larger P600 effect in FC1 [F (1, 14) = 5.24, p = 0.038] and CP4 [F (1, 14) = 9.37, p = 0.008]. (Fig.5, see color page 1)

Anomaly effect in the unique structure (AO)

Analysis of mean activity in the N400 time window found no significant N400 effect, while analysis of mean activity in the P600 time window showed that the P600 effect was significant in AF3 [F (1, 14) = 6.48, p = 0.023], F3 [F (1, 24)=5.28, p = 0.038], F5 [F (1, 14) =

5.52, $p = 0.034$], Fp2 [F (1, 14) = 4.71, $p = 0.048$], Fpz [F (1, 14) = 6.14, $p = 0.027$], CPz [F (1, 14) = 4.87, $p = 0.044$] and PZ [F (1, 14)=5.21, $p = 0.039$]. (Fig.6, see color page 1)

7.3.2.2 Slow speed

There were 84.44% artifact-free segments in SV sentences and 79.56% in AO. Similar analyses were performed. The mean latency and amplitudes around peak of the ERP components are shown in Table 11. Mean latencies revealed that the peak amplitudes for the slow speed presentation was delayed. Thus, the two sets of ANOVAs were run on mean neural activities in about 100ms around peak, the first corresponding to the early N400 time window (348 to 448ms poststimulus) and the second corresponding to a P600 time window (560 to 660ms poststimulus).

Table 11 Mean latencies and peak amplitudes of ERP components for the slow speed

	Condition	acceptability	Latency	Fz	Cz	Pz
N400	SV	acceptable	387.47	−0.9	−0.98	0.74
		unacceptable	373.47	−1.68	−1.72	0.14
	AO	acceptable	400	−0.71	−1.34	0.25
		unacceptable	396.13	−0.68	−0.63	1.31
P600	SV	acceptable	598.4	1.74	2.35	1.94
		unacceptable	635.47	1.4	1.65	1.24
	AO	acceptable	620.13	1.63	2.09	1.98
		unacceptable	617.2	1.9	2.52	2.63

Anomaly effect in the different structure (SV)

Analysis of mean activity in the area relative to time 348.00-448.00ms (the N400 time window) showed the unacceptable sentences evoked more negative waves than the acceptable sentences in FC4 [F (1, 14) = 5.91, $p = 0.029$]. Analysis of mean activity in the area relative to time 560.00-660.00ms (the P600 time window) indicated more frontal P600 effects in F1 [F (1, 14) = 4.92, $p = 0.044$], F3 [F (1, 14) = 7.62, $p = 0.015$] and CP1 [F (1, 14) = 5.30, $p = 0.037$].(Fig.7, see color page 2)

Anomaly effect in the unique structure (AO)

Analysis of mean activity in the area relative to time 348.00-448.00ms showed no significant N400 effect. Analysis of mean activity in the area relative to time 550.00-

660.00ms found significant P600 effects in FC1[F (1, 14) = 6.03, p = 0.028], FC3 [F (1, 14) = 7.89, p = 0.014], FC5 [F (1, 14) = 6.43, p = 0.024], C2 [F (1, 14) = 4.68, p = 0.048], and C5 [F (1, 14) = 8.58, p = 0.011]. (Fig.8, see color page 2)

7.4 Discussion

The aim of the present study was to examine the ERP waveform characteristics of Chinese-English bilinguals when processing two different syntactic properties at different processing speeds. Using experimental paradigm of our previous study (Xue et al., 2013), we investigated patterns of brain activation of later bilinguals when they made grammatical judgment at slow or fast processing speed.

As predicted on the previous studies (e.g., Mclaughin et al., 2010; Tokowicz & MacWhinney, 2005; Xue et al., 2013), for the fast speed experiment, the more widely-spread P600 effects were observed in AO than in SV. The results on the fast speed experiment replicate the findings in Xue et al. (2013), indicating that conflicting features between L1 and L2 will impede new language acquisition. The P600 effects in AO revealed in both fast and slow processing speeds experiments confirm that new syntactic features are acquirable both explicitly and implicitly.

The most significant finding is that L1 and L2 remain potentially active during online L2 syntactic processing. As show in the ANOVA analysis for SV, more widely spread P600 effects were found in the slow speed than in the fast speed. The map view also reveals more obvious N400 effects for SV in the fast speed, although they are not significant statistically. The results indicate the N400 and the P600 are both active during on-line processing. It is well established that the N400 is elicited in L1 Chinese morphosyntactic violation (Liu & Perfetti, 2003). Some reports the N400 effect when Chinese natives process syntactic properties in L2, and the researchers attributed the N400 effect to the influence of L1 (Chen et al., 2007; Liu & Perfetti, 2003). Thus, the above results could be alternatively interpreted as a return of the dominant processing pattern, when participants process an L2 syntactic property with taxed cognitive resources. Theoretically, the findings could be explained by the competitive hypothesis (Tokowicz & MacWhinney, 2005). When the L1 and L2 provide contrasting interpretations of a given structure, the stronger pattern will typically dominate, especially at times when the language system is taxed and processing resources are limited. Since the participants are intermediate-to-advanced learners of English. Thus, the present findings suggest the competition between L1 and L2 processing patterns is likely to persist even in later stages of language learning.

The most important outcome of the study was the revelation of different strategies adopted during grammaticalizing different L2 syntactic properties. On the one hand, the neural processing pattern for AO in the two different speeds is distinct from that for SV. On the other, more obvious P600 effects were observed for AO in the fast speed than in the slow speed. The P600 effect difference could not be explained by language proficiency effect, since the participants are randomly selected from the same grade and the on-line judgment accuracies are equivalent for the two groups ($p > 0.05$). The P600, indexing the grammaticalization (Ullman, 2002), seems to be dominant despite the cognitive resource is taxed and accuracy is lower in the fast-speed presentation. The possible explanation is that when grammaticalizing an L2-unique syntactic rule, L2 learners are likely to adopt a different strategy from that in learning conflicting properties. In other words, the L2 learners are likely to accommodate the neural system to different learning process (Xue et al., 2013). The bilingual's language system may create optimal conditions for learning grammar in a new language and the enhanced cognitive control enables effective selection of the syntactic rules during on-line processing (Kroll, Bogulski & McClain, 2012).

7.5 Conclusion

Several conclusions could be drawn. First, language similarity plays an important role in L2 syntactic grammaticalization. The rate of L2 grammaticalization is dependent on the online computation cost. Second, L1 and L2 processing patterns remain potentially active during the process of L2 syntactic grammaticalization. Finally, distinct strategies might be adopted when the L2 learners grammaticalize different syntactic rules.

Chapter 8 The role of age of acquisition on Chinese native learners' English word processing: An ERP Study

Abstract: The present study was aimed at distinguishing processing of an early from a late learned L2 words for Chinese natives who learns English as a foreign language. The behavior data and ERP data were collected when 28 Chinese native adult learners of English performed a semantic related judgment task. Analysis on accuracy and reaction time showed that early learned words had an advantage in processing accuracy and speed. ERP results showed earlier acquired words are easier and quicker to process, compared with later acquired words; there was a larger AoA effect for characters from low-predictive families than for characters from high-predictive families. More important, early acquired words had more negative-going N400 effects activation than late acquire words in the central lobe. The results indicate early acquired words have more semantic interconnections than late acquired words and the locus of AoA effects might derive from the way word forms are stored related to the semantic concepts.

Key words: AOA Event-related potentials semantic processing Chinese-native learners of English

8.1 Introduction

Age of acquisition (AoA) refers to the age at which a concept or a skill is learned (Hernandez & Li, 2007). AoA is an important variable for lexical processing (Brysbaert, van Wijnendaele & De Deyne, 2000). Early-learned (early AoA) words have advantage over late AoA words in processing accuracy and speed (Belke, Brysbaert, Meyer & Ghyselinck, 2005; Brysbaert, et al., 2000; Hernandez, Hofmann & Kotz, 2007; Zevin & Seidenberg,

2002). The AoA effect on language processing has cognitive and neuronal bases (Belke et al., 2005; Chen, Zhou, Dunlap & Perfetti, 2007; Hernandez & Li, 2007). However, little research is devoted to the cognitive and neuronal mechanisms underlying the AoA effect on L2 English word acquisition in Chinese speakers. According to current policies in China, the second or foreign language (L2) English is usually offered in the public schools at the age of 9 (about Grade 3 or 4 of elementary school). The present study is aimed at distinguishing processing of an early from a late learned L2 words for Chinese natives who learn English as a foreign language.A large body of research has detected age-related developmental changes in language processing. For instance, the left lateralization of the neuronal networks involved in word recognition changes with age (Spironelli & Angrilli, 2009). To be more specific, the functional lateralization of linguistic neuronal networks involved in automatic word recognition and in phonological processing is not yet developed in linguistically competent children aged 10 years, whereas the observed lateralization is relatively stable and not degraded in moderately aged subjects. On the other hand, a delayed AoA is associated with differential neuronal activation patterns during language processing (Hernandez et al., 2007). In an ERP (event-related potential) study, the N400 effect is significantly smaller and later for older adults when target words in strongly constrained contexts are compared with weakly constrained contexts (Federmeier & Kutas, 2005). The authors attributed the results to the decreased ability for older adults to make use of the richer information available from strongly constraining contexts to guide semantic processing. In a fMRI study on deaf adults with AoA of sign language acquisition ranging from birth to 14 years, AoA was found to be linearly and negatively related to activation levels in anterior language regions and positively related to activation levels in posterior visual regions for both grammatical judgment and phonemic-hand judgment tasks (Mayberry, Chen, Witcher & Klein, 2011). Specifically, deaf native signers, whose age-onset of language acquisition was from birth, activated the classic left hemisphere language regions. However, signers with older age-onset of language acquisition showed neuronal activation patterns that deviate from the classic one. In the case of second language processing, evidence has also indicated differences in cortical organization for L1 and L2, especially for "late bilinguals" (Kim et al., 1997; Weber-Fox & Neville, 1996). AoA is significantly correlated with the cortical thickness of the inferior frontal gyrus (IFG). Later acquisition of an L2 seems to be associated with significantly thicker cortex in the left IFG and thinner cortex in the right IFG (Klein, Moka, Chen & Watkins, 2014). Weber-Fox and

Neville (1996) examined how early and late L2 learners processed sentences with semantic or syntactic anomalies when ERPs were compared. Regarding syntactic processing, the results revealed differences between native speakers and early L2 learners who began L2 acquisition between 1 and 3 years of life; in contrast, for semantic processing, differences between monolinguals and L2 speakers were observed only in individuals who learned L2 after the age of 11. Wartenburger et al. (2003) found there were no differences in semantic judgements between early and late high proficiency subjects. Whereas, for syntactic anomalies, there were significant differences between different AoA groups, but very subtle differences between the two late AoA groups that differed on proficiency. These findings indicate AoA of L2 has an effect on later language processing, and the neuronal patterns with grammatical rules are influenced by L2 AoA to a greater extent than those associated with semantic processing. Further, neuronal activity is greater for irregular grammatical items than regular items and differential recruitment of brain areas associated with grammatical processing in late L2 learners (Wartenburger et al., 2003). Hernandez, et al. (2007) found that when early and late learners were compared when they made gender decisions to regular and irregular words, increased activity was found in left BA 44 for irregular words. Specifically, processing of irregular grammatical gender led to increased activity in left BA 44 and adjacent areas in the left IFG. Further, within group-comparison analysis showed that neuronal activity for irregular words extended into left BA 47 for late learners and into left BA 6 for early learners. Direct comparisons between-groups revealed increased activity in left BA 44/45 for irregular items indicating the need for more extensive syntactic processing in late learners.As is well-established, metalinguistic awareness regarding radical and phonetic rules has a facilitative effect on Chinese character development (Ku & Anderson, 2001), since in Chinese writing system, about 81% of characters in modern Chinese are semantic-phonetic compounds consisting of a semantic radical and a phonetic component (Li & Kang, 1993). In contrast with Chinese, the alphabetic scripts like English have the grapheme-phoneme correspondence rules. It is relevant to know whether Chinese natives take advantage of English grapheme-phoneme correspondence rules at different stage of language acquisition. Thus, the present study addressed the issue of whether late-acquired English words might have different neuronal representation as compared to early-acquired words for Chinese natives who learned English as a foreign language relatively very late in life. Particularly, the present study investigated how the different word AoAs was related to the regularity in orthography-phonology mapping rules during Chinese natives' L2 processing. Not much research has investigated L2 AoA-related effects on the regularity of orthography-phonology mapping; thus, this study aims at contributing to this research topic. The present study addressed two research questions; whether early versus late learned L2 words elicited different neuronal processing patterns, and how orthography-phonology mapping regularity was modulated by word AoAs during on-line word processing. A 3 (AoA: early vs intermediate vs. late words) × 2 (regularity: regular and irregular) × 2 (semantic context: related vs unrelated) × 2 (hemisphere: left vs right) × 3 (lobe: frontal vs. central vs. posterior) within-subjects design was adopted. We employed a semantic judgment task, in which participants were required to judge whether the two words in a word pair were related in meaning (***). The semantic relatedness task was thought to evoke print-to-meaning mapping to retrieve the semantic relationship, and thus would be a suitable task to examine the semantic processing. This task also manipulated the orthography-phonology mapping rules. EEG data was collected and data analysis focused on the N400 component as semantic unrelatedness or incongruities elicit a negative-going ERP which peaks around 400ms, known as the N400, following the onset of the anomalous word and is largest over central-parietal electrode sites (Kutas & Hillyard, 1984). Findings from the current study will provide further understanding of AoA-related influence on the neuronal patterns underlying L2 word processing as well as shed light on the locus of the AoA effects. We hypothesized that the neuronal processing patterns might be modulated by task conditions differentially with respect to AoA words. When the orthography-phonology (O-P) was highly predictable, as it was for consistent words, AoA effects would be reduced; In contrast, when the O-P mapping was unpredictable, as it was for exception words, AoA effects would be comparably much larger. Therefore, later acquired words should cause larger N400 amplitude in irregular words. It was predicted that early acquired word should be more accessible than late-acquired words in the semantic judgment task. Accordingly, the semantic context should be stronger for semantic relatedness of early acquired words than for late-acquired words, and semantic context effects on semantic relatedness judgment latencies and N400 amplitudes should be more pronounced for early-acquired words.

8.2 Methods

8.2.1 Participants

The participants were 28 English major students from Beijing International Studies University of China, whose first language was Chinese and second language was English. The participants' average age was 20.7 years old, ranged from 18 to 22 (SD = 0.85). They have studied English for an average of 8.4 years (SD = 3.11). The mean AoA of L2 English was 8.36 (SD = 2.70). According to a 10-point self-rating scale (describe the anchors; e.g., 1 = not proficient and 10 = highly proficient??), their mean English proficiency was 7.7 (SD = 1.42). All participants had normal or corrected to normal vision and received compensation for their participations.

8.2.2 Materials

Early acquired words, intermediate acquired words and late acquired words were, respectively, selected from the third-year primary school English textbook, the second-year junior school English textbook and the second-year senior school English textbook. All selected words were part of compulsory education in primary and middle schools so as to ensure simplicity and familiarity of the chosen words to the participants. The stimuli comprised 90 English words, with 30 early AoA words (15 regular and 15 irregular words), 30 intermediate AoA words (15 regular and 15 irregular words) and 30 late AoA words (15 regular and 15 irregular words). Regularity was defined on the orthography-phonology predictability. Two sets of semantic related vs. unrelated word pairs were generated for the 90 words. There were another 180 English word pairs were generated as fillers with half of them being semantically related and the other half being unrelated (see Table 12). The frequency and numbers of letters were strictly matched across the three AoA word groups. The word frequency was based on the *Corpus of Contemporary* American English (COCA, http://corpus.byu.edu/coca/). ANOVA analysis found there were no significant frequency differences between regular and irregular words across the three AoA groups, F (2, 87) = 1.28, p = 0.28. T-tests indicated that there was no difference on frequency, for early AoA, regular vs irregular, t (14) = 0.93, p = 0.36; for intermediate AoA, regular vs irregular, t (14) = 0.39, p = 0.69; for late AoA, regular vs irregular, t (14) = −0.98, p = 0.34. Since these experimental words were selected from textbooks of primary school Grade 3, junior and senior middle school Grade 2 respectively, they represent the actual language input situation in the foreign language context. Despite a thorough perusal of the textbooks, we failed to control the number of letters [for early AoA, $M = 3.93$, $SD = 0.78$; for intermediate AoA, $M = 4.43$, $SD = 0.68$; for late AoA, $M = 5.63$, $SD = 1.03$; $F(2, 87) = 32.03$, $p < 0.001$] or phonemes [for early AoA, $M = 2.87$, $SD = 0.86$; for intermediate AoA, $M = 3.50$, $SD = 0.82$; for late AoA, $M = 4.70$, $SD = 1.06$; $F(2, 87) = 30.89$, $p < 0.001$] in words across the three AoA word groups. However, word frequency, number of word letters, and phonemes were controlled for regular vs. irregular words. ANOVA results showed regular and irregular words were matched on word frequency, $F(1, 88) = 1.04$, $p = 0.31$, on number of letters, $F(1, 88) = 2.38$, $p = 0.13$, and on number of phonemes, $F(1, 88) = 0.13$, $p = 0.72$.

Table 12 Sample of the experiment materials

AoA	Regularity	Targets	Prime 1	Prime 2
			Semantic related	*Semantic unrelated*
Early	Regular	pen	pencil	cup
	Irregular	eye	ear	light
Intermediate	Regular	lake	river	sock
	Irregular	read	write	cheat
Late	Regular	dust	ash	closet
	Irregular	source	origin	feature

The word-pairs across experimental conditions were controlled for the level of semantic relatedness as rated by 15 native Chinese learners of English on a 1-5 point scale. ANOVA analysis with AoA groups of words (early vs. intermediate vs. late) and semantic relation (related vs. unrelated) as two within-subject factors showed there was a main effect of semantic relatedness, $F(2, 58) = 895.22$, $p < 0.001$, but there was no AoA effect on semantic relatedness, $F(2, 58) = 2.67$, $p > 0.05$ or interaction between AoA and semantic relatedness, $F(1, 29) = 0.01$, $p = 0.99$.

8.2.3 Procedure

Each participant read 180 experimental word pairs (either of the two versions, 30 sentences for each AoA word groups) and 180 filler word pairs in random ordering. The

360 word pairs were presented on the screen via the E-Prime software. There were two versions of the materials and the ordering of experimental word pairs and fillers was pseudorandomized. During the process, the participants were seated one meter away from the computer screen. The room was sound-proof to establish a quiet environment so that the participants could concentrate. The experiment lasted for nearly one hour with 3 breaks of 5 minutes each. All participants were tested individually. The participants could see the fixation "+" at the center of the screen for 300ms first, and then the fixation will disappear. The word pairs were presented 500ms for each word, followed by intervals between words for 300ms. After the word pair, a "?" would appear, which would last for 2s. The participants were required to make judgment on the semantic relatedness of the word pairs. Participants gave their responses by pressing one of two buttons with their left or right index finger. The response buttons were counterbalanced across participants. When a response was given, a new trial started. Each participant had a short practice before the ERP experiment.

8.2.4 Data Collection

Continuous EEG was recorded from 64 active electrodes (Act-iCap, Brain Products GmbH, Munich) at standard international 10-20 system, referenced to bilateral mastoids and grounded to forehead. To control for vertical eye movements, a vertical electro-oculogram (VEOG) was recorded from Ag/AgCI electrodes placed closely above and below the left eye. Horizon eye movements were measured by a horizon electro-oculogram (HEGO) recorded from Ag/AgCI electrodes that placed at the outer canthus of each eye. All impedances were kept below 20Ω during the experiment. EEG signals were bandpass filtered between 0.01 and 100Hz, and amplified and digitized at a rate of 500-Hz using a BrainAmp amplifier (Brain Products GmbH, Munich). All EEG data were collected using Brain Vision Recorder (Brain Products GmbH, Munich).

8.2.5 Data Analysis

The EEG data were processed offline using Brain Vision Analyzer 2. They were re-referenced to the mean of the left and right mastoids, and filtered with a 0.1Hz high-pass filter to remove drifts and a 30-Hz filter to eliminate line noise. Based on the findings of prior neuroimaging studies, we selected the following regions to examine the AoA effects. Electrode sites from midline site (3 levels corresponding to Fz, Cz, Pz), frontal area (in both left/right hemispheres: F1/F2, F3/F4, F5/F6, F7/F8), central area (in both left/right hemispheres: C1/C2, C3/C4, C5/C6, C7/C8) and posterior area (in both left/right hemispheres: P1/P2, P3/P4, P5/P6, P7/P8) were selected for analysis of the N400 time window (350-450ms post stimulus). Effects of anomalies were assessed by measuring the mean amplitude (average of non-rejected epochs from 0 to 800ms after the onset of the key words, calculated relative to a baseline from −200 to 0ms) of ERPs for each participant. We performed repeated-measures ANOVAs with grade, semantic relatedness, regularity, hemisphere and lobe as within-subject factors. The primary concern of the analysis on EEG data was whether AoA had effects on neuronal processing of second language words. Thus, analyses focused on the AoA factor. For all analyses, original degrees of freedom were reported. A Greenhouse-Geisser correction for sphericity was applied to p-values when more than two levels of a factor were present (Greenhouse & Geisser, 1959). Any main effects not reported below were all non-significant (all $ps > 0.05$).

8.3 Results

8.3.1 Behavioral results

After excluding those participants whose accuracy rate was below chance level (50%), there were 28 effective participants. The participants had a rather high accuracy rate when making semantic related judgments.

The mean ACC (accurate rate) for early, intermediate, and late AoA were 0.78 ($SD = 0.24$), 0.72 ($SD = 0.21$), and 0.66 ($SD = 0.21$) respectively. ANOVA results of ACCs showed significant difference on ACC across the AoA groups, $F(2, 52) = 4.44$, $p = 0.013$. Accuracy results indicate that earlier acquired words were easier to process than the later acquired words.

The mean RT (reaction time) for early, AoA, and late AoA words were 288.00 ($SD = 129.53$), 314.29 ($SD = 146.14$), and 331.43 ($SD = 160.72$) respectively. ANOVA analysis on RTs showed no significant difference across the AoA groups, $F(2, 52) = 1.256$, $p = 0.287$. The average RT for the late AoA words was the longest; however, it was not statistically different from the RTs for early and intermediate AoA words. Such null result, we believe, could be due to participants being required to judge the semantic relatedness of the words without the condition of being as fast and accurate as possible.

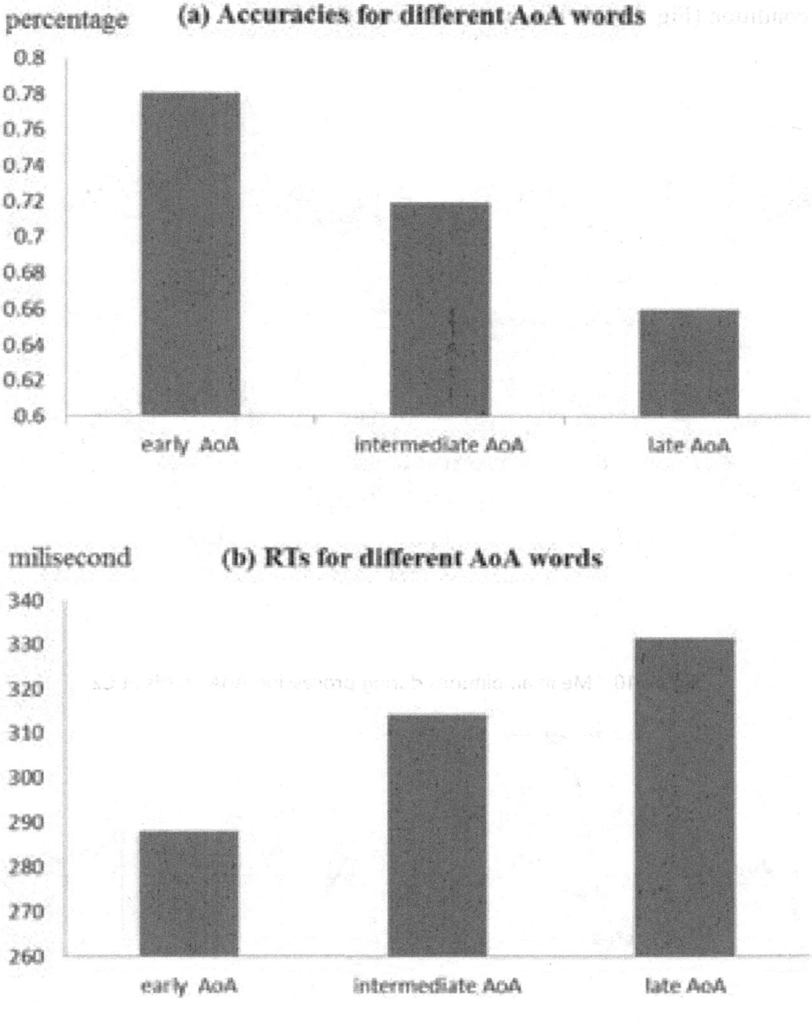

Figure 9 Accuracy rates (a) and reaction times (b) for the three AoA word groups

8.3.2 ERPs results

Visual inspection revealed negative-going waves in the N400 time window (350-450ms post stimulus) and that ERPs for word processing were more negative-going in the frontal and central areas. EEG data were exemplified in the Cz electrode. For earlier acquired words, N400 amplitudes were more negative going than that of later acquired words (Fig.

10) and semantic unrelated word pairs evoked more negative going than the semantic related condition (Fig. 11), so the materials were reliable.

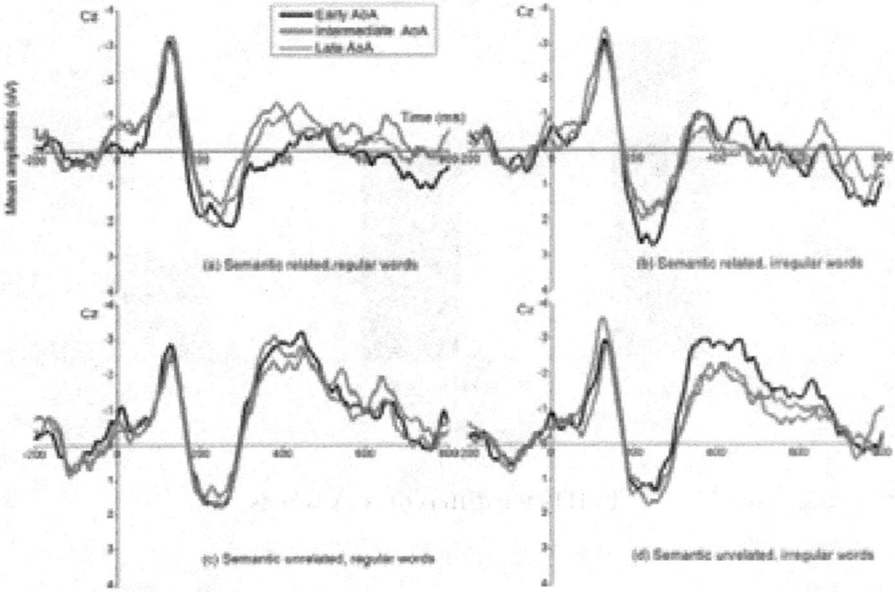

Figure 10　Mean amplitudes during processing AoA words at Cz

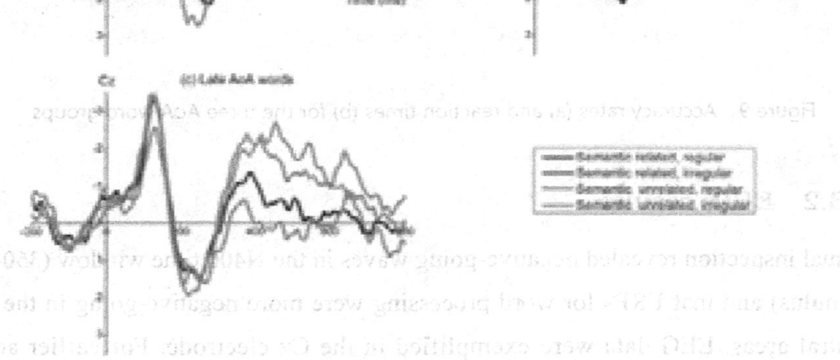

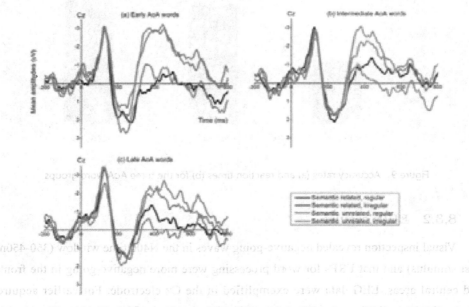

Figure 11　Early, intermediate and late AoA words in different conditions at Cz

Mean N400 amplitudes were, respectively, $M = 0.39$, $SD = 0.21$ for early AoA words, $M = 0.50$, $SD = 0.21$ for intermediate AoA, and $M = 0.74$, $SD = 0.23$ for late AoA; F (2, 52) = 3.44, $p = 0.04$. The analysis on mean N400 amplitudes also showed a main effect of hemisphere, F (1, 26) = 7.25, p=0.012 and a main effect of lobe, F (2, 52) =25.55, $p <$ 0.001. There was a main effect of semantic context, for semantic related, $M = 1.06$, $SD =$ 0.21, and for semantic unrelated, $M = 0.21$, $SD = 0.22$, F (1, 26) = 53.32, $p < 0.001$. There was an interaction between regularity and lobe, F (2, 52) = 7.31, $p = 0.009$ and a marginal two-way interaction between semantic and hemisphere, F (1, 26) = 4.06, $p = 0.054$. There was a three-way interaction between regularity, hemisphere and lobe, F (2, 52) = 3.67, $p =$ 0.044.There was an interaction effect between AoA and regularity, F (2, 52) = 5.94, $p =$ 0.005. Simple effect analysis on the AoA and regularity interaction showed that the mean amplitudes across conditions were for early AoA, regular words, $M = 0.54$, $SD = 0.20$ vs irregular words $M = 0.23$, $SD = 0.25$, for intermediate AoA, regular words, $M = 0.31$, $SD =$ 0.20 vs irregular words $M = 0.69$, $SD = 0.25$, and for late AoA, regular words, $M = 0.66$, $SD =$ 0.22, vs irregular words $M = 0.81$, $SD = 0.25$. There was a significant difference between regular words and irregular words for intermediate AoA words, F (1, 27) = 5.66, $p =$ 0.025 and marginal significant difference for early AoA words, F (1, 27) = 3.63, $p = 0.068$. However, there was no significant difference between regular words and irregular words for late AoA words, F (1, 27) = 1.21, $p = 0.28$.

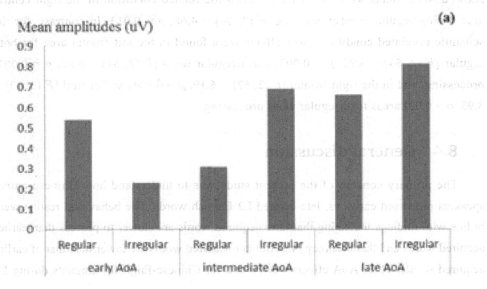

(a)

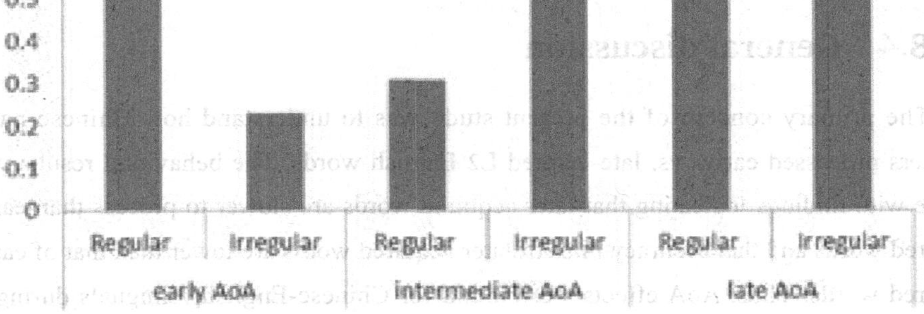

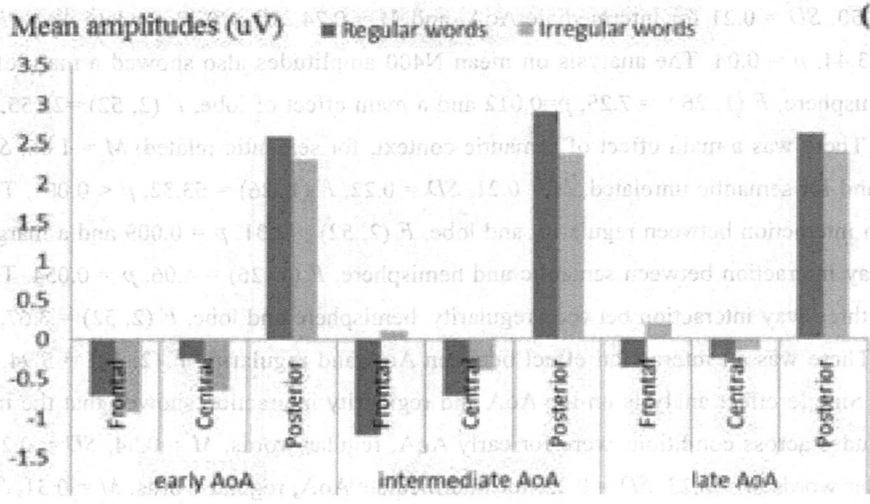

Figure 12 Interaction between (a) AoA and regularity and (b) between AcA, regularity and lobe

There was a marginal three-way interaction between AoA, regularity and lobe, F (4, 104) = 2.91, p = 0.06 (Fig. 12b). ANOVA analysis found a four-way interaction between AoA, hemisphere, regularity and semantic relatedness, F (2, 52) = 4.79, p = 0.02. Simple effect analysis on the above mentioned three-way and four way interactions showed AoA effects were found for the semantic related condition in the right central area during regular word processing, F (2, 54) = 4.68, p = 0.013. In contrast, for the semantic unrelated condition, AoA effects were found in the left frontal area for both regular [F (2, 54) = 3.75, p = 0.003] and irregular word [F (2, 54) = 5.57, p = 0.001] processing, and in the right frontal [F (2, 52) = 6.19, p = 0.004] and central [F (2, 52) = 3.95, p = 0.03] areas for irregular word processing.

8.4 General discussion

The primary concern of the present study was to understand how Chinese native speakers processed early- vs. late-learned L2 English words. The behavioral results were in line with findings indicating that later acquired words are slower to process than earlier acquired words and that accuracy rates of later acquired words are lower than that of earlier acquired words. Thus, AoA effects were found for Chinese-English bilinguals during L2 word processing. In terms of mean N400 amplitudes, the AoA effects were more pronounced for the semantic unrelated conditions and for irregular word processing. Early AoA words activated more negative going amplitudes than intermediate and late AoA words, especially in the frontal and central lobes. In order to tap into how orthography-phonology mapping rules influenced the AoA effects, the AoA and regularity was manipulated in semantic related judgment task. An interesting finding in the present study is that the regularity effect did not become larger when AoA increased, whereas a significant regularity effect was found only for intermediate AoA words but not for early and late AoA words. Specifically, for early AoA words, the irregular words were more difficult to process than regular words (reflected in more negative going N400 during processing irregular words); comparatively, the irregular words were easier to process than regular words for intermediate and late AoA words. The findings indicate that different AoA words might be reflected in different neurocognitive processing strategies.

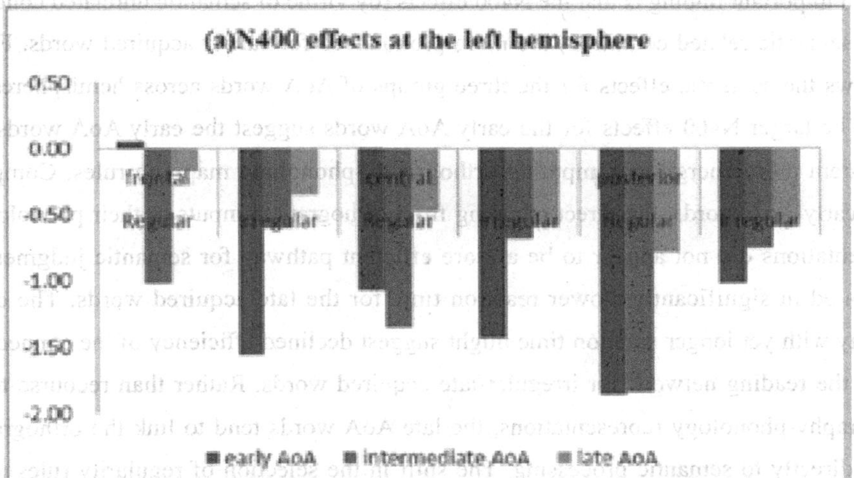

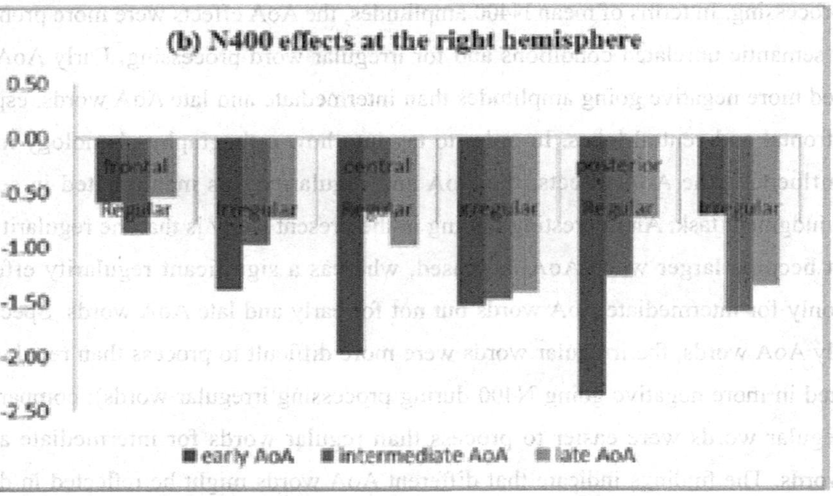

Figure 13 Semantic context effects for the early, intermediate and late AoA groups of words

An important finding is that the N400 effects (by virtue of semantic unrelated condition minus semantic related condition) are more pronounced for earlier acquired words. Figure 13 shows the semantic effects for the three groups of AoA words across hemispheres and lobes.The larger N400 effects for the early AoA words suggest the early AoA words cost the system more energy in computing orthography-phonology mapping rules. Compared to the early AoA words, the direct mapping from orthographic inputs to their phonological representations did not appear to be a more efficient pathway for semantic judgment, as implicated in significantly slower reaction time for the late acquired words. The direct pathway with yet longer reaction time might suggest declined efficiency of the connections within the reading network for irregular/late acquired words. Rather than recourse to the orthography-phonology representations, the late AoA words tend to link the orthographic inputs directly to semantic processing. The shift in the selection of regularity rules might reflect neurocognitive changes during processing different AoA words.

Further ANOVA analysis found a main effect of AoA in the right central area, F (2, 54) = 4.52, $p < 0.05$. There was more negative-going N400 in the frontal-central areas for early acquired words than intermediate acquired words, F (1, 27) = 6.36, $p = 0.018$, and the effect was also found between early and late acquired words, F (1, 27) = 6.59, $p = 0.016$. As the frontal-central areas plays an important role in semantic processing (Tang et al., 2001), the results indicate earlier acquired words had more semantic activation than later acquired words. In other words, early acquired words have more semantic interconnections than late acquired ones. At least two important hypotheses have been proposed in the literature for the locus of AoA effects. Two dominant theories underlying the mechanism of the AoA effects are the Arbitrary Mapping Hypothesis (Chen et al., 2007; You, Chen & Dunlap, 2009) and the Semantic Hypothesis (Belke et al., 2005; Brysbaert et al., 2000). The Arbitrary Mapping Hypothesis assumes the AoA effect reflects the arbitrary nature of the mapping between input (e.g., orthography) and output (phonological or semantic) representations during the development of the lexical network. The nature of the mapping between the input and output determines the size of the AoA. When the mapping between input and output is inconsistent, or arbitrary, AoA effects will be increased. According to Arbitrary Mapping hypothesis, irregular words could take less advantage of the shaped brain pattern than regular words, so irregular words should be more difficult to process. This theory attributes the AoA effect to the organization of the input-output mapping system. The Semantic Hypothesis proposes early acquired concepts are more accessible than late acquired concepts (Belke et al., 2005; Brysbaert et al., 2000). This is because the concepts of late acquired words are constructed on the basis of the concept of early acquired words. According to this theory, the order of acquisition determines the speed with which the semantic representations of concepts can be activated. This theory explains the larger AoA effects for the picture-naming task (involving Semantic-Phonology mapping) than reading aloud the printed names of the same objects, and no AoA effect in a word-naming task (involved Orthography-Phonology mapping) (Belke et al., 2005). The Arbitrary Mapping Hypothesis attributes the source of AoA effects to the nature of input-output mapping and the Semantic Hypothesis explains the locus from semantic representation.

Current findings may have implications for the neuronal-cognitive mechanism underlying the AoA effects. The present findings indicate both of the above sources should contribute to AoA effects, since word processing usually involves the establishment of associations in between three types of representation: phonological, orthographic and semantic representations. As proposed in the Semantic Hypothesis, concepts of early acquired words have more connection than late acquired ones. Although the highly connected conceptual knowledge is easier to be activated by virtue of reduced RT, the access to the early AoA words are energy consuming, which was reflected in more negative going N400 effects. Thus, the current findings are consistent with the semantic hypothesis. The findings are also supported from the simulating organization structure of semantic networks in the mathematical model proposed by Steyvers and Tenenbaum (2005). According to that model, the order of meaning acquisition determines the connection strength of Nodes in the semantic network. The new concept Nodes in the semantic network would connect to the existed concept Nodes (the early acquired concept) and the concept Node which had more connection was easy to be connected. The present results also suggest AoA effects should arise from mapping between conceptual knowledge onto linguistic units (Belke et al., 2005). During this process, orthography-phonology mapping rules contribute to the word processing. The size of the contribution is determined by the way of word acquisition. To sum, the locus of AoA effects might derive from the way word forms are stored and the way the word forms are related to the semantic concepts in the mental lexicon.

8.5 Conclusion

This study examined how English words of different AoA manifested on the neuronal representation patterns during word processing. Several conclusions could be drawn. First, during semantic processing, earlier acquired words are easier and quicker to process, compared with later acquired words. Second, the regularity of orthography-phonology mapping rules are differentially associated with words of different AoAs, which reflects neurocognitive changes during the processing of different AoA words. Last, the locus of AoA effects might derive from the way word forms are stored and related to the semantic concepts.

The present study has some limitations nonetheless. First, the selection of early, intermediate vs. late acquired words followed a general demarcation based on authoritative mandated textbooks for each age group. It still cannot provide a complete picture of words AoA for learners. Second, even though some variables such as word frequency, number of letters etc. were controlled, some variables such as image ability and concreteness might have some influence. Thus, future research is necessary to replicate the present findings.

Despite the limitations, the present study paves the way for the future studies on the AoA effect of Chinese-English bilinguals and the second language acquisition at early stage. A strong implication of this paper is that the early acquired second language is easier and faster to process than the late acquired second language. For Chinese-English bilinguals, second language acquisition might be relatively fast and successful when they are acquired at an early stage, because the semantics of late acquired second language concepts are constructed on the basis of that of early acquired second language concepts. Neuronal processing patterns are in an AoA-dependent way.

Chapter 9 Chinese-English bilinguals processing temporal-spatial metaphor[1]

Abstract: The conceptual projection of time onto the domain of space constitutes one of the most challenging issues in the cognitive embodied theories. In Chinese, spatial order (e.g., "大树*前*"/da shu *qian*/, *in front of* a tree) shares the same terms with temporal sequence ("三月*前*", /san yue *qian*/, *before* March). In comparison, English natives use different sets of prepositions to describe spatial and temporal relationship, i.e., "before" to express temporal sequencing and "in front of" to express spatial order. The linguistic variations regarding the specific lexical encodings indicate that some flexibility might be available in how space-time parallelisms are formulated across different languages. In the present study, ERP (Event-related potentials) data were collected when Chinese-English bilinguals processed temporal ordering and spatial sequencing in both their first language (L1) Chinese (Experiment 1) and the second language (L2) English (Experiment 2). It was found that, despite the different lexical encodings, early sensory-motor simulation plays a role in temporal sequencing processing in both L1 Chinese and L2 English. The findings well supports the Embodied Theory that conceptual knowledge is grounded in sensory-motor systems (Gallese & Lakoff, 2005). Additionally, in both languages, neural representations during comprehending temporal sequencing and spatial ordering are different. The time-spatial relationship is asymmetric, in that space schema could be imported into temporal sequence processing but not vice versa. These findings support the weak view of the Metaphoric Mapping Theory.

Key words: temporal sequence spatial order metaphor ERP bilingual

---

[1] This paper was published in *Cognitive Processing*, 2014, 15 (3): 269-281.

9.1 Introduction

9.1.1 Space-time parallelism relationship

People often use spatial terms to talk about temporal sequencing (e.g., *a long night*). Language from a concrete domain of space (i.e., *long*) is used to talk about the more abstract domain of time (i.e., *night*). The language phenomenon coincides with the systematic space-time parallelisms across languages. For example, those prepositions in expressing spatial relationships (*on* the wall, *in* the box) are also used to indicate an event occurred with a particular time (*on* Monday, *in* this year). Such linguistic patterns suggest that people apparently conceptualize abstract semantic domains in more concrete terms. The conceptual projection between time domain and space domain constitutes one of the most challenging issues in cognitive embodied theories.

Empirical studies regarding a fundamental link between spatial and temporal perception accrued positive evidence (see Walsh, 2003, for a review). Casasanto and Boroditsky (2003) showed that spatial displacement biased temporal judgments: Longer movements seem to last longer. Semantic processing of the abstract domain of time activates the more concrete domain of space (Torralbo, Santiago & Lupianez, 2006). Recent work by Vallesi, McIntosh and Stuss (2011) found that spatial attention and spatial representations can also influence temporal processing. Specifically, elapsing time is represented from left to right, and this left-to-right time representation generates corresponding response codes that influence performance. These results support that spatial schemas are systematically used in the comprehension of the abstract time concepts.

9.1.2 The Metaphoric Mapping Theory: Asymmetrical projection and cross-linguistic flexibility

Consistent with the most available behavioral data, the Metaphoric Mapping Theory is one compelling theory among the different explanations for the time-space parallelisms (for details, see Haspelmath, 1997). The theory proposes that the abstract domain of time is structured by metaphorical mappings from the more concrete and experiential space domains (Boroditsky, 2000; Casasanto & Boroditsky, 2008). By virtue of the theory, humans have a cognitive predisposition to structure temporal concepts in terms of spatial schemas through the application of a TIME IS SPACE metaphor. The structure of space, characterized by a high degree of specification, is imported into the abstract domain of time. Thus, time is represented as a material object with specific physical and spatial parameters. Besides, the metaphoric mapping between time and space is a computational ability for human being to conceptualize time in terms of space in certain preferential ways (e.g., Kemmerer, 2005).

The Metaphoric Mapping Theory entails an asymmetrical relationship between the conceptual domains of space and time. The spatial meanings should "always be chronologically primary, and temporal meaning should emerge from them gradually through a process of semantic extension" (Kemmerer, 2005). This is supported by research on the semantic change in languages over the course of history in that the temporal sense is developed historically from the spatial sense (Hopper & Traugott, 2003). For example, German *vor* "before" is based on *vor* "in front of" . Further evidence comes from language development in children. The spatial meanings of prepositions are typically acquired before temporal meanings (Lossifova & Marmolejo-Ramos, 2012). In their study, three groups of children (typical developing children, children with vision-motor impairments and blind children) were asked to point at space and time locations in relation to their body. It was found that typical developing children were almost two times more likely to perform spatial deixis than temporal deixis. There was an increasing trend of performing more spatial deixis than temporal deixis such that typical development children < children with visual-motor impairments < blind children was detected. A significant association between temporal deixis and spatial dexis was found.The results also indicated that vision plays an important role in performing both spatial and temporal concepts. These findings are consistent with the view that there should be a metaphorical relationship between time and space. In addition, the metaphorical relationship between temporal and spatial processing is asymmetric.

To account for the asymmetric relationship, two different hypotheses concerning the Metaphoric Mapping Theory have been proposed: the weak view versus the strong view (for details, see Kemmerer, 2005). To put it simple, the strong view maintains that when people process temporal sequencing, the relational structures of spatial ordering are always activated. Consequently, there is a cross-domain alignment and projection (e.g., Lakoff & Johnson, 1999). Alternatively, the weak view proposes that the metaphoric mapping between time and space is not obligatory in that the temporal meanings are presented and processed independently of the corresponding spatial meaning, even though the metaphor is available as an optional processing strategy (e.g., Boroditsky, 2000; Kemmerer, 2005). Thus, understanding temporal sequencing does not necessarily involve the on-line application of time-space metaphor. Nevertheless, on-line research on the asymmetric time-space metaphorical relationship is still scant.

Additionally, some flexibility is available in how time-space metaphoric mapping is formulated. For instance, Boroditsky (2001) found that the time-space metaphorical mapping was influenced by cross-linguistic differences. English speakers often used horizontal terms oriented along the egocentrically grounded anterior/posterior axis (e.g., back-front). However, Chinese speakers used vertical terms, for instance, up ("上" /shang/) for earlier and down ("下" /xia/) for later). Thus, the Metaphoric Mapping Theory should maintain a certain degree of cross-linguistic variation in time-space mapping.

9.1.3 The present research

The above findings lead naturally to an interesting question of how the time-space metaphorical relationship plays a role in the representations and processing of temporal sequencing and spatial ordering for bilingual adult speakers, especially when the two languages (i.e., Chinese vs. English) have different lexical encoding systems on the same concepts. An intriguing feature of Chinese Mandarin is that, spatial order and temporal sequence share same terms. For instance, the temporal sequence term "前" in "两天*前*" (/liang tian *qian*/, two days *before*) is the same with the spatial order term"前" in "大树*前*"(/da shu *qian*/, *in front of* a tree). In comparison, English natives use different sets of prepositions to describe spatial and temporal relationships, i.e., "in front of" to express spatial order and "before" to express temporal sequence in most cases. The linguistic variations regarding the specific lexical encodings on the same temporal and spatial concepts indicate that some flexibility might be available in how space-time parallelisms are formulated across different languages. The cross-linguistic difference provides a good venue to understand the space-time metaphorical mapping. Thus, the present study is concerned with how Chinese-English bilinguals apply their time-space associations of the first language Chinese, which are stored in their long-term semantic memory, to their second language English.

On the other hand, on-line evidence showing how temporal sequence is related to spatial order is scant. ERPs provide an on-line measure with millisecond accuracy on a specific stimulus on the brain (Kutas & Hillyard, 1980; Osterhout & Holcomb, 1992). Thus, ERP technique is effective in tracking the multiple cognitive processes of space-time metaphorical mapping as they unfold in time. ERPs are labeled by their latency with respect to stimulus onset. The amplitudes of the ERP waveform relative to the baseline can be interpreted as the degree of engagement in a task. The positive and negative deflections (components) are found to be correlated with sensory, motor and cognitive processing (e.g., Kutas & Federmeier, 2000). Three components are relevant with temporal sequencing and space ordering in the present study: P200, N400 and P600.

According to the limited numbers of online studies on spatial metaphor during temporal comprehension, a simulation of spatial perception occurs in an early time window (Kiefer, Sim, Herrnberger, Grothe & Hoenig, 2008; Pulvermuller, Hauk, Nikulin & Ilmoniemi 2005; Yang & Xue, 2011). This stage is important for understanding spatial knowledge and has the similar neural substrate to actual spatial processing (Barsalou, 1999; Gallese & Lakoff, 2005). In ERP, this stage is indexed by P200. P200 (or P2 for short) is a positive-going wave around 200ms after stimulus onset. It is an early component related to visual spatial processing, such as spatial memory retrieval (Tlauka et al., 2009), spatial discrimination (O'Donnell et al., 1997), spatial attention (Niu et al., 2008), and stimulus spatial-orientation (Song et al., 2007).

At a later stage, the recognition of spatial metaphor occurs. The recognition can be achieved through an integration of spatial terms and time terms contained in the temporal sequencing concepts. This integration may occur in a semantic level (integrating the meaning of the spatial and the temporal terms). A recent study on Chinese temporal sequencing confirms that the mapping from spatial knowledge domain to event-order knowledge domain includes a semantic integration in a middle time window, indexed by the N400 (Yang & Xue, 2011). The N400 is a negative deflection, occurring approximately 400ms after stimulus onset (Friederici, 2002). It is an index of difficulty in semantic integration (Hagoort, 2008) and the amplitude is larger when words semantically disassociate with each other (Rugg, 1984). N400 could also reflect the process of retrieving images from memory. For instance, an N400 effect occurs during mental rehearsal imagery tasks (van Petten & Luka, 2006).

The understanding of temporal sequencing may also involve the P600, which reflects the structure mapping between temporal sequencing and spatial ordering. The P600 is late centro-parietal positivity (Friederici, 2002). The effect is in the late time window, and indicates a prolonged semantic integration and a late structural integration. The P600 pattern has been found in a large number of syntactic structures (verb agreement; verb-, case-, pronoun-inflection; verb argument) evoked by either syntactic violations, or syntactic ambiguity, or syntactic integration difficulty (e.g., Kaan, Harris, Gibson & Holcomb, 2000). P600 has lately been reported to index grammatical complexity or an encounter with uncanonical less preferred syntactic structures, not necessarily calling for the existence of an overt syntactic violation (e.g., Mueller et al., 2005).

In this study, two experiments were devoted to providing on-line processing evidence of the time-space metaphorical relationships from a cross-linguistic and neuropsychological perspective. Experiment 1 examined the Metaphoric Mapping Theory with Chinese materials. The research question for Experiment 1 was whether Chinese natives processed spatial order terms (e.g., "大树前"/da shu *qian*/, *in front of* a tree) in the same way as they performed temporal sequence terms ("三月前", /san yue *qian*/, *before* March). Experiment 2 was a further study on the Metaphoric Mapping Theory. The research question was about how Chinese natives processed the same temporal sequence and spatial order concepts in their second language English.

9.2 Experiment 1

Experiment 1 examined the time-space metaphorical relationship with Chinese materials. Temporal sequence and spatial order in Chinese share the same terms. For instance, the spatial order "前" in "大树前" (/da shu *qian*/, *in front of* the tree) is the same with the temporal sequence "前" in "三月前" (/san yue *qian*/, *before* March). This provides a good venue to examine the difference between the on-line processing of time sequence and space order. It is predicted that the semantic difference (temporal vs. spatial) would induce an N400 effect. According to the Metaphoric Mapping Theory, spatial scenarios are dominant and temporal abstract domains are likely to be projected in terms of spatial structures. Thus, it was further predicted that there would be a P200 effect for both temporal sequence processing and spatial order processing. Additionally, there would be a P600 effect when temporal sequence processing was compared with spatial order processing.

9.2.1 Methods

9.2.1.1 Participants

Twenty-four right-handed Chinese readers from Beijing International Studies University

(2 men, Mean age = 23.58 years, *SD* = 1.72) participated in the study. One was left-handed and 23 were right handed. All reported Mandarin as their first language and English as their second language. According to a 10-point self-rating scale, the means for their Chinese listening, speaking, reading and writing were 8.21 (*SD* = 1.02), 7.83 (*SD* = 1.27), 8.13 (*SD* = 1.23, and 7.38 (*SD* = 1.27), respectively. Their self-ratings on English listening, speaking, reading and writing were 7.00 (*SD* = 1.29), 6.63 (*SD* = 1.44), 7.33 (*SD* = 1.27), and 6.79 (*SD* = 1.35). All participants had normal or corrected to normal vision and got compensation for their participation. All gave their informed consent prior to their inclusion in the study.

9.2.1.2 Design and materials

For Experiment 1, the critical stimuli consisted of 60 Chinese sentences, which fell into two conditions (see Table 13): temporal correct (TC) and spatial correct (SC). In all example sentences, critical fragments were bold and italicized. In temporal and spatial conditions, the sentences shared common terms. The only difference in the two conditions was that the context constraining would enable the readers to comprehend the terms as either temporal sequencing or spatial ordering. To distract participants' attention from the manipulation of the temporal/spatial phrases and to balance the "yes" and "no" responses, 120 filler sentences consisted of correct sentences, sentences with semantic anomaly, and sentences with syntactic anomaly were included. Thus, 180 sentences were used in Experiment 1.

Table 13 Examples of the Chinese conditions

Conditions	Examples
temporal, correct (TC)	这台洗衣机在三月前就买了。 **Zhe tai xi yi ji zai san yue *qian* jiu mai le。** The washing machine had been bought before March.
spatial, correct (SC)	壮汉站在老式农舍大门***前***。 **Zhuang han zhan zai lao shi nong she da men *qian*。** A strong man stood ***in front of*** the gate of the old farm house.
semantic, correct (SEC)	主人招待客人，把西瓜***切了***。 **zhu ren zhao dai ke ren, ba xi gua *qie* le。** To cater to the guest, the host ***cut*** the water melon.
semantic, incorrect (SEI)	主人招待客人，把西瓜***轧***了。 **zhu ren zhao dai ke ren, ba xi gua *zha* le。** To cater to the guest, the host ***rolled*** the water melon.

Note: Chinese characters, Chinese morpheme-by-morpheme glosses and English translations are provided for each sample. The bold and italicized parts are the critical words.

9.2.1.3 Procedure

Experiment 1 and 2 followed an identical procedure. The participants were comfortably seated in a dimly lit and sound-attenuated chamber, at about 1 meter in front of a computer. They were asked to attentively read each sentence and perform a sentence acceptability task. Each sentence was presented segment-by-segment in a rapid serial visual presentation paradigm, in black font at the center of a write screen. The sentence was divided into 4 to 8 segments.

In Experiment 1, a fixation appeared on the screen for 500ms, and then a sentence was presented by fragment in each trial. Each fragment was presented for 500ms followed by a blank interval of 300ms. When the sentence was finished, a question mark appeared, and participants decided whether the sentence was "acceptable" or not by pressing one of two buttons with their index fingers. The response buttons were counterbalanced across participants. When a response was made, another trial began. Each participant had a short practice before the experiment. The ordering of experimental sentences and filler sentences was pseudorandomized.

9.2.1.4 Data acquisition

The EEGs were recorded with 64 Ag/AgCl electrodes (AF7, AF3, FP1, FPZ, FP2, AF4, AF8, F7, F5, F3, F1, Fz, F2, F4, F6, F8, FT7, FC5, FC3, FC1, FCZ, FC2, FC4, FC6, FT8, T7, C5, C3, C1, CZ, C2, C4, C6, T8, TP9, TP7, CP5, CP3, CP1, CPZ, CP2, CP4, CP6, TP8, TP10, P7, P5, P3, P1, PZ, P2, P4, P6, P8, PO7, PO5, PO3, POZ, PO4, PO6, PO8, O1, Oz, O2) mounted in an elastic cap (EASYCAP GmbH, Germany), referenced online to the nose tip and re-referenced offline to the arithmetic average of the left and right mastoids (TP9 and TP10). The vertical electrooculogram (VEOG) was monitored from electrodes located below the right eye and the horizontal electrooculogram (HEOG) from electrodes located at the outer canthus of the left eye. Electrode impedances were maintained below 5 kΩ. The EEG and EOG were amplified by BrainAmps (Brain Products GmbH, Germany) using a band-pass filter from 0.016 to 100Hz and were digitized online at a sampling rate of 1 000Hz.

9.2.1.5 Data analyses

The EEGs were processed offline with Analyzer 2.0 software (Brain Products GmbH, Germany).Those contaminated by ocular or other artifacts (exceeding a threshold of 50μV) were excluded from further analysis, resulting in 80% artifact-free trials for Experiment

1 and 78.89% artifact-free trials for Experiment 2. The filter cutoff was set between low frequency of 0.1 and high frequency of 32. ERPs were computed for each participant and each electrode over an epoch from 200ms before to 1 000ms after the onset of the critical words for Experiment 1, and the post-critical words for Experiment 2. The 200ms pre-stimulus interval was used for baseline correction of the critical words.

For each type of effect, repeated measure ANOVAs were performed with within subject factors of Sentence Type and Electrode site from midline site (3 levels—corresponding to Fz, Cz, Pz), medial site (with 2 levels of hemisphere—left and right—and 5 anterior-posterior levels—F3/F4, FC1/FC2, C3/C4, CP1/CP2, P3/P4) and from lateral sites (with 2 levels of Hemisphere—left and right—and 5 anterior-posterior levels—F7/F8, FC5/FC6, T7/T8, CP5/CP6, P7/P8). In comparing Chinese temporal and spatial processing, the sentence type (temporal vs. spatial) was the factor included in the above mentioned repeated measure ANOVAs. For all analyses, original degrees of freedom were reported. A Greenhouse-Geisser correction for sphericity was applied to p-values when more than two levels of a factor were present (Greenhouse & Geisser, 1959). Reliable main effects and interactions were followed by simple effect analysis when appropriate. Main effects and interactions that involved Sentence Type were reported here, because they were of most theoretical interest. Any main effects or interactions not reported below were all non-significant (all *p*s > 0.05). Marginally significant main effects and interactions ($p < 0.1$) were only reported when at least one other significant main effect or interaction existed at another column.

Based on our hypothesis, three main time windows were defined: 190-250ms, 300-500ms, and 500-800ms, respectively. The sentence type effects were compared between the two conditions through a statistical analysis of three time windows.

9.2.2 Results

9.2.2.1 Behavioral performance

The accuracy rates in the acceptability judgment were computed as the percentage of yes-responses in the four conditions by the participants. The acceptability ratios of sentences in temporal correct (TC) and spatial correct (SC) were 0.91 and 0.82, respectively. Results from paired-samples t-test showed that the acceptability ratio of Chinese temporal processing sentences did not differ from that of spatial ordering sentences [$t(29) = 1.92, p = 0.065$].

9.2.2.2 Electrophysiological data

Temporal processing vs. spatial processing

Grand-averaged ERPs time-locked to the onset of the critical words TC and SC were showed at electrode sites FC1, CP2, F7, F8, FC5, FC6, and CP5 (Fig. 14), and the waves represent the mean signal evoked by TC and SC (dark vs. light grey lines). Significant ERP differences were observed on the critical words, i.e., temporal sequencing terms (TC) ("三月前", /san yue ***qian***/, *before March)* vs. spatial ordering terms (SC) ("大树前", /da shu ***qian***/, *in front of* a tree). Visual inspection also showed a positive going wave around the first 300ms after stimulus onset. A clear negative-going component with a peak around 400ms post word onset (N400) was found in the central sites, followed by a late positive-going component in the frontal-central sites. These effects were compared between the two conditions through a statistical analysis on the mean amplitudes in the three time windows: 190-250ms, 300-500ms, and 500-800ms, respectively.

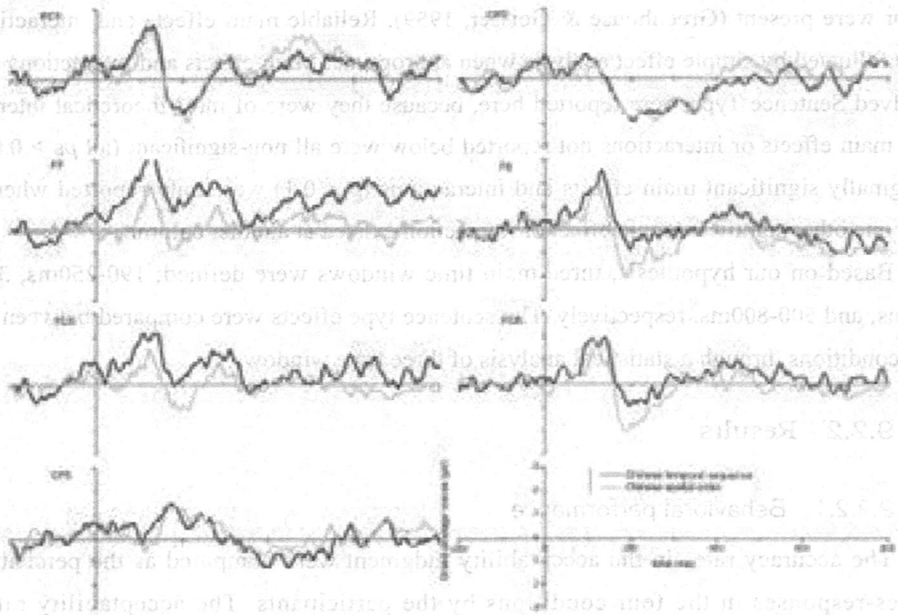

Figure 14 Grand-average ERPs during processing temporal sequencing and spatial ordering

In the 190-250ms time window, ANOVA revealed that there was a main effect of hemisphere in medial site [$F(1, 23) = 15.60$, $p = 0.001$]. No other effect was found.

In the 300-500ms time window, ANOVA revealed a significant effect related to Electrode Site [F (4, 92) = 3.52, p = 0.037] and a Sentence Type × Electrode Site interaction [F (4, 92) = 2.83, p = 0.041] in medial site. Simple effect analyses indicated a reliable main effect of Sentence Type in the electrode sites FC1 [$M_{\text{temporal sequence}}$ = 1.81, SD = 1.09; $M_{\text{spatial order}}$ = 2.13, SD = 1.07, F (1, 23) = 5.35, p = 0.03] and CP2 [$M_{\text{temporal sequence}}$ = 2.17, SD = 1.32; $M_{\text{spatial order}}$ = 1.77, SD = 1.09, F (1, 23) = 9.38, p = 0.006]. In lateral site, ANOVA revealed main effects related to Sentence Type [F (1, 23) = 4.73, p = 0.04] and Electrode Site [F (1, 23) = 9.80, p = 0.001]. For instance, the main effect of Sentence Type was found in F8 [$M_{\text{temporal sequence}}$ = 2.67, SD = 1.66; $M_{\text{spatial order}}$ = 1.97, SD = 1.43, F (1, 23) = 5.61, p = 0.02] and FC6 [$M_{\text{temporal sequence}}$ = 1.97, SD = 1.19; $M_{\text{spatial order}}$ = 1.61, SD = 1.04, F (1, 23) = 5.83, p = 0.02]. No other effect was found.

One participant had equipment failure in T7 in the 500-800ms time window. Thus, the ANOVA analysis on the lateral site included only 4 levels (i.e., F7/F8, FC5/FC6, CP5/CP6, and P7/P8). In the 500-800ms time window, in lateral site, ANOVA showed a main effect of Sentence Type [F (1, 22) = 5.75, p = 0.03]. Specifically, the main effect of Sentence Type was found in F7 [$M_{\text{temporal sequence}}$ = 2.76, SD = 2.90; $M_{\text{spatial order}}$ = 1.60, SD = 0.79, F (1, 23) = 4.16, p = 0.053], FC5 [$M_{\text{temporal sequence}}$ = 1.87, SD = 0.86; $M_{\text{spatial order}}$ = 1.32, SD = 0.67, F (1, 23) = 8.95, p = 0.007] and CP5 [$M_{\text{temporal sequence}}$ = 1.84, SD = 1.00; $M_{\text{spatial order}}$ = 1.38, SD = 0.73, F (1, 23) = 11.31, p = 0.003]. There was a main effect of Electrode Site [F (3, 69) = 3.92, p = 0.03]. No other effect was found.

9.2.3 Discussion

According to the ERP grand averages, the positive going waves (the P200) were activated around 200ms after stimulus onset for both the space order terms and temporal sequence terms, although the P200 was marginally more positive for space order. Since the P200 is an index of visual spatial processing (Niu et al., 2008; O'Donnell et al., 1997; Song et al., 2007; Tlauka et al., 2009), we took it as evidence that a projection from space schema to temporal domains occurred during processing temporal sequence. This finding supports the Metaphoric Structuring Theory that temporal scenarios are structured in terms of on-line mapping from the domain of space. The Sentence Type main effects found in the N400 and P600 reflect differences existing in both semantic and syntactic processes between temporal sequence processing and space order processing.

9.3 Experiment 2

Experiment 2 was aimed at exploring how L2 English inputs were neutrally enacted in comprehending the same temporal sequence and spatial order concepts as in L1 Chinese. The L1 processing pattern might be applicable to their L2 if the habitual time-space metaphorical relationship plays an important role in processing temporal sequence. Thus, when manipulating the prepositions expressing the time and space crdering (for details, see Design and Materials section), similar neural processing patterns as induced for L1 Chinese materials should be evoked for L2 English materials. Similarly, the exchange may disrupt the semantic integration between the spatial order and the temporal sequence, and hence anomalies would evoke an N400 effect that indicates difficulty in semantic integration (Hagoort, 2008). According to the Metaphoric Mapping Theory, the spatial schema should be employed in understanding temporal sequence. Thus, it was further predicted that during temporal sequence comprehension, exchanging temporal prepositions with spatial prepositions should not cause differences in P2 or P600. However, during spatial order comprehension, if the spatial order terms were replaced by temporal sequence terms, the sensor-motor simulation was expected to be disrupted in the early time window, resulting in the P200 differences. The exchanging was also expected to cause difficulty in spatial structure analysis. This difficulty may evoke a late positive shift (the P600) related to structure integration (Osterhout & Holcomb, 1992).

9.3.1 Methods

9.3.1.1 Participants

The participants in Experiment 2 were the same with Experiment 1.

9.3.1.2 Design and materials

In Experiment 2, the critical sentences included 120 English sentences, which fell into four conditions: temporal correct condition (TC), temporal incorrect condition (TI), spatial correct condition (SC), and spatial incorrect condition (SI) (see examples in Table 14). For instance, the temporal meaning of "before" is the salient meaning, if not the only meaning. According to "A Grammar of Contemporary English" (Quirk, Greenbaum, Leech & Svartvik, 1972: 318), the word "before" occur almost exclusively as prepositions of time and are followed by either (a) a temporal noun phrase (eg: before next week), (b) a subjectless V-ing clause (eg: since leaving school, or (c) a noun phrase with a deverbal noun or noun phrase interpreted as equivalent to a clause. As for English teaching in the context of China, students are usually taught according to the above-mentioned grammar rules. Followed by the grammar rules, "before" in the TI condition was followed exclusively by a place, and "in front of" in the SI condition was followed exclusively by a temporal noun in order to ensure the stimuli examine the temporal sequence and spatial order.

In each type of temporal/spatial concepts, the sentences in the correct and the incorrect conditions in each set shared a common sentence structure: Subject ＋ Verb ＋ object ＋ temporal sequence/spatial order prepositions ＋ time terms/space terms. In addition, the critical temporal sequence/spatial order prepositional phrases in correct and incorrect conditions in each set shared the same Chinese concepts as in Experiment 1. For instance, in the temporal incorrect (TI) condition, the spatial preposition "in front of" replaced the temporal preposition "before". Similarly, in spatial incorrect (SI) condition, the temporal preposition "before" replaced the spatial preposition "in front of", and "after" replaced "behind". Besides, the key stimuli "in front of" and "before" could be translated into the same Chinese character "前"/qian/, which has concepts of both temporal sequence and spatial order. To minimize the repetition effect, we used various time and spatial terms during stimuli construction. In the temporal sequencing phrases, time terms like *morning, day, week, month*, and *year* were used. Additionally, different numerals were used to modify the time terms and to vary the length of the described time period. Similar consideration was taken during spatial stimuli construction.

Table 14 Examples of the English conditions

Conditions	Description	Examples
temporal, correct (TC)	The sentence contains a temporal sequencing phrase in which a temporal term is correctly used.	Tom went to the shop ***before*** dark.
temporal, incorrect (TI)	The sentence is similar in TC condition, but a spatial term replaces the temporal term and thus causes anomaly.	Tom went to the shop ***in front of*** dark.
spatial, correct (SC)	The sentence contains a spatial order phrase in which a spatial term is correctly used.	Tom found his book ***in front of*** the TV.
spatial, incorrect (SI)	The sentence is similar in SC condition, but a temporal term replaces the spatial term and thus causes anomaly.	Tom found his book ***before*** the TV.

Note: The bold and italicized parts are the critical words.

9.3.1.3 Data acquisition and analysis

Data acquisition and analysis were the same with Experiment 1, except that each fragment was presented for 700ms, followed by a blank interval of 300ms.

9.3.2 Results

9.3.2.1 Behavioral performance

The acceptability ratios of sentences in English temporal correct (TC), English temporal incorrect (TI), English spatial correct (SC), and English spatial incorrect (SI) conditions were 0.87, 0.90, 0.83, and 0.71, respectively. Results from paired-samples t-test showed that no reliable difference was found between TC and TI sentences [t (30) = −1.52, p = 0.49]. SC sentences were more acceptable than SI sentences [t (30) = 2.86, p = 0.008]. The behavioral results showed that the participants finished the judgement task in the English temporal incorrect (TI) with an accuracy of 0.90 and in English spatial incorrect (SI) with an accuracy of 0.71, meaning the participants followed the contemporary English grammar rules quite well. In other words, the stimuli examined the temporal sequence and spatial order well enough.

9.3.2.2 Electrophysiological data

Temporal anomaly effect

Since the anomaly could be identified only after the participants read the critical words (i.e., TC and TI), analysis on ERP data would locate at one segment after the critical words. Significant ERP differences were observed on the two segments post the critical words. Fig.15 displayed grand-averaged ERPs at electrodes Fz, Cz and Pz, time-locked to the onset of the segments post the critical words. The waves represent the mean signal evoked by TC and TI (dark vs. light grey lines). Visual inspection revealed not much difference between TC and TI over the first 200ms after stimulus onset (the P2 effect). However, visual inspection revealed that TC elicited evoked stronger positive effects than TI in from about 300ms after stimuli onset until 800ms after stimuli onset.

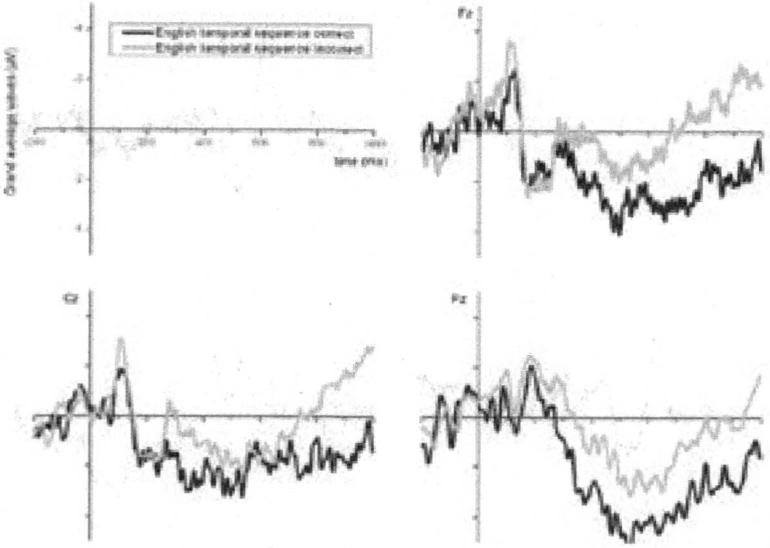

Figure 15 Grand-average ERPs during processing English TC and English TI

In the 190-250ms time window, ANOVA revealed a main effect of Electrode Site [*F* (4, 88) = 4.04, *p* = 0.021], the main effect of Hemisphere [*F* (1, 22) = 6.93, *p* = 0.02] in lateral site. No other effect was found.

In the 300-500ms time window, ANOVA revealed a main effect for Electrode site [*F* (4, 88) = 3.10, *p* = 0.051] in lateral site. No other effect was found.

In the 500-800ms time window, ANOVA revealed a main effect for Electrode site [*F* (4, 88) = 4.10, *p* = 0.02] in lateral site. No other effect was found.

Spatial anomaly effect

Grand-averaged ERPs in SC and SI were presented at Fz, Cz, and Pz electrode sites in Fig. 16, and the waves represent the mean signal evoked by SC and SI (dark vs. light grey lines). A N1-P2 complex over the first 300ms was visible, and then a negative-going component with a peak around 400ms following word onset (N400) appeared, following by a later positive-going component.

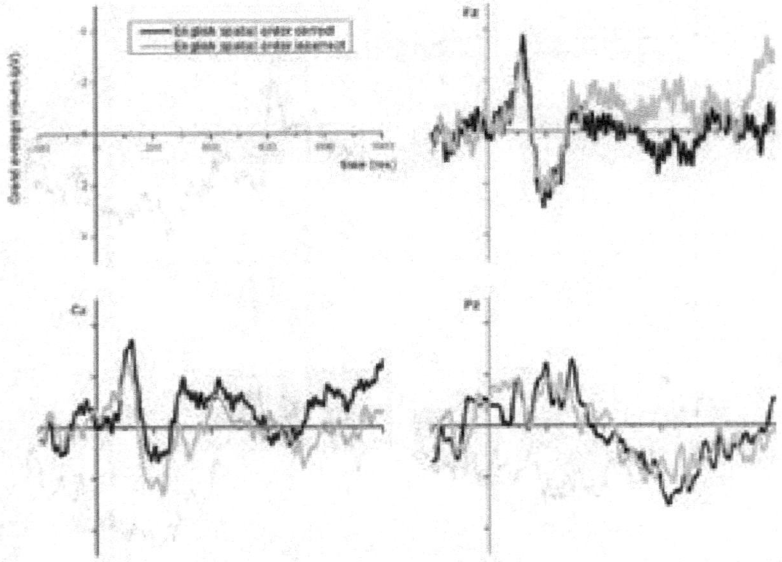

Figure 16 Grand-average ERPs during processing English SC and English SI

In the 190-250ms time window, ANOVA revealed that a main effect of Sentence Type in midline [F (1, 23) = 10.27, p = 0.004] and in medial site [F (1, 22) = 8.82, p = 0.007]. In lateral site, there was a main effect of Sentence Type [F (1, 22) = 7.85, p = 0.01], a main effect of Electrode Site [F (4, 88) = 4.34, p = 0.02] and a main effect of Hemisphere [F (1, 22) = 5.37, p = 0.03].

In the 300-500ms time window, ANOVA revealed a Sentence Type × Electrode Site interaction in midline [F (2, 44) = 4.02, p = 0.03]. Simple effect analysis indicated that there was a main effect of Sentence Type in electrodes Fz [F (1, 22) = 4.88, p = 0.038]. There was a main effect of Electrode Site in the lateral Site [F (4, 88) = 5.12, p = 0.01]. No other effect was found.

In the 500-800ms time window, ANOVA revealed a main effect of Electrode Site [F (4, 88) = 7.88, p = 0.002] in lateral site. No other effect was found.

9.3.3 Discussion

In Experiment 2, we compared the two types of anomaly effects to examine the neural representations for L2 English temporal ordering and spatial processing. We calculated each anomaly effect by subtracting the brain potentials of the correct condition from the potentials of the incorrect condition. Overall, we observed that the exchange between spatial terms and temporal terms in English elicited different patterns of anomalous effects between temporal sequence processing and spatial order processing for Chinese-English bilinguals.

Specifically, we subtracted the potentials in TC from the potentials in TI to obtain the temporal anomaly effects. In temporal sequencing concepts, the sentences in the correct and the incorrect conditions in each set shared a common sentence structure and described a same event. In addition, the critical temporal sequencing phrases in the correct and the incorrect conditions in each set shared the characters as in Experiment 1 if translated into Chinese. Thus, the contrast between TI and TC excluded potential confounding factors unrelated to the processing of temporal sequencing. According to the ANOVA analysis, the spatial order terms (TI) replacing the temporal sequence (TC) did not activate any Sentence Type effect. The results indicate that the violation did not interrupt the temporal order processing. This implies that during temporal sequence comprehension, spatial order preposition could make up for the semantic and structure representations for temporal prepositions. In other words, spatial schemas can be used to think about time.

Similarly, we subtracted the potentials in SC (spatial order terms) from the potentials in SI (temporal sequence terms) to obtain the spatial anomaly effect. Interestingly, anomaly effects in the P2 time window and the N400 time window were found. The results indicate that anomaly conditions might cause difficulty in spatial simulation as represented in P2. Besides, the anomaly also induces the difficulty in semantic integration as represented in the N400 effect.

9.4 General discussion

The primary purpose of the present study was to examine the Metaphoric Mapping Theory. Chinese temporal sequencing and spatial ordering share the same terms (e.g., "大树*前*", /da shu ***qian***/, ***in front of*** the tree vs. "三月*前*", /san yue ***qian***/, ***before*** March). This provides a good venue to the study. In Experiment 1, when comparing Chinese temporal sequence processing patterns with spatial order, we found that the two conditions evoked similar P200 effects but different N400 and P600 effects. P200 was well established as an ERP component reflecting spatial memory retrieval (Tlauka et al., 2009), spatial orientation (Song et al., 2007), spatial attention (Gao et al., 2002; Niu et al., 2008) and visual-spatial discrimination (Kong, Zhang, Zhang, Kang, 2012; Liu Perfetti & Hart, 2003; O'Donnell et al., 1997; Russo, Aprile, Spitoni & Spinelli, 2008). For instance, O'Donnell et al. (1997) showed that the P2 were sensitive to stimulus location and orientation, and that it can be influenced by task demand. Song et al. (2007) showed that the P2 amplitude was increased over posterior sites during a visual perceptual learning in grating orientation discrimination. Russo, Aprile, Spitoni and Spinelli (2008) examined impaired visual processing of contralesional stimuli with patients of right brain damage and spatial neglect. High-resolution EEG was recorded using focal stimuli located in the four visual quadrants. Results showed P2 (180-220ms) components were delayed and/or reduced in amplitude for stimuli located on the neglected side. For the relation between the event-related potential component P200 and orthographic processing in reading Chinese words, it has been found that P200 was sensitive to orthographic similarity and can be modulated by orthography alone in reading Chinese word. Liu, Perfetti and Hart (2003) found that P200 was reduced when the character shared a radical with the preceding character and interpreted it as a graphic processing component. Similarly, in Kong, Zhang Zhang, Kang (2012), participants performed a semantic judgment task on pairs of words (prime-target pairs) presented sequentially and the P200 elicited by the second target word was examined and compared across different prime conditions. The critical pairs were single characters similar in orthography but unrelated in phonology or semantics. Results showed that visually similar primes led to reduced P200 than control primes. Additionally, the processing of scale of visual attention was mainly concerned with P2 components. Gao, Wei & Peng (2002) asked 14 healthy young participants to perform a search task in which the search array was preceded by Chinese characters cues (large, medium, and small). The targets evoked P2 amplitudes and latency have significant differences with the different cues of large, middle and small.

In order to provide further evidence that P200 is specific to spatial processing, two sets of fillers in Experiment 1 (the semantic correct vs. semantic incorrect) were analyzed. Visual inspection revealed that Chinese semantic correct (SEC) and incorrect sentences (SEI) did not evoke distinct patterns of positive going waves around 200ms (the P200), even though the characters in the two conditions were different. ANOVA further showed no effect related to sentence type for the 190-250ms and 500-800ms time window, despite there was a main effect of sentence type and an interaction between Sentence Type and Electrode site [F (4, 88) = 5.53, p = 0.03] in medial site in the 300-500ms time window (i.e. the N400 effect). The above ANOVA results showed Chinese semantic violation induced exclusively N400 effect instead of P200 or other ERP components. Although the Chinese characters were different between SEC and SEI, the difference was not significant enough in arousing differential spatial representation or attention, thus resulting in no P200 difference. The results further support that N400 effects reflect the semantic processing and provide indirect evidence that P200 is robust in indexing space-related processing.

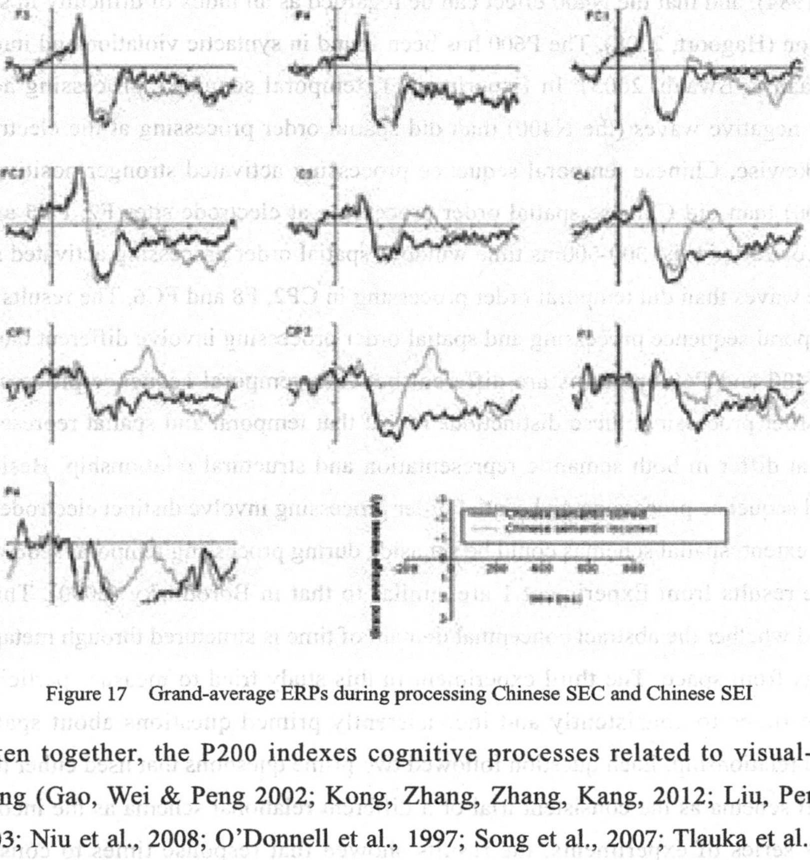

Figure 17 Grand-average ERPs during processing Chinese SEC and Chinese SEI

Taken together, the P200 indexes cognitive processes related to visual-spatial processing (Gao, Wei & Peng 2002; Kong, Zhang, Zhang, Kang, 2012; Liu, Perfetti & Hart 2003; Niu et al., 2008; O'Donnell et al., 1997; Song et al., 2007; Tlauka et al., 2009). The similar P200 effects in the present study are taken as evidence that temporal sequence processing share relational information on-line with spatial order. The results support the Metaphoric Structuring Theory that the spatial schema is imported during understanding temporal sequence. As P200 represents cognitive processes at the neurophysiological level, the results further indicate that temporal sequence representation involves a spatial simulation in the brain. This is consistent with the embodied semantic theory that linguistic meaning or conceptual knowledge is fundamentally tied to sensory-motor representations (e.g., Barsalou, 1999; Gallese & Lakoff, 2005).

N400 reflects semantic processing (Hagoort, 2008) and P600 indicates a prolonged semantic integration and a late structural integration in the late time window (e.g., Friederici, 2002; Kaan, Harris, Gibson & Holcomb, 2000). Previous studies have indicated that the N400 amplitude is larger when words semantically disassociate with each other (Rugg, 1984), and that the N400 effect can be regarded as an index of difficulty in semantic integration (Hagoort, 2008). The P600 has been found in syntactic violation and integration (e.g., Kaan & Swaab, 2003). In Experiment 1, temporal sequence processing activated stronger negative waves (the N400) than did spatial order processing at the electrode site FC1. Likewise, Chinese temporal sequence processing activated stronger positive waves (the P600) than did Chinese spatial order processing at electrode sites F7, FC5 and CP5. On the contrary, in the 300-500ms time window, spatial order processing activated stronger negative waves than did temporal order processing in CP2, F8 and FC6. The results suggest that temporal sequence processing and spatial order processing involve different electrodes. Since N400 and P600 patterns are different between temporal sequence processing and spatial order processing, these distinctions reveal that temporal and spatial representations somewhat differ in both semantic representation and structural relationship. Besides, the temporal sequence processing and spatial order processing involve distinct electrodes. Thus, to some extent, spatial schemas could be set aside during processing temporal sequence.

The results from Experiment 1 are similar to that in Boroditsky (2000). This study evaluated whether the abstract conceptual domain of time is structured through metaphorical mappings from space. The third experiment in this study tried to measure participants' response times to consistently and inconsistently primed questions about spatial and temporal relationship. Each question followed two prime questions that used either the same relational schema as the consistent trial or a different relational schema as the inconsistent trial. By series of experiments, the results showed that response times to consistently primed targets in the time-to-space condition did not differ from those to inconsistently primed targets, while the effect of consistency was statistically different from that in the control space-to-space condition. The results suggest that the shared relational structures between time and space are asymmetric. Moreover, a recent study on four brain-damaged subjects with left perisylvian lesions found that the subjects exhibited the dissociations on spatial tests and temporal tests (Kemmerer, 2005). Two subjects failed a test that assessed knowledge of the spatial meanings of prepositions, but passed a test that assessed knowledge of the corresponding temporal meanings of the same prepositions, while two other subjects performed better on the spatial test than on the temporal test. The researcher suggested that spatial and temporal meanings may normally be represented and processed independently of each other in the brains of modern adults. As Kemmerer (2005) put it, "Although the spatial and temporal meanings of prepositions are historically linked by virtue of the TIME IS SPACE metaphor, understanding the temporal meanings of prepositions does not necessarily require establishing structural alignments with their spatial correlates". In Experiment 1, the temporal sequence and spatial order processing evoked different N400 and P600 effects and got distinct electrodes involved, indicating that the two conditions do not share semantic representations or structural relationship. Therefore, the present findings contradict the strong claim that spatial schemas are necessary to understand time.

The second purpose of the present study was to examine how different linguistic encodings influence the time-space mappings. Experiment 2 provided cross-linguistic evidence on processing the same temporal sequence and space order concepts as in Experiment 1. Chinese-English bilinguals were recruited, because the Chinese and English languages have a sharp contrast in temporal and spatial expressions. English temporal sequence and spatial order expressions are two sets of prepositions (*in front of* vs. *before*). The differences in lexical encoding in the two languages are insightful in describing the nature of how bilinguals process temporal sequence and spatial order.

In Experiment 2, the contrast between SI and SC showed significant differences in early time window (190-250ms after stimuli onset) and later time window (300-500ms after stimuli onset). In other words, a spatial simulation occurred in an early time window (the P2 effect), and then a semantic and structural integration followed (the N400 effect), though both the spatial and the temporal prepositions imply similar sequence (front-back). The obvious anomaly effect as reflected in spatial order anomaly sentence is similar to what we found in L1 Chinese (Yang & Xue, 2011). P2 is involved in mapping from spatial knowledge domain to event-order knowledge domain, a simulation of spatial-orientation perception. The P2 component was found related to spatial processing, such as spatial orientation, spatial location and spatial frequency (O'Donnell et al., 1997). P2 was also sensitive to visual discrimination, spatial memory retrieval, spatial congruity of audio-visual stimulus and spatial attention (e.g., Tlauka, Clark, Liu & Conway, 2009; Niu, Wei & Luo, 2008; Song et al., 2007). Thus, the P2 effect found in Experiment 2 during L2

English temporal sequence processing provides evidence for spatial representation in the brain. Since N400 captures the semantic integration process, the N400 difference induced between SC (spatial preposition) and SI (temporal preposition) indicates that the neural representations on concepts of temporal sequencing distinguish from spatial ordering in L2 English.

However, the English temporal sequence anomaly in Experiment 2 did not evoke similar P2 and N400 effects as observed in spatial order anomaly processing. When temporal prepositions were replaced by spatial terms as in TI condition, the exchange was supposed to disrupt the semantic integration. For instance, when the temporal terms "before" (TC) in "Tom went to the shop before dark" were replaced by a spatial term "in front of" (TI), it was expected the semantic and structural relationship of temporal sequence should be violated by spatial term. However, the exchange elicited neither significant P200 nor N400 effects. This means that subjects were more likely to use the spatial schema when processing TC. The results indicate that temporal sequence processing is somewhat dependent on spatial schema.

It is argued that Chinese-English subjects might translate the English TI sentence (e.g., *in front of*) into Chinese ("前" meaning both temporal sequence and spatial order). So the similar processing patterns for TS and TI in Experiment 2 cannot be taken as evidence that spatial scenario were involved in temporal sequence processing. Luckily, ERP components are good at revealing the cognitive processes. As illustrated above, P200 indexes visual-spatial processing. It has been found that a simulation of spatial perception occurs during temporal processing (e.g., Kiefer, Sim, Herrnberger, Grothe & Hoenig, 2008; Yang & Xue, 2011). In Experiment 2, the positive going waves around 200ms were obvious at the sites of Fz and Cz for both English temporal sequence correct and temporal incorrect sentences. Meanwhile, during processing temporal sequence, when temporal terms (e.g., *before*) were replaced by spatial terms (e.g., *in front of*), spatial terms in the TI sentences aroused similar P200 as temporal terms did in TC sentences. This could be taken as evidence that both temporal sequencing terms (i.e., *before*) and spatial order terms in TI (i.e., *in front of*) were involved in visual-spatial processing. Although it is not clear whether the subjects interpreted the English sentences into Chinese, the similar P200 pattern for TC and TI indicates that spatial scenario would be constructed for temporal order processing.

Overall, Experiment 2 shows that the patterns between temporal and spatial anomaly effects are different. On the one hand, Chinese-English bilinguals have different neural representations in comprehending their L2 English temporal and spatial terms in that anomaly effects during temporal sequence processing are distinct from those during spatial order processing. On the other hand, there is an asymmetric relationship in time-space mapping. Spatial schema is likely to be activated during temporal sequencing comprehension as spatial terms did not disrupt the meaning and structure representations during processing TI sentences, but temporal schema might not be activated during spatial order comprehension. In other words, temporal scenarios can be structured in terms of on-line mappings from the domain of space but spatial schemas are not necessary to be structured from the domain of time.

9.5 Conclusions

Although how the different lexical encodings in bilinguals' two languages interfere with time-space metaphorical processing needs further evidence, the present study would be among the first few studies which provide neural evidence for the temporal-spatial metaphorical relationship in bilingual processing. The experiments lead to several conclusions. First, despite the different lexical encodings, early sensory-motor simulation plays a role in temporal sequencing processing in both L1 Chinese and L2 English. The findings well supports the Embodied Theory that conceptual knowledge is grounded in sensory-motor systems (Gallese & Lakoff, 2005). Second, in both languages, neural representations during comprehending temporal sequencing and spatial ordering are different. Besides, the time-spatial relationship is asymmetric, in that space schema or structures could be activated and imported into temporal sequence processing but not vice versa. These findings support the weak view of the Metaphoric Mapping Theory.

Part 3 Characteristics, Presentation and Causes for ESL Reading Difficulty

内容简介

这部分共包括5个研究，探讨汉语母语背景下英语学习者阅读困难特点、表现形式和困难的根源。研究中结合横断研究和追踪研究，分析①汉英双语阅读困难的表现形式和发生率；②英语学习者阅读中理解、解码和阅读速度缺陷情况；③英语阅读困难者认知缺陷和元认知缺陷情况，以及缺陷对二语英语阅读的影响。同时，使用脑电技术，考查阅读能力差异的两组读者在字词加工、语义整合的大脑神经机制。具体研究内容如下：

（1）研究1（第10章）题为"Trajectory of Reading disability for Chinese speakers of English"（汉语母语者英语阅读困难的表现形式），筛选英语解码困难、阅读理解困难、速度缺陷三种不同类型，并考察汉英双语阅读情况。本研究通过对照阅读困难者和普通读者的汉英双语阅读技能，来探讨双语的语言文字特性和阅读技能发展之间复杂关系。研究中从257个汉英双语者中筛查出英语字词阅读困难组（$N=26$）和控制组（$N=26$）。两组被试参加标准化的汉英双语字词阅读、字词阅读流畅性、篇章阅读流畅性、阅读理解测验。方差分析发现，困难组在英语阅读各种技能加工显著落后于控制组，但两组被试在汉语各阅读技能上并不存在显著差异。相关分析发现，两组被试在汉英双语的流畅性相关都显著，但困难组的双语字词阅读和流畅性、理解之间的关系更密切。

（2）研究2（第11章）题为"Cognitive deficits underlying Chinese EFL reading comprehension difficulty"（英语学习者阅读理解困难的认知缺陷），考察导致阅读理解困难的语言技能和认知因素上的根源，以及这些因素和阅读理解困难之间的关系。本研究旨在考察汉语母语者在英语阅读理解困难的语言和认知根源。研究从英语专业学生中筛查出英语阅读理解困难组和控制组，使用标准化测验测查了智力、英语阅读理解、词汇、语法、语音意识、语素、记忆广度、快速命名。方差分析发现，英语阅读理解困难者在语素、语音和快速命名上显著落后于年龄控制组。缺陷比例和阅读关系的进一步分析也发现，英语阅读理解困难组的语言和认知缺陷比例更高。研究结果对外语英语阅读困难的诊断有启示作用。

（3）研究 3（第 12 章）题为“Study on the relationship between Chinese-English bilingual reading and working memory deficits”（工作记忆缺陷和汉英双语阅读关系的研究），更深入考察工作记忆缺陷和汉英双语者的两种语言阅读的三个层面解码、流畅性和阅读理解之间的关系。国内外实证研究也表明，工作记忆对阅读理解具有较强的预测性。然而，国内极少数的研究考察英语阅读的另外两个技能（字词阅读和阅读流畅性）和工作记忆的关系。本研究以汉英双语者为研究对象，考察工作记忆和汉英双语的关系；在此基础上，探测高、中、低三种工作记忆能力的被试在英汉字词阅读、英汉阅读流畅性和英汉阅读理解上是否呈现差异。研究中以某大学英语专业低年级学生为研究对象，测查了汉语 / 英语单词阅读，汉语 / 英语阅读理解，以及汉语 / 英语句子流畅性以及英语工作记忆。研究中分别根据总体被试的工作记忆的回忆正确率的总体标准分为筛选依据，筛选出高工作记忆组、普通工作记忆组和工作记忆缺陷组三组被试。相关分析和方差分析结果发现，工作记忆与汉语字词阅读呈显著相关关系，但是与阅读理解和汉语阅读流畅性无显著相关性。工作记忆与英语阅读理解和阅读流畅性呈显著相关关系，但是与英语字词阅读无显著相关性。高工作记忆组、普通工作记忆组和工作记忆缺陷组三组被试在英语阅读理解，英语阅读流畅性上存在显著差异性。研究结果证实工作记忆对阅读理解的贡献；研究也说明，第二语言工作记忆对汉英双语阅读不同技能的作用存在差异，工作记忆缺陷，更大程度上影响了句子和篇章阅读。

（4）研究 4（第 13 章）题为“A revisit on L1 automatic activation during L2 reading: An ERP study on Chinese-English bilinguals”（再论二语阅读中的一语的自动激活），使用 ERP 技术，分析阅读能力差异对字词加工的大脑神经机制的影响。本研究考察汉英双语者阅读中，字形、语音和语义表征如何被激活。研究中要求汉英熟练双语者对相继出现的一组词进行语义相关性判断，并收集脑电数据。采用语言（2 水平：一语汉语外显加工 / 二语英语内隐加工）* 条件（4 水平：语义相关 / 语义不相关 / 语音重复 / 字形重复）* 半球（2 水平：左半球 / 右半球）* 部位（3 水平：前 / 中 / 后）的实验设计。对于被试来说，二语英语是内隐条件中，词对在语义不相关的词对，其汉语对译词在语音或者在字形上相近（即，词对的两个单词的汉语对译词在字形或语音重复）。研究中也把上述 6 个感兴趣区（左右半球的前中后脑区）的 N400 效应的大小和英语阅读水平做回归分析。研究发现，无论是汉语母语的外显任务，还是二语英语的内隐任务，语音和字形重复启动对 N400 波幅起调节作用。相比之下，语音重复启动的N400效应比字形重复启动的效应更小。不仅如此，一语汉语和二语英语的加工在脑区激活上存在差异。阅读成绩可以有效解释字形重复启动条件下的前部脑区的N400效应量。研究结果重复了前人关于二语理解中，无意识地、自动通达一语表征。研究结果对双语词汇通达机制有启示作用。

（6）研究5（第14章）题为“An ERP Study on the semantic unification mechanism of Chinese native learners of English during L2 English reading comprehension”（汉语母语的英语学习者在二语英语阅读理解中的语义整合机制），考察二语英语阅读困难者和普通读者句子阅读中字词语义整合机制的差异。阅读中利用各种手段进行语义整合从而理解文义是一个复杂的过程。词语语义分析能力和语境整合能力是阅读理解过程中进行语义整合不可或缺的能力。前人对阅读的研究多从母语角度进行理论探究，对正常阅读水平的阅读者关注较多，本研究利用事件相关电位（ERP）就英语水平不同的两组英语学习者的词语语义分析能力和利用语境能力进行探究。28名北京第二外国语学院大二的英语专业学生参加实验。根据阅读成绩把被试分为两组，即阅读困难组（$N = 14$）及正常阅读组（$N = 14$）。实验中要求被试阅读句子，并判断句子可接受性；收集被试行为数据及脑电数据。实验以组别（阅读困难组，实验控制组）为组间变量，语义频率（高，低），语境（相关，不相关）为组内变量，进行方差分析。行为结果显示，熟练读者和阅读困难者都呈现词频效应，但是总体数据并不呈现出语义频率效应。行为结果的语境效应也不显著。脑电结果显示，在N400的潜伏期上，组间效应边缘显著，这种效应在普通读者呈现在左脑中区，而对于阅读困难者，语境效应右脑中区。本研究表明，阅读水平差异导致阅读理解中语义整合过程中涉及的脑区存在差异。研究进一步表明：①不同英语水平的汉英双语者，在字词分析能力和语境利用能力方面确实存在差异。词频对阅读困难者影响更大。②正常阅读者表现为更大的语境依赖，而阅读困难者的语境、词频利用模式则更为复杂。

Chapter 10 Trajectory of reading disability for Chinese speakers of English

Abstract: This study examined reading difficulty in bilinguals and the complex relationship between reading-related cognitive skills and reading. Readers with word decoding and reading comprehension difficulties were screened from Chinese-English bilinguals and were matched with a control group. Two groups of subjects were measured on Chinese-English bilingual word reading, word reading fluency, reading fluency, and reading comprehension. ANOVA analysis found that readers with difficulty in English reading skills lagged behind the control group, but the two groups were comparable in Chinese reading skills. Results also showed that English words decoding difficulties were usually associated with difficulties in reading comprehension and reading fluency.

Key words: Chinese-English bilingual reading difficulties the difference mode

10.1 Introduction

Reading difficulty in native language exists in three forms: decoding difficulty, comprehension difficulty and reading fluency deficit (e.g., Limbos & Geva, 2001). Research at home and abroad mostly focuses on decoding difficulties. And definition of dyslexia is often based on word reading (e.g., Ho & Lai, 1999; Limbos & Geva, 2001; Lyon, Shaywitz & Shaywitz, 2003; Shu et al., 2006).

10.1.1 Word reading

Based on the simple view of reading, word decoding and comprehension are two components of reading components (Gough & Tunmer, 1986). Studies on native language have confirmed the important role of decoding in reading comprehension (e.g., Katzir et al.,

2006). Word recognition also becomes the core of reading difficulty defects (e.g., Snowling, 1997). Psudoword decoding is usually used to detect the ability in manipulating units smaller than syllables (August and Shanahan, 2006). Standardized tests, such as Word attack (WA) in the Woodcock Reading Mastery Test, are known as a task for word decoding. Many studies have found that a high correlation between decoding and phonological awareness (Quiroga, Lemos-Britton, Mostafapourm & Berninger, 2002). However, one line of research suggests that Chinese adults may take the form of whole word reading method (Wang, Koda & Perfetti, 2003). Children are to some extent also with whole word reading strategies (Knell, 2010), but this is not the best way to read English.

10.1.2 Reading fluency

Reading is a main way of access to outside information. For an adult, word reading and effective access to information can be acquired by fluent reading. Reading fluency needs to quickly extract morphological transformation rules, quickly identify word forms, rapid extraction of semantic information. Reading fluency is a component of language proficiency. It is an automated skill (Schmidt, 1992: 357). During this process, orthographic knowledge, the knowledge of relationships between shapes, sounds, facilitate skilled reader to automate analyze language structures (Ehri, 1998: 3). Thus, decoding efficiency, context information and orthographic structures may affect reading fluency (Katzir et al., 2006; Liu Dandan, 2002).

10.1.3 Reading comprehension

Reading comprehension is a part of language skills. In the reading comprehension process, word recognition is the premise (Lundberg, 2002). According to Carver (2000), reading comprehension is a bi-directional capability, reflected in the interactions between the depth of understanding and processing speed. Although research shows that the decoding and understanding could explain most of the variation in reading comprehension (Savage, 2006), but this is still controversial (彭鹏 & 陶沙, 2009).

Word decoding and Difficulty in reading comprehension is often found to be associated with decoding. There are still cases of dissociation between decoding and reading comprehension (Cain, Oakhill, Barnes & Bryant, 2001; Catts, Adlof & Weismer, 2006). Some researchers suggest readers with reading comprehension difficulty may have defects in oral skills (Catts et al., 2006), although some evidence found they did not have problems in phonological processing (Catts et al., 2006; Wong, Kidd, Ho & Au, 2010). From this view, reading difficulties are differentially rooted.

Research on second language reading difficulty is relatively scarce. There exists transfer between the two languages for the bilinguals. The transfer is manifested in both behavioral and neural responses (Leij & Morfidi, 2006; Oren & Breznitz, 2005). Previous studies also found dissociation of difficulties in native language vs. the second language (Wydell & Butterworth, 1999; Lundberg, 2000).

In the study of Chinese native learners of English, word reading test on reading difficulties are limited mainly to decoding. The study explores the relationship between development of bilingual language and reading skills. In particular, the present study focuses on the difference and consistency in different reading components for difficult readers. Research questions are as following: Did readers with the second language English word decoding difficulty have problems in English reading speed and English reading comprehension? Did readers with the second language English word decoding difficulty have problems in Chinese reading skills? Did the reading difficulty group and the control group have similar relationship in terms of the different reading components?

10.2 Research methods

10.2.1 Subjects

English majors (n = 257) participated in this study. Based on the previous research (Ho et al., 2004), screening criteria are the normal intelligence and reading scores and at least one cognitive task 1 *SD* below the grade mean. Given that the present subjects were college students, we did not measure their ID. According to the screening criteria, the word-decoding-difficulty group had 26 subject, screening rates of 10.11%. The result was in line with previous studies (Lyon, 1995). A control group (n = 26) were selected with word reading scores being 1 SD higher than the grade mean.

10.2.2 Experimental procedures

English reading comprehension (approximately 30 minutes) is a group test; Individual tests include English word reading and Chinese characters (approximately 20 minutes). All tasks were tested randomly.

10.2.3 Measures

Characters/words reading in English reading

Chinese characters reading consists of 240 Chinese characters, and English words have a total of 106 words. Subjects were asked to read the words on the cards as much as possible. The correlations between twice measurements are 0.55 in Chinese and 0.48 for English, $ps < 0.001$, indicating good reliability.

Chinese/English word reading fluency

Chinese characters/English word (in total 104 words) were printed in a card. Participants were asked to read the words as quickly as possible. The correlations between twice measurements are 0.56 in Chinese and 0.62 for English, $ps < 0.001$, indicating good reliability.

Chinese/English reading comprehension

English reading comprehension used Gates MacGinitie Reading Comprehension (Form 4, Level f), with 14 articles. Chinese reading materials were in a similar design. Cronbach alpha for Chinese was 0.68 and that for English was 0.70, respectively, indicating good reliability.

10. 3 Results and discussion

10.3.1 Differences between the two reading groups

In order to compare the reading group and control group, we used ANOVA. The following table showed the results of ANOVA. The results showed significant differences in English word reading, including reading comprehension, word reading and reading fluency. Whereas, in Chinese tasks, there is no significant difference between the two groups. The marginal difference was found in Chinese reading comprehension, $p = 0.06$.

The results indicate a double dissociation in reading skills in the two languages. The results are in line with the script-dependent hypothesis (Breznitz, Oren & Shaul, 2005). This double dissociation may be derived from the bilingual language differences, although reading involves similar processes (Snowling et al., 1997).

Table 15 Comparison between the word–reading–difficulty and the control group

	Groups	*N*	Mean	*SD*	*F*	Sig.
English word reading	Difficult	26	60.62	17.92	98.21	0.001
	Control	26	95.96	3.10		
English reading fluency	Difficult	25	72.52	7.48	45.45	0.001
	Control	26	84.54	5.06		
English reading comprehension	Difficult	20	19.55	5.15	37.01	0.001
	Control	24	32.08	7.92		
Chinese character reading	Difficult	25	221.16	10.88	0.32	0.57
	Control	26	222.54	5.92		
Chinese reading fluency	Difficult	25	100.76	5.66	0.03	0.87
	Control	26	100.50	5.84		
Chinese reading comprehension	Difficult	25	35.20	5.76	3.84	0.06
	Control	24	37.96	3.87		

10.3.2 Correlation analysis

To further analyze the relationships between the components of bilingual reading skills, Pearson's correlation analysis was performed. The following table showed the correlation results for the reading-difficulty group. The coefficients between Chinese reading comprehension, character reading and reading fluency were respectively $r = 0.59$ and $r = 0.71$, $ps < 0.01$. The results indicate reading comprehension achievement relies on word reading, similar to the relationship between English reading skills. On the relationship between Chinese and English reading skills, both Chinese character reading and reading fluency have the correlation coefficient of 0.44, $p < 0.05$. The correlation between Chinese reading comprehension and English word reading fluency is 0.47, $p < 0.05$. The correlation between Chinese and English reading comprehension is marginally significant, $r = 0.43, p < 0.08$.

Table 16 Correlation analysis for the word–reading–difficulty group

	2	3	4	5	6
1. English word reading	−0.31	−0.36	−0.01	−0.15	−0.27
2. English reading fluency		0.23	0.44*	0.44*	0.47*
3. English reading comprehension			0.20	0.16	0.43#
4. Chinese character reading				0.59**	0.71**
5. Chinese reading fluency					0.71**
6. Chinese reading comprehension					

Notes: ** $p < 0.01$; * $p < 0.05$; # $p < 0.08$.

The following table showed the correlation results for the control group. The English word reading fluency is significantly related to Chinese character reading fluency, $r = 0.64$, $p < 0.01$; in addition, the correlation between bilingual word reading is not significant. Reading fluency is a component of language proficiency, and it is an automated program-technical skill (Schmidt, 1992). The higher efficiency level of word identification fluency, the more cognitive resources could be allocated to reading comprehension.

It can be seen from the comparison between the two groups, there are three major differences between the two groups: first, the correlations between word reading, reading fluency, reading comprehension are significant for the difficult group, but not for the control group. Second, bilingual reading comprehension is correlated with each other for the difficult group, but not for the control group. Third, English reading fluency is correlated with Chinese words reading and Chinese reading comprehension, but not for the control group.

Table 17 Correlation analysis for the control group

	2	3	4	5	6
1. English word reading	−0.01	0.37	0.05	−0.10	0.28
2. English reading fluency		0.28	0.17	0.64**	0.01
3. English reading comprehension			0.37	0.10	0.34
4. Chinese character reading				0.13	0.02
5. Chinese reading fluency					−0.01
6. Chinese reading comprehension					

Note: **, $p < 0.01$.

10.4 Conclusion

Research draws two main conclusions: Readers with English word reading difficulty rely more on lower-level word decoding, and decoding difficulty becomes the key to deficits in reading fluency and reading comprehension; second, reading efficiency in both languages is interdependent. Results of the study on bilingual teaching and difficulty reading mechanisms have important implications. Theoretically, the results also support the assumptions and hypothesis of Central Processing Hypothesis (Breznitz, Oren & Shaul, 2005). Additionally, for second language learners, teachers often ignore words in second language reading difficulties (Limbos & Geva, 2001). English reading instruction in China focuses on metacognitive training (e.g., 李俊 , 倪杭英 , 2007; Liu Li, 2002; 孟悦 , 2004). From the results of this study, word recognition is the premise and foundation of understanding (Lundberg, 2002), and decoding difficulty is typical of dyslexia (Snowling et al., 1997). Therefore, intervention on English reading comprehension difficulty needs to consider the source of comprehension difficulties.

Chapter 11 Cognitive deficits underlying Chinese EFL reading comprehension difficulty

Abstract: The present research is aimed at exploring the linguistic and cognitive sources for reading difficulty. English reading difficulty group and control group were screened from English majors. They were measured on IQ, reading comprehension, vocabulary, grammar, phonological awareness, morphological awareness, sentence span, rapid naming in English. ANOVA analyses found that the reading difficulty groups were more impaired on morphological awareness, phonological awareness and RAN. Further analysis on the relation between deficit percentage and reading performance revealed that the degree of linguistic and cognitive deficits was proportional to English reading difficulty. The findings would be insightful for the diagnosis of EFL reading difficulty.

Key words: EFL reading comprehension cognitive impairment

11.1 Introduction

Developmental dyslexia is a special difficulty in learning to read and write. The occurrence rate is about 5%-10% population. It affects the individual's academic achievement, cognitive, emotional and social development (Lyon, 1995; 孟祥芝 & 舒华, 1999). For the latest 20 years, the componential approach has been taken to tap into the relationship between cognitive skills and reading and help to reveal the causes of dyslexia (Koda, 2007). Studies have found that most reading difficulties will accompany the low-level cognitive impairment (e.g., Ho et al., 2004; Manis, 1996; Shu et al., 2006). Specifically, for alphabetic languages, impairment in phonological processing skills (short-time memory and phonological awareness, naming speed) becomes the core to dyslexia (Leij & Morfid, 2006; Goswami, 2003). Chinese dyslexia children have deficits in phonological skills, morphological awareness, orthographic processing skills and rapid naming (Ho et al., 2002; Ho & Lai, 1999; 李虹 & 舒华, 2009; Shu et al., 2006).

However, relatively little research was devoted to the reading disability in a foreign or second language. In China domestic studies, it has found poor vocabulary and grammar, inefficient reading speed, low ability in syntactic analysis lead to difficulties in reading English for Chinese speakers of English (刘丹丹, 2002). On the lower level of cognitive skills, researchers have identified deficits in phonological awareness contribute to English reading disability for the sample of Chinese native speakers (董燕, 段建平 & 邵波, 2004; 郭楠 et al., 2009; 陶沙, 2009). And the deficits have neural bases. For instance, the Chinese natives with English reading difficulties are poor in inhibiting interference stimulus in both left and right hemispheres, and there exists insufficient activation in the left hemisphere (董燕 & 段建平, 2004; 董燕, 段建平 & 邵波, 2004).

It is to be noted that this cognitive diagnostic studies are aimed at primary school children. As proposed by August and Shanahan (2006), most research on the second language reading disability focused on children in the primary school, and it is necessary to aim at older subjects. In defining reading disability, the equal chance of education should be ensured (Lyon, 1995; 席旭琳, 2009). However, for the second language English education in China, the primary school children have English classes for about 6 hours per week, which does not provide enough language input.

Therefore, the present study examined English majors in China, who learned English as a foreign language for more than six years. The research questions of this study were: Were the language skills (grammar, vocabulary, morphemes) and cognitive skills (rapid naming, phonological awareness, working memory) impaired for the subjects who had difficulty in English reading comprehension? How were the impairments related to the performance of English reading comprehension?

11.2 Method

11.2.1 Participants

212 English majors in China (Grade 2 in a university) participated in the study. They completed the English reading comprehension test (selected from national tests for non-English majors). There were 4 passages with a total of 20 questions (2 points per question).

According to Shu et al. 2006, the criteria for reading disability include normal IQ, and reading scores and at least one cognitive skills being 1SD lower than mean. The selection was based on the Z-score. The reading difficulty group was matched with the control group ($M = 25.29$, $SD = 4.72$) at the age (as shown in the following table).

Table 18 Demographic information of the reading difficulty group and the control group

	Group	*M*	*(SD)*	Comparison
Age (year)	D	20.56	(1.01)	C=D
	C	20.18	(0.87)	
IQ	D	24.75	(6.50)	C=D
	C	28.33	(3.03)	
English reading comprehension	D	18.33	(2.06)	C>D
	C	26.18	(2.89)	

Notes: D = The reading comprehension difficulty group; C = The control group; $p < 0.05$.

11.2.2 Procedures

All of the individual tests took place in a large conference room in the university. The individual assessment was done on a one-to-one basis, including English phonological awareness, English working memory, and rapid naming. Five postgraduate research assistants participated as examiners to collect the data. They were all English majors and were highly proficient bilinguals. The individual tests took about 30 minutes.

The group assessment tasks, including Matrix Analogies Reasoning, English reading comprehension, English vocabulary, English morphology and English grammar subtests, were administered in the classroom by their course teachers. The group tests took approximately 3 hours to complete, and thus was administered in two sections.

11.2.3 Materials

Matrix Analogies Reasoning (MAT)

Section 2 and 4 of MAT were administered (Naglieri 1985). There were 32 items, and Cronbach alpha = 0.85.

English Reading Comprehension

For testing English reading comprehension, the Gates MacGinitie Reading Comprehension (Form 4, Level F) were adopted with fourteen passages in total for both the first-year students and the second-year students for answering the question. Each passage had several questions with five -answer multiple choices and there were 48 questions in total with a full score of 48. The students were asked to finish this part within 30 minutes and the total scores they got were regarded as the index of their reading performance (Conbach alpha = 0.70).

English Vocabulary

The task used Gates-Macgintie Vocabulary Knowledge Test, Level E Form 4, Second Canadian Edition. There were 65 items in total and Cronbach alpha = 0.82.

Phonological Awareness

The task was subtest from Comprehensive Test of Phonological Processing (CTOPP) Elision Subtest (Wagner, Torgesen & Rashotte, 1999). There were 20 test items. The participants were asked to listen a word, which was present by MP3, e.g.,/toothbrush /, the participants were required to take of the sound /tooth/. The sounds deleted included 3 syllables and 17 phonemes, which located at the beginning or the mid of the word. Cronbach alpha = 0.68.

English Word Decoding

The subtest of Word Attack (Wookcock) was adopted. There were 45 pseudowords. The subjects were asked to read the words. Cronbach alpha = 0.77.

English Working Memory

Working memory capacity was tested by WM (Daneman & Carpenter, 1980). It consisted of unrelated sentences range from two sentences at least to five sentences at most, and each one ended with a different word. All of the sentences were grammatically correct. The subjects were requested to make a true-false judgment to the sentences and recall the very last word of each sentence. The numbers of the correctly recalled sentences was regarded as the quota of working memory. The total score of this test is 42; Cronbach alpha = 0.87 for the judgment task and Cronbach alpha = 0.87 for the repetition task.

Rapid Naming

Two versions (for both digital and picture respectively) were used. They were 4*9 matrixes for each version. The subjects were asked to read as quickly and accurately as possible the digits (or pictures) in the cards. The correlations between the two versions were 0.85, $p < 0.001$ for the digital rapid naming, and 0.81, $p < 0.001$ for the picture rapid naming.

English Derivational Morphology

Participants' English Morphological Awareness included two sections. One section was compound words and the other was the derivation. For the compound task, the subjects were asked to reading (and listen) a second, and filled in the blank an appropriate word form. The total score was 15. For the derivation task, the subjects were presented with a root word and a sentence with a word missing, and were required to produce a derived form of the root word to complete the sentence, with a total score of 31 and Cronbach alpha = 0.70.

English Syntactic Awareness

Two tasks were included: syntactic judgment task and morpho-syntax task. For the syntactic judgment, the subjects heard sentences, some sentences were grammatically correct and others are not. They were asked to judge whether the sentence was grammatically correct or not. They only heard each sentence twice. There are three major types of errors: subject-verb agreement (e.g., The boy being sad.), word order (e.g., The child the letter wrote.), and function word usage (e.g., Very much we thanked him.). There were 36 in total and Cronbach alpha = 0.58. For the morpho-syntactic task, the subjects listened (and read) a sentence, and chose the appropriate word form to fill in the blank of the sentence.

11.3 Results and discussion

The following table showed that the reading comprehension difficulty group lagged behind the control group in English reading comprehension, $F = 4.74$, $p = 0.04$. The results confirmed the reliability of the selection criterion for the two groups.

Table 19 Comparison between the two groups on language and cognitive skills

Measures	Group	*M*	*SD*	Min.	Max.	*F*	Sig.
Reading comprehension	D	0.56	0.07	0.46	0.67	4.74	0.04
	C	0.64	0.09	0.42	0.77		
Vocabulary	D	0.36	0.09	0.22	0.51	4.87	0.04
	C	0.48	0.16	0.26	0.77		
Phonological awareness	D	0.68	0.15	0.30	0.90	4.72	0.04
	C	0.82	0.16	0.55	1.00		
Decoding	D	0.52	0.22	0.14	0.86	6.20	0.02
	C	0.70	0.13	0.52	0.86		
Working memory (judgment)	D	24.25	6.37	18.00	36.00	1.84	0.19
	C	27.50	5.33	23.00	37.00		
Working memory (repetition)	D	20.50	3.90	16.00	27.00	2.94	0.10
	C	25.33	8.96	13.00	42.00		
Rapid naming (digit)	D	14.72	1.73	12.30	18.39	12.44	0.00
	C	12.02	2.00	8.60	14.65		
Rapid naming (pictutre)	D	21.77	2.67	18.55	27.85	0.98	0.33
	C	20.84	1.81	17.55	23.80		
Morphological awareness (compound)	D	0.35	0.24	0.00	0.82	0.22	0.65
	C	0.29	0.24	0.00	0.73		
Morphological awareness (derivation)	D	0.56	0.08	0.39	0.68	20.93	0.00
	C	0.70	0.07	0.58	0.81		
Syntactic judgment	D	0.67	0.13	0.44	0.86	0.90	0.35
	C	0.71	0.09	0.56	0.86		
Morpho-syntax	D	0.65	0.24	0.24	0.95	3.87	0.06
	C	0.81	0.14	0.62	1.00		

Notes: D = The reading comprehension difficulty group; C = The control group.

11.3.1 Comparison between the two reading groups on language and cognitive skills

Results showed that the reading difficulty group significantly lags behind the control group in series of skills such as vocabulary, phonological awareness, rapid naming, morphological awareness (derivation), and morphosyntax. The comparison results as shown in Table 19 prove that the reading comprehension difficulty group has difficulty in several phonological processing tasks (phonological awareness, naming speed and working memory). The results are consistent with the findings in alphabetic languages (e.g., van Daal & van der Leji, 1999; Vellutino et al., 2004). This result is also consistent with the findings on Chinese-English bilinguals who had deficits in English word reading (陶沙 , 2009). It seems to be cross-language universal that accurate recognition, memory, quick access to phonological representation plays an important role in the development of second language reading.

11.3.2 Analysis on the cognitive deficits percentage

The present study used Fletcher et al.'s (2002) criterion of "deficit", namely, 1 *SD* below the average, as the point of defining the reading difficulty. First, base on the sample mean and standard deviation, all test scores are calculated; then, those skills that were 1 *SD* below the overall average scores were defined as the deficit skills.

The percentages of the deficit skills were shown in the following table. Generally, the reading difficulty group had more percentage of deficit skills. Specifically, 38% of the reading difficulty group showed difficulty on morphological awareness (compound), whereas only 8% of the control group showed deficits in morphological compounding. 17% of the reading difficulty group had deficits in derivations, while no deficits were found for the control group. And for phonological awareness, 17% was for the reading difficulty group, and 8% was for the control group. In the decoding task, 25% was for the difficulty group, whereas no case was found for the control.

These results confirmed that for the group of reading comprehension difficulty, morphological awareness was more impaired, followed by the phonological processing skills, including phonological awareness, working memory, and rapid naming. This result is consistent with the findings on Chinese natives, where morphological awareness was found to be the core deficit Chinese dyslexia (Shu et al., 2006). As well, phonological deficits and rapid naming deficits were the two independent factors that contributed to dyslexia (Wolf et al., 2002).

Table 20 Analysis results on cognitive deficits for the two reading groups

Deficits types	Percentage in the difficulty group	Percentage in the control group
Morphology		
Compound	38%	8%
Derivation	17%	0%
Phonology		
Phoneme	17%	8%
Decoding	25%	0%
Working memory		
Judgment	17%	0%
Repetition	0%	8%
Rapid naming		
Digit	17%	0%
Picture	8%	0%
Syntax		
Judgment	25%	8%
Morph-syntax	42%	0%
Vocabulary	8%	8%

11.3.3 Impact of cognitive deficits on reading

Dyslexia may be caused by more than one cognitive deficit (Ho et al., 2004). The following analyzed the heterogeneity of the reading difficulty and how the number and degree of cognitive deficit combinations contributed to reading difficulty. If a subject in two or more cognitive skills that were 1 *SD* lower than the mean, the number and degree (Zscore) were added up. The following table showed the results.

Comparative analysis on the combination of defects found that the reading comprehension difficulty group was a heterogeneous group. They had different cognitive deficits. And combinations of different kinds of cognitive deficits also affect reading performance. It is worth mentioning that some reading comprehension difficulties individuals found no language and cognitive deficiencies, but they did not perform well in reading comprehension. This type of reading difficulty may arise from a number of unknown factors, such as Metacognition, motivation and experience. In addition, the language and cognitive factors may change with the improvement of English language ability (闫嵘 & 霍健才, 2013).

Table 21 Combination of the cognitive deficits and reading scores

Deficit types	Number	Percentage	Reading comprehension scores（Z-score）
0 deficit	2	16.67%	0.23
1 deficit	2	16.67%	1.11
morphology (compound)	1	8.33%	
rapid naming（digit)	1	8.33%	
2 deficits	3	25.00%	−0.53
decoding + rapid naming	1	8.33%	
working memory (repetition) + morphology	2	16.67%	
3 deficits and above	5	41.67%	−1.41
morphology + decoding + syntax	1	8.33%	
vocabulary + morph-syntax + morphology + syntax	1	8.33%	
IQ + phonology + morph-syntax working memory（judgment）	1	8.33%	
morphology + IQ + syntax + morph-syntax	1	8.33%	
Morphology + IQ + phonology + decoding + syntax + morph-syntax + rapid naming	1	8.33%	

11.4 Conclusion

First, in the context of Chinese native language, readers with English reading comprehension difficulty lagged behind the control groups in a series of language and cognitive skills, including vocabulary, morphological awareness, phonological awareness, rapid naming etc. The results indicate reading comprehension difficulty is modulated by the deficits in the lower level of cognitive abilities. Second, the degree and the number of language and cognitive deficits are in proportion to the success of reading performance. Accordingly, deficits in language awareness or cognitive processing skills may cause comprehension difficulties. Third, the group of the second language learners with English reading comprehension difficulty is a heterogeneous group. They are different in cognitive deficits. The present findings have insightful implications for the diagnosis of reading difficulty for Chinese native adults.

Chapter 12　Study on the relationship between Chinese-English bilingual reading and working memory deficits

Abstract: Working memory (WM) plays an important role in reading comprehension. However, few studies have focused on the relationship between the second language WM (L2 WM) and reading components (i.e., word recognition and reading fluency). This study investigated the relationship between Chinese-English bilingual reading and working memory deficits. English majors from a university in China were examined on word recognition, reading fluency, reading comprehension and WM capacity. Subjects were grouped in to good vs. poor WM groups. Correlation analysis showed that WM was significantly correlated with Chinese word recognition and Chinese reading comprehension, but it has no significant correlation with Chinese reading fluency. WM was found to be correlated with English reading fluency and reading comprehension, but there was no significant correlation with English word recognition. ANOVA found significant difference between L2 WM groups on English reading fluency and English reading comprehension. The results revealed that L2 WM is significantly correlated with bilingual reading development; participants with good WM and average WM capacity have better performance than those with poor WM in bilingual reading tasks.

Key words: WM deficiency　Chinese-English bilingual　reading components

12.1　Introduction

Baddeley and Hitch (1974) put forward the concept of working memory (working memory). Just & Carpenter (1992) and Baddeley & Hitch (1974) claimed that working memory was a limited resource, used for temporary processing and storage of information.

However, reading comprehension skills for normal adults are not dependent on temporary storage of information of the article, but rely on a more complex working memory operation. King (1991) compared subjects with high vs. low reading spans, and found that subjects with low reading span test used a longer period of time. Daneman and Merikle's (1996) research focused on individual differences in working memory. Daneman and Carpenter (1980) found that the breadth of reading (reading span) was associated with reading comprehension. Domestic research also found evidence of individual differences in working memory capacity (Cui et al., 1996; Jing, 2003; Li, 2004).

Despite the findings, little evidence has shown how good vs. poor WM is related to different levels of reading comprehension. Few studies have focused on the relationship between second language WM (L2 WM) and reading components (i.e., word recognition and reading fluency). This study investigated the relationship between different components of Chinese-English bilingual reading and working memory deficits.

12.2 Research methods

12.2.1 Participants

106 participants who were English majors participated in the experiment. They were 60 Grade 1 and 46 Grade 2 students whose ages ranged from 19 to 21 years. All the students learned English as a second language for about 8 years.

12.2.2 Procedure

Participants were assessed in a quiet classroom. The tests were administered by trained graduate research assistants who majored in English linguistics.

12.2.3 Measures

The experiment contained two parts: collective tests and individual tests. The collective tests last for one hour, including Chinese and English reading fluency tests and reading comprehension tests. The individual tests lasted half an hour, including WM, Chinese word recognition and English word recognition.

Working Memory

WM capacity was tested by using WM (Daneman & Carpenter, 1980). The subjects were requested to make a judgment on the sentences and recall the very last word of each sentence. The total score of this test was 27; Conbach alpha = 0.64.

Chinese/English Word Recognition Test

The Chinese word recognition test was self-developed materials, including 240 Chinese characters. The Woodcock Reading Mastery Test-Revised (WRMT-R: Woodcock, 1987) was adopted for the English word recognition test. There were 106 English words in total. The subjects were requested to read aloud the words on the card. The test would be suspended if there were 6 mistakes in a consecutive order. Conbach alpha for Chinese characters = 0.76. Conbach alpha for English wording recognition = 0.83.

Chinese/English Reading Fluency

The reading fluency task was presented by the E-Prime. The subjects were required to read the sentence as fast and as good as possible, and then made the judgment. In the pre-test we found that the accurate rate was as high as 95%, partially because they are very simple sentences. The average reaction time was taken as the index of reading fluency. The test-retest correlation coefficient measured for English reading fluency was = 0.50, while that of the Chinese sentence reading fluency was = 0.30, p = 0.5. Accordingly, the reliabilities for both tests were acceptable.

Chinese/English Reading Comprehension

The English reading comprehension task used Gates MacGinitie Reading Comprehension (Form 4, Level F 14 texts), while the Chinese reading comprehension tasks were the translation version of the English tasks mentioned above. There were 48 questions. The duration for the tests was both 30 minutes. Conbach alpha of the Chinese reading comprehension test was 0.87, while that of the English reading comprehension was 0.72.

12.3 Results

Table 22 Descriptive statistics of all measures

Variables	*M*	*SD*	Min.	Max.
WM	22.09	8.47	8.00	6.00
CWR	221.44	10.82	173.00	235.00
EWR	80.29	7.06	66.00	96.00
CRF	4 058.38	651.20	2 547.65	5 520.95
ERF	2 763.05	671.61	1 751.90	4 560.6
CRC	37.29	5.41	26.00	45.00
ERC	27.19	8.22	5.00	41.00

Notes: WM = working memory; EWR = English word recognition; ERF = English reading fluency; ERC = English reading comprehension; CWR = Chinese word recognition; CRF = Chinese reading fluency; CRC = Chinese reading comprehension. **p* < 0.05, ***p* < 0.01.

The descriptive statistics were shown in the above table. ANOVA was used to examine whether readers with better WM achieve higher scores in Chinese word recognition, reading fluency and reading comprehension. In order to find out the relationship between L2 WM and Chinese-English word recognition, reading fluency and reading comprehension, Spearson correlation analysis was used.

Table 23 Correlation analysis between WM and bilingual reading

	WM	EWR	ERF	ERC	CWR	CRF	CRC
WM	—						
EWR	0.06	—					
ERF	0.42*	−0.12	—				
ERC	0.44**	−0.17	−0.38**	—			
CWR	0.23**	0.00	−0.41**	0.28**	—		
CRF	0.01	−0.01	0.27**	−0.22*	−0.05	—	
CRC	0.41*	−0.05	−0.25*	0.43**	0.48**	−0.09	—

Notes: WM = working memory; EWR = English word recognition; ERF = English reading fluency; ERC = English reading comprehension; CWR = Chinese word recognition; CRF = Chinese reading fluency; CRC = Chinese reading comprehension. **p* < 0.05, ***p* < 0.01.

The above table showed correlations between L2 WM and bilingual reading. It revealed that participants' WM was strongly associated with English reading fluency ($r = 0.42$, $p < 0.05$), with English reading comprehension ($r = 0.44$, $p < 0.01$), with Chinese word recognition ($r = 0.23$, $p < 0.01$) with Chinese reading comprehension ($r = 0.41$, $p < 0.05$), but not with English word recognition and Chinese reading fluency.

The results above indicated that L2 WM is significantly related with English reading fluency, English reading comprehension, Chinese word recognition and Chinese reading comprehension. The correlation coefficients of English reading fluency, English reading comprehension and Chinese reading comprehension are higher than Chinese word recognition. These results showed that L2 WM plays a very important role for students to comprehend complex sentences and text both in Chinese and in English.

In order to find out whether there is a significant difference between different WM capacity groups and Chinese word recognition, reading fluency and reading comprehension, ANOVA was employed to further examine their relationship. The participants were matched on grade and gender. The following table showed no difference across WM groups in terms of Chinese reading skills.

Table 24 ANOVA analysis on Chinese reading across different WM groups

	Grouped by WM	*M*	*SD*	*F*	*p*
CWR	Poor	219.07	16.43	1.08	0.35
	Average	220.60	6.06		
	Good	221.44	6.59		
CRF	Poor	4327.12	551.08	1.85	0.17
	Average	3826.43	714.68		
	Good	4101.44	605.07		
CRC	Poor	36.87	5.90	0.16	0.85
	Average	37.08	5.92		
	Good	38.00	4.56		

Notes: WM = working memory; EWR = English word recognition; ERF = English reading fluency; ERC = English reading comprehension; CWR = Chinese word recognition; CRF = Chinese reading fluency; CRC = Chinese reading comprehension. $^*p < 0.05$, $^{**}p < 0.01$.

In order to find out whether readers with better WM capacity achieve higher scores in English word recognition, reading fluency and reading comprehension, ANOVA was employed to further compare the differences between groups.

Table 25 ANOVA analysis on English reading across different WM groups

	WM	*M*	*SD*	*F*	*p*
EWR	Poor	80.80	7.26	0.29	0.75
	Average	79.13	7.86		
	High	80.93	6.33		
ERF	Poor	3311.96	825.53	6.06	0.00**
	Average	2490.93	513.00		
	Good	2633.82	448.74		
ERC	Poor	22.60	7.52	4.57	0.00**
	Average	28.64	7.48		
	Good	30.92	5.06		

Notes: Notes: WM = working memory; EWR = English word recognition; ERF = English reading fluency; ERC = English reading comprehension; CWR = Chinese word recognition; CRF = Chinese reading fluency; CRC = Chinese reading comprehension. $*p < 0.05$, $**p < 0.01$.

The above table showed that there was no significant difference was observed across WM groups on English word recognition [F (2, 45)= 0.29, $p > 0.05$]; But significant difference was revealed across WM groups on English reading fluency [F (2, 45) = 6.06, $p < 0.01$] and English reading comprehension [F (2, 45) = 4.57, $p < 0.01$]. The results demonstrated that participants with different L2 WM capacity showed different performance in English reading. Specifically, when grouped by L2 WM capacity, participants with good WM capacity performed better than those with average and poor WM capacity groups in English word recognition tasks and English reading comprehension tasks. But average WM group performed better than good WM group in the English reading fluency tasks.

12.4 Discussion

Experimental results show that working memor, Chinese word reading, reading comprehension, English reading fluency and reading comprehension are significantly related. These are consistent with findings in Daneman & Carpenter (1980), Daneman & Merikle (1996) and Seigneuric, Ehrlich, Oakhill & Yuill (2000), namely reading span test can predict the adult reading comprehension. According to Kintch's (1978) model of text comprehension, comprehension follows a process of decomposition-integration-new proposition-to consolidate the cyclical process of decomposition. Working memory plays a key role in reading comprehension. After the selective processing of information,

information can be stored into long-term memory. Baddeley (1986) noted that the language learning relies on working memory. Working memory capacity not only affects short term memory, but also long-term memory retrieval speed of information processing. According to expertise effects in memory, Dehn (2008) notes that when a task is overlearned, information is retrieved automatically and directly from the long-term memory. Daneman and Carpenter (1986) propose that processing and storage are competing, due to the limited capacity of working memory. Low reading skills will demand more resources in semantic processing. Therefore, readers with high working memory process information faster.

One interesting finding is that WM capacity does not affect Chinese reading skills. The result is divergent with those found in English reading. The results indicate WM in English might have different components related to Chinese reading skills.

12.5 Conclusion

English WM is an important cognitive factor that may have influence on English reading. English WM has a high and positive correlation with Chinese word recognition, Chinese reading comprehension and English reading fluency and reading comprehension. Readers with higher WM capacity tend to spend less time in English reading fluency tests and achieve higher scores in reading comprehension.

Chapter 13 A revisit on L1 automatic activation during L2 reading: An ERP study on Chinese-English bilinguals

Abstract: The present study examined how orthographic, phonological, and semantic representations become activated in Chinese-English bilingual reading. EEG data were collected when fluent Chinese (L1)-English (L2) bilinguals made semantic relatedness judgment in Chinese and English. An experiment design of language (2 levels: L1 Chinese explicit/L2 English implicit)* condition (four levels: semantic related/semantic unrelated/sound repetition/spelling repetition), hemisphere (2 levels: left/right) and lobe (3 levels: frontal/central/posterior) were adopted. Implicit to the participants, L2 English word pairs were not related in meaning but shared a radical component or sound when translated into Chinese (implicit radical or sound priming through Chinese translation). Further, N400 effects measured on the difference waves at 6 Regions of Interest were regressed against English reading scores. It was found both explicit and implicit sound and spelling repetition modulated behavioural accuracies and attenuated the N400 amplitudes. Comparatively, sound repetition priming elicited less N400 effect than spelling repetition. Additionally, some variation in the scalp topography was found for the L1 explicit vs. L2 implicit access. Reading scores accounted for significant variances in N400 effects in the frontal areas for L1 explicit and L2 implicit reading with the spelling repetition condition. The results replicate previous findings on unconscious and automatic access to L1 representations during L2 comprehension. The results shed light on the mechanism of bilingual lexical access.

Key words: bilingual lexical access ERP topography variation

13.1 Introduction

How bilinguals have access to lexical items in the two languages is a heated topic in psycholinguistic research. Earlier studies indicate bilinguals language processing is language-selective (e.g., Altenberg & Cairns, 1983; Scarborough, Gerard & Cortese, 1984). Bilinguals seem to be insensitive to the non-target. For instance, Scarborough, Gerard & Cortese's (1984) study on Spanish-English bilinguals found practice on one language did not speed word recognition of the translation on the other language. Recently, an increasing number of studies reveal that information in the other language is simultaneously accessed. Bilinguals activated their native language translations no matter whether they were required an explicit (e.g., Guo et al., 2012; Schwartz & Kroll, 2006; Sunderman & Kroll, 2006) or implicit language processing (Wu & Thierry, 2010; Wu, Cristino, Leek & Thierry, 2013; Thierry & Wu, 2007). Accordingly, language non-selective lexical access is well established in bilinguals.

Despite, previous research mostly focuses on access to spelling of the native language (L1) (e.g., De Groot, Delmaar & Lupker, 2000; Dijkstra & van Heuven, 2002; Lemhofer, K. & Dijkstra, 2004). Bilingual performance in L2 was shown to be differentiated by words that share spellings with translations in L1. For instance, in the processing of non-native (L2) English homographs, there was significant native language (L1) semantic priming in the reaction times (RTs) and modulations in the N200 and N400 components for participants who viewed the L1 German movie (Elston, Gunter & Kotz, 2005). Generally, this line of study indicates bilinguals are sensitive to the interlingual status of homographs. However, previous research findings are controversial. Some found inhibitory effects (e.g., Doctor & Klein, 1992), and others facilitation effects for interlingual homophones in the lexical decision tasks (Brysbaert et al., 1999; Lemhofer & Dijkstra, 2004). Comparatively, relatively fewer studies were devoted to the nature of access to the L1 sound representation during L2 reading. In a latest study (Spalek et al., 2014), participants were asked to produce L2 English adjective-noun sequences. It was found phonological priming in English (e.g., green-goat) modulated event-related brain potentials over the frontocentral scalp region from around 440ms after picture onset. Phonological priming in L1 German (e.g., blue flower-"blaue blume") was detectable even earlier, from 300ms, even though German was never produced. Further, it is also argued that most alphabetic languages have strong alphabetical overlap and similar grapheme-phoneme correspondence rules. The relative interdependence between spelling and sound makes it difficult to tease apart the relative contribution of spelling and sound in cross-language interactions. Thus, the nature of the information (e.g., meaning, spelling or sound) that is accessed is still an open question.

In recent years, a number of studies have examined Chinese-English bilinguals' lexical access. Chinese characters have different grapheme-phoneme correspondence rules from alphabetic languages (e.g., English). Chinese characters are typically composed of one or more than one radical components. These characters are developed in six principles including pictographic, ideographic, logical aggregates, semantic-phonetic compound, transference, and loan. Except the regular semantic-phonetic compound character, there is no systematic sound-spelling correspondence, avoiding the confounding between speed and sound. Chinese-English bilinguals provide a good venue for examining bilingual lexical access.

Most studies on Chinese-English bilinguals have shown a strong lexico-semantic link between L1 and L2 can exist (Kroll et al., 2010), even for relatively high proficiency speakers (Guo et al., 2012). In Thierry & Wu's (2007) study, proficient Chinese (L1)-English (L2) bilinguals were asked to judge whether or not English words presented in pairs were related in meaning. Participants were unaware that some of the unrelated English words concealed character repetition via translation in Chinese. Although the data failed to find spelling (character) repetition affected the behavioral performance, the hidden factor modulated the brain potentials during L2 English comprehension in both the visual and auditory modality. However, even using similar experiment tasks, findings in Wu & Thierry (2010) entail a modality driven effect on lexical access to Chinese L1 during L2 English comprehension. L1 processing activated the sound of L1 translations, instead of the spelling. The experimental design might possibly attribute to the above controversial results. In the above two studies, different conditions were subjected to a between-stimulus comparison. For instance, ANOVA was performed with semantic related (related/unrelated), spelling repetition (repeated/ unrepeated) as within-subject factors. For instance, for semantically related, haven ("天堂" /**Tian Tang**/) vs. hell ("地狱" /**Di Yu**/); for semantic unrelated, sports ("体育" /**Ti Yu**/) vs. wealth ("财富" /**Cai Fu**/); for spelling repetition, accountant ("会计" /**Kuai Ji**/) vs. conference ("会议" /**Hui Yi**/). The different targets in word pairs across conditions might reduce the effect size of the experiment factor. Thus, the present study employed a within-stimulus comparison (for details, see "Materials" section).

The present study attempted to determine the relative magnitude of phonological vs. orthographic activation of L1 Chinese information during L2 English comprehension. The followed research questions were addressed: first, whether Chinese-English bilinguals automatically accessed L1 Chinese word representation when they performed semantic related judgment in their L2 English. The results were expected to replicate the previous studies on automatic access to L1 representation during L2 comprehension. Second, whether implicit access to different properties (spelling vs. sound vs. semantics) through L1 translation exerted similar priming effects. Third, whether the mechanism for L2 implicit lexical access was similar to L1 explicit effects. A experiment design of language (2 levels: L1 Chinese explicit/L2 English implicit)* condition (four levels: semantic related/semantic unrelated/sound repetition/spelling repetition), hemisphere (2 levels: left/right) and lobe (3 levels: frontal/central/posterior) were adopted. The present study collected both behavioral and ERP (Event-related potential) data when Chinese-English bilinguals performed a semantic relatedness judgment task.

ERPs can capture neural activities throughout a time period, and they are quite sensitive in revealing second language processing that may not emerge in behavioral studies (e.g., ratings and reaction times) (e.g., Tokowicz & MacWhinney, 2005; McLaughlin J, Osterhout L, Kim, 2004; Mueller, 2005). The N200 and N400 are two ERP components related to the present study. The N200 component is used to investigate if items in the non-target language produced interference in a lexical decision task (Moreno, Rodriguez-Fornells, Laine, 2008). A recent study showed N200 of implicit and automatic translation priming (e.g., Wu & Thierry, 2012). The N400, a negative deflection, occurs approximately 400ms after stimulus onset (Friederici, 2002). This late ERP component is associated with the completion of cognitive processing and it has been reported as an index of difficulty in semantic integration (Hagoort, 2008; Kutas & Hillyard, 1984). The character repetition priming is indexed by an amplitude reduction of the N400 component, which is known to be sensitive to overt (Kutas & Hillyard, 1984) and unconscious (Luck, Vogel & Shapiro, 1996) semantic priming and to repetition priming (Liu, Perfetti & Hart, 2003). Specifically, N400 is modulated by character repetition or sound repetition, no matter whether words are presented in their first or their second language and no matter whether they are presented visually or auditorily (Liu, Perfetti & Hart, 2003; Thierry & Wu, 2007; Wu & Thierry, 2010).

It was generally predicted that L1 Chinese explicit and L2 English explicit sound/

spelling repetitions should both modulate response accuracy, RT, and N200 and N400 amplitudes during processing the subsequent word. The priming effects should be attenuated in L2 implicit access. Sound priming effects on the subsequent word comprehension should be different from those of spelling repetition, considering sound and spelling representations are different language properties. Finally, due to the different nature of L1 Chinese and L2 English bilingual properties, sound/spelling repetition effects on lexical access should involve a distinct brain mechanism.

13.2 Methods

13.2.1 Participants

A total number of 28 Native speakers of Chinese (L1) volunteered for the experiment. They majored in English (L2) and had an experience of English immersion class for more than two years in a university in China. They acquired English after mean age of 8.35 (*SD* = 2.7). Thus, they were late beginning to intermediate bilinguals. According to the self-evaluation on the 10-point scale, their language proficiency was *M* = 7.70, *SD* = 1.21 for Chinese, and *M* = 6.36, *SD* = 0.95 for English. The participants gave their informed consent to participate in this study. They were compensated by money for their participation.

13.2.2 Materials

A total of 180 word pairs, falling into four conditions as illustrated in Table 26, were critical stimuli for the experiment. For each word pair, the first word (prime) was manipulated to establish semantic (un)relatedness for the second word (target). The semantic related condition was for "Yes" response; semantic unrelated, spelling repetition and sound repetition conditions were for "No" response. The target words were the same across the four conditions. Another 180 semantic (un)related word pairs were created as fillers to balance the "yes" and "no" responses, as well as distracting participants from the targets.

For Chinese semantic related condition, the word pair was related in meaning but differed in both spelling and sound, for instance, 疵 (/ci/, flaw) vs. 瑕 (/xia/, flaw). For Chinese semantic unrelated condition, the word pairs were not related in meaning and differed in both spelling and sound, for instance, 蜡 (/la/, wax)/ vs. 瑕 (/xia/, flaw). For Chinese sound repetition condition, the word pairs shared word pronunciation but differed in spelling and meaning, for instance, 霞 (/xia/, cloud) vs. 瑕 (/xia/, flaw). For Chinese spelling repetition, the word pairs shared a radical but differed in pronunciation and meaning). for instance, 王 (/wang/, king) vs. 瑕 (/xia/, flaw). Chinese-English bilinguals perceived spelling or sound repetitions explicitly. The priming effect in semantic related, spelling repetition and sound repetition conditions would reveal explicit lexical access in Chinese semantic relatedness task.

Table 26 Examples of stimuli used in the semantic–relatedness tasks

Conditions	Chinese word pairs		English word pairs	
	primes	targets	primes	targets
semantic related	疵 (/ci/, flaw)	瑕 (/xia/, flaw)	pencil(铅 笔 , /qian/)	pen(笔 , /bi/)
semantic unrelated	蜡 (/la/, wax)/	瑕 (/xia/, flaw)	cup(杯 , /bei/)	pen(笔 , /bi/)
sound repetition	霞 (/xia/, cloud)	瑕 (/xia/, flaw)	must(必 , /bi/)	pen(笔 , /bi/)
spelling repetition	王 (/wang/, king)	瑕 (/xia/, flaw)	fur(毛 , /mao/)	pen(笔 , /bi/)

Notes: Each cell contains one example of a word pair used in the semantic-relatedness task, it's the corresponding Chinese Pin Yin (alphabetic transposition of the phonological form), English/ Chinese translation.

Similar considerations were taken for English word pairs, except that the participants perceived spelling and sound repetitions implicitly. For English spelling repetition condition, the word pair did not share word meaning or sound, for instance, fur(" 毛 ", /mao/) vs. pen(" 笔 ", /bi/). Participants were unaware that the English words concealed radical component repetition via translation in Chinese. Likewise, for English sound repetition condition, the word pair concealed sound via translation in Chinese, for instance, must(" 必 ", /bi/) vs. pen(" 笔 ", /bi/). To verify the Chinese translation used in the experiment, 15 Chinese-English bilinguals performed a translation task. These participants were randomly drawn from the same population as the bilingual participants tested in the study to minimize the differences attributable to levels of proficiency and everyday use of English. The "first translation" method (Tokowicz & Kroll, 2007) was used, in which participants provide the first translation that comes to their mind and cannot change their responses. Participants generated over 99% consistency in the translation. Thus, any effect of spelling or sound repetition would then reveal implicit access to the native language during second language processing.

To avoid possible eye movements during the reading experiment, no English word had more than 5 letters and all Chinese translations featured less than two Chinese characters. The word-pairs across experimental conditions were controlled for the level of semantic relatedness as rated by 15 native Chinese learners of English on a 1-5 point scale. For Chinese word pairs, there was a main effect of experiment condition, F (3, 176) = 276.53, all ps < 0.001; ratings on semantic relatedness showed significant difference between semantic related condition vs. other three conditions, all ps < 0.001, and no difference across spelling repetition, sound repetition and unrelated conditions. For English word pairs, there was a main effect of experiment condition, F (3, 176) = 163.91, p < 0.001; Post hoc analysis on ratings on semantic relatedness showed significant difference between semantic related condition vs. other three conditions, all ps < 0.001, and no difference across spelling repetition, sound repetition and unrelated conditions.

13.2.3 Tasks

Chinese and English word pairs were run in two separate sections. For each section, there were two blocks. In both Chinese and English sections, participants viewed 180 word pairs (45 pairs for each condition, see Table 26 in Material Section) and 180 pairs of fillers. They were presented in a pseudo-randomized order. Participants were required to decide whether words presented in pairs were related in meaning or not.

After a prestimulus interval of 300ms, the first word was flashed for 500ms at fixation followed by the second word after an interstimulus interval of 300ms. The duration of the second word presentation was also 500ms. After the offset of the second word, a blank screen appeared for 300ms, followed by a question mark "?" that served as a prompt for 1 500ms. When the prompt appeared, participants were supposed to respond by pressing either "1" or "2". Right and left hand response types were counterbalanced. Each participant first completed 10 practice trials, consisting of five semantic related and five semantic unrelated word pairs. All practice stimuli were similar to the experimental items.

13.2.4 Data acquisition

Continuous EEG was recorded from 64 active electrodes (ActiCap, Brain Products GmbH, Munich) at standard international 10-20 system, referenced to bilateral mastoids and grounded to forehead. To control for vertical eye movements, a vertical electro-oculogram (VEOG) was recorded from Ag/AgCl electrodes placed closely above and below the left eye. Horizontal eye movements were measured by a horizontal electro-oculogram (HEOG) recorded from Ag/AgCl electrodes that placed at the outer canthus of each eye. All impedances were kept below 5kΩ during the experiment. EEG signals were bandpass filtered between 0.01 and 100Hz, and amplified and digitized at a rate of 500Hz using a BrainAmp amplifier (Brain Products GmbH, Munich). All EEG data were collected using Brain Vision Recorder software from Brain Products.

13.2.5 Data analyses

The analyses were conducted on data from 28 participants. The EEG data were processed offline using Brain Vision Analyzer 2. They were re-referenced to the mean of the left and right mastoid, and filtered with a 0.1Hz high-pass filter to remove drifts and a 30Hz filter to eliminate line noise. Independent component analysis (ICA) was employed to remove artifacts caused by eye movements, eye blinks, and muscular activity (Onton & Makeig, 2006). Epochs were removed from analysis if there was significant artifact in the EEG signal. The artifacts were removed based on visual inspection.

Peak detection was performed automatically, time-locked to the latency of the peak at the electrode of maximal amplitude on the grand-average ERP. Temporal windows for peak detection were determined at ±50ms around the peak. Electrode sites from frontal area (2 levels of hemisphere-left and right —F1/F2, F3/F4, F5/F6, F7/F8), central area (2 levels of hemisphere—left and right —C1/C2, C3/C4, C5/C6, C7/C8) and posterior area (2 levels of hemisphere—left and right —P1/P2, P3/P4, P5/P6, P7/P8) were selected for analysis. N400 were assessed by measuring the mean amplitude (average of non-rejected epochs from 0 to 800ms after the onset of the target, calculated relative to a baseline from −200 to 0ms) of ERPs for each participant. Thus, six regions of interests (ROIs) were identified. N400 effects involved calculating 3 main-effect contrasts (semantic related: semantically unrelated-semantically related; sound repetition: sound repetition-semantically related; spelling repetition: spelling repetition-semantically related). The 3 sets of N400 effects were subjected to a repeated-measure ANOVA. To examine the relationship between the neuropsychological data obtained for each participant (English reading scores) and the ERP measures of interest, the N400 effects measured on the difference wave at 6 ROIs were correlated with, as well as regressed against, English reading scores measured on the standardized Reading test-Gates MacGinitie Reading Comprehension (Form 4, Level F).

For all analyses, original degrees of freedom were reported. A Greenhouse-Geisser correction for sphericity was applied to p-values when more than two levels of a factor were present (Greenhouse and Geisser, 1959). Any main effects not reported below were all non-significant (all *ps* > 0.05).

13.3 Results

13.3.1 Behavioral performance

The acceptability ratios of Chinese related, unrelated, sound repetition and spelling repetition conditions were 0.83, 0.87, 0.81 and 0.46, respectively. ANOVA results with the within-subject factor of conditions showed a significant main effect of condition on the acceptability ratios [F (3, 78) = 19.81, $p < 0.001$]. Post hoc analysis revealed that the acceptability for spelling repetition word pairs were lower than other conditions (all $ps <$ 0.05). No other effects were found. The RTs of the four conditions were 285.52, 305.84, 320.08 and 323.71, respectively. Results from ANOVA on the within-subject factor of conditions showed a significant main effect of condition on RTs [F (3, 78) = 2.79, $p < 0.05$]. Post hoc analysis revealed that semantic related word pairs were responded to faster than other conditions (all $ps < 0.05$). No other effects were found.

The acceptability ratios of English related, unrelated, sound repetition and spelling repetition conditions were 0.74, 0.78, 0.84 and 0.82, respectively. Results from ANOVA on the within-subject factor of conditions showed a significant main effect of condition on the acceptability ratios [F (3, 81) = 3.78; $p < 0.001$]. Post hoc analysis revealed that the acceptability for spelling and sound repetition word pairs were higher than semantic related condition (all $ps < 0.05$). No other effects were found. The RTs of English related, unrelated, sound repetition and spelling repetition conditions were 321.72, 344.17, 316.80 and 334.84, respectively. ANOVA results showed no significant main effect of condition on RTs [F (3, 81) = 0.92, $p = 0.44$].

13.3.2 Electrophysiological data

Grand-averaged ERPs time-locked to the onset of the target were exemplified at electrode sites F1, F2, Fz, FC1, FC2, Cz, CP1, CP2, CPz (for Chinese word pairs, Fig. 18A; for English word pairs, Fig. 19A), and the waves represent the mean amplitudes evoked. Visual inspection also showed little negative going wave around the first 200ms after stimulus onset (N200), whereas a clear negative-going component with a peak around 400ms post word onset (N400) was found in the central sites for both Chinese and English conditions. Significant ERP differences were observed on the four conditions, although the wave differences across conditions were attenuated for English word pairs. Since N200 was not contrastive across conditions, statistical analyses were performed on the mean amplitudes in the N400 time window.

A repeated-measure ANOVA was performed on N400 effects including language (L1explicit/L2 implicit) as a between-subject factor, and condition (3 levels: semantic unrelated/sound repetition/spelling repetition), hemisphere (2 levels: left/right) and lobe (3 levels: frontal/central/posterior) as within-subject factors. The ERP results showed a main effect of condition [F (2, 108) = 14.41, $p < 0.001$], a language and lobe interaction effect [F (2, 108) = 7.52, $p = 0.006$] and a three-way interaction effect between condition, lobe and hemisphere [F (4, 216) = 4.76, $p = 0.004$]. In order to further verify how different conditions exerted effects on L1 vs. L2, separate analysis were run on Chinese vs. English tasks.

Chinese explicit effects

N400 effects from the Chinese task were subjected to a repeated-measure ANOVA with condition (3 levels: semantic unrelated/sound repetition/spelling repetition), hemisphere (2 levels: left/right) and lobe (3 levels: frontal/central/posterior) as within-subject factors. The results showed a significant main effect of condition [F (2, 54) = 15.49, $p < 0.001$] and a condition and lobe interaction effect [F (4, 108) = 15.49, $p = 0.37$]. Simple effects analysis showed a main effect of condition in frontal, central and parietal lobes (all $ps < 0.05$). Paired sample T-test revealed a significant N400 effect difference between semantic unrelated and sound repetition conditions in the left parietal lobe ($p = 0.016$), the right central ($p = 0.004$) and the right parietal lobes ($p = 0.001$). In contrast, the N400 effect between semantic unrelated and spelling repetition was significantly different in all the ROIs except the left parietal lobe. The significant difference between N400 effects indicated experiment conditions resulted in differential priming effects (all $ps < 0.05$) (as shown in the following Fig. 18B).

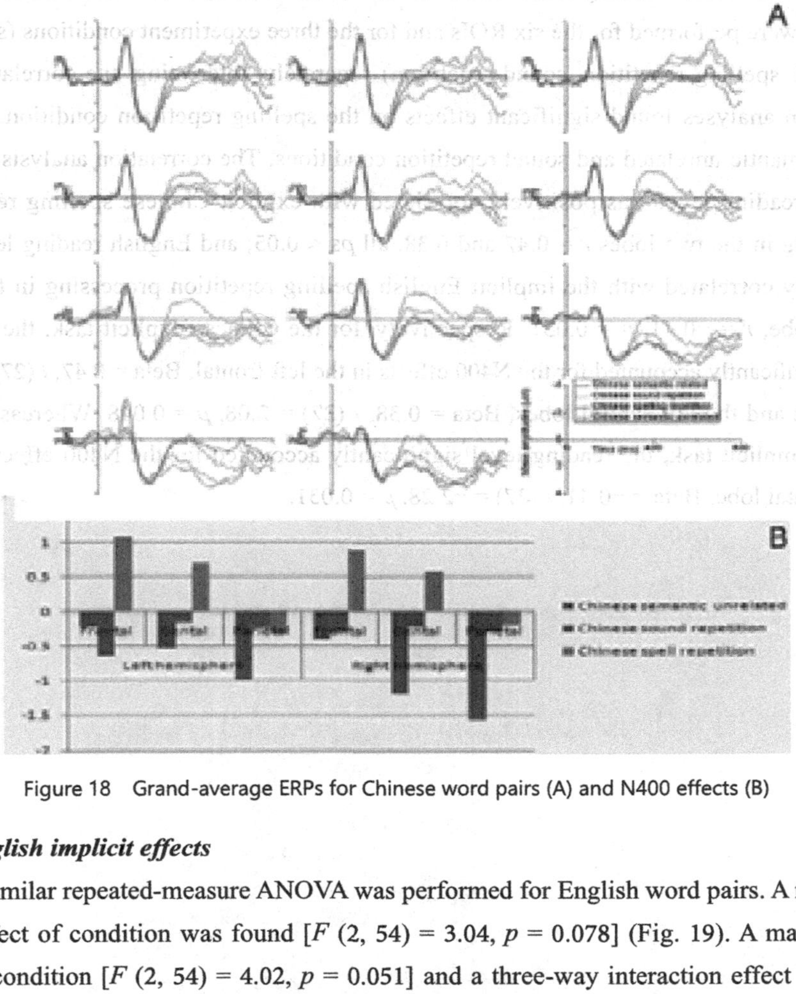

Figure 18 Grand-average ERPs for Chinese word pairs (A) and N400 effects (B)

English implicit effects

A similar repeated-measure ANOVA was performed for English word pairs. A marginal main effect of condition was found [F (2, 54) = 3.04, p = 0.078] (Fig. 19). A main effect of lobe condition [F (2, 54) = 4.02, p = 0.051] and a three-way interaction effect between condition, hemisphere and lobe were found [F (4, 108) = 3.31, p = 0.034]. Simple effects analysis showed a main effect of condition in the left parietal [F (2, 54) = 3.75, p = 0.036], the right central [F (2, 54) = 6.90, p = 0.005] and the right parietal lobes [F (2, 54) = 4.34, p = 0.034]. No other effects were found. Paired sample T-test showed a significant N400 effect difference between semantic unrelated and sound repetition in the right central (p = 0.005). Comparatively, there was a significant N400 effect difference between semantic unrelated and spelling repetition in the left central (p = 0.037), the right central (p = 0.01) and parietal lobes (p = 0.01) (Fig. 19B). No other effects were found.

To look at how reading level modulates the N400 effects, correlation and regression analyses were performed for the six ROIs and for the three experiment conditions (semantic unrelated, spelling repetition, sound repetition) separately. Interesting, the correlation and regression analyses found significant effects on the spelling repetition condition, instead of the semantic unrelated and sound repetition conditions. The correlation analysis showed English reading level was positively correlated with explicit Chinese spelling repetition processing in the two lobes $r = 0.47$ and 0.38, all $ps < 0.05$; and English reading level was negatively correlated with the implicit English spelling repetition processing in the right frontal lobe, $r = -0.41$, $p = 0.031$. Respectively, for the Chinese explicit task, the reading level significantly accounted for the N400 effects in the left frontal, Beta = 0.47, $t\ (27) = 2.72$, $p = 0.012$ and the left central lobes, Beta = 0.38, $t\ (27) = 2.08$, $p = 0.048$. Whereas, for the English implicit task, the reading level significantly accounted for the N400 effects in the right frontal lobe, Beta = −0.41, $t\ (27) = -2.28$, $p = 0.031$.

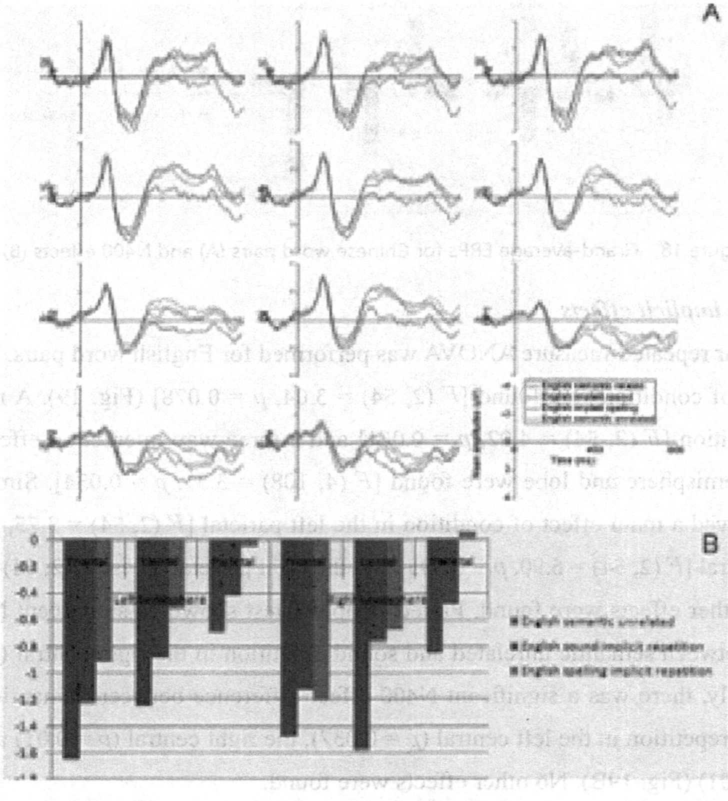

Figure 19 Grand-average ERPs for English word pairs (A) and N400 effects across conditions (B)

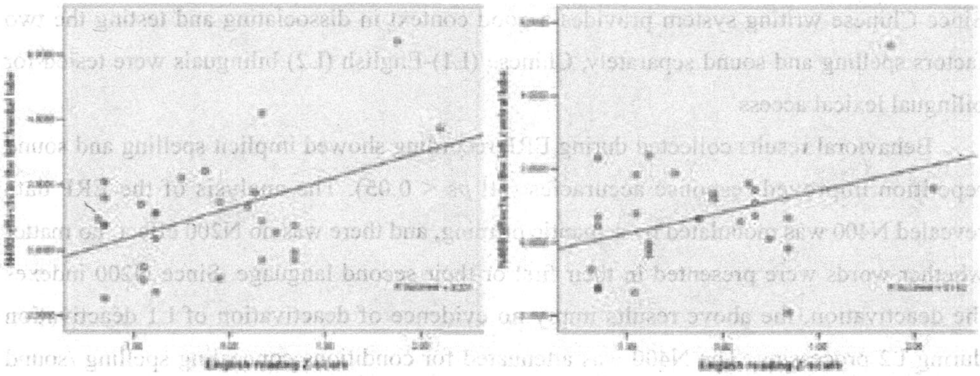

Figure 20 The simple scatter between English reading level and N400 effects in the left frontal and central lobes for Chinese explicit priming task

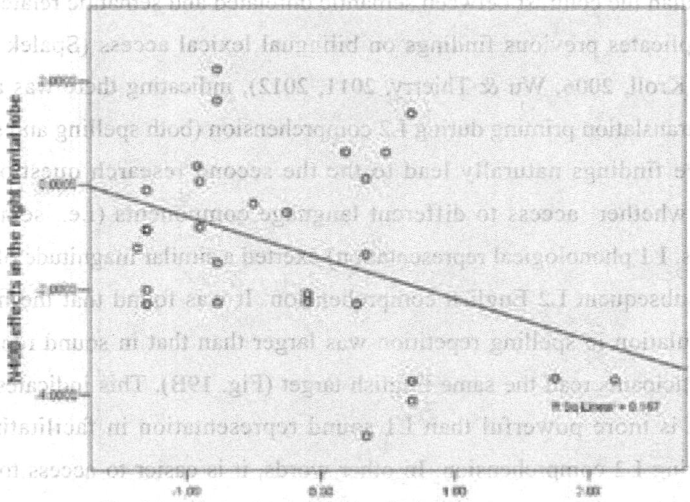

Figure 21 The simple scatter between English reading level and N400 effects in the right frontal lobe for English implicit priming task

13.4 Discussion

The primary goal of the present study was aimed at tapping into how L1 representations (spelling, sound and meaning) were automatically accessed during L2 comprehension. This was achieved by comparing the behavioral responses and brain potentials elicited by semantic related, semantic unrelated, sound implicit access and spelling implicit access. Since Chinese writing system provides a good context in dissociating and testing the two factors spelling and sound separately, Chinese (L1)-English (L2) bilinguals were tested for bilingual lexical access.

Behavioral results collected during ERP recording showed implicit spelling and sound repetition improved response accuracies (all *ps* < 0.05). The analysis of the ERP data revealed N400 was modulated by semantic priming, and there was no N200 effect, no matter whether words were presented in their first or their second language. Since N200 indexes the deactivation, the above results imply no evidence of deactivation of L1 deactivation during L2 processing. The N400 was attenuated for conditions concealing spelling /sound repetition via translation in L1 Chinese (Fig. 19A). The main-effect contrasts (i.e., N400 effects: sound repetition vs. semantic related; spelling repetition vs. semantic related) were more reduced than the contrast between semantic unrelated and semantic related (Fig. 19B). The results replicates previous findings on bilingual lexical access (Spalek et al., 2014; Sunderman & Kroll, 2006; Wu & Thierry, 2011, 2012), indicating there was an automatic (and implicit) translation priming during L2 comprehension (both spelling and sound).

The above findings naturally lead to the the second research question addressed in this study: whether access to different language components (i.e., semantic vs. L1 orthographic vs. L1 phonological representation) exerted a similar magnitude of the priming effect on the subsequent L2 English comprehension. It was found that the magnitude of the N400 modulation in spelling repetition was larger than that in sound repetition, even though the participants read the same English target (Fig. 19B). This indicates L1 spelling representation is more powerful than L1 sound representation in facilitating semantic integration during L2 comprehension. In other words, it is easier to access to L1 Chinese spelling than Chinese sound during L2 English word reading for the present sample. In a latest study Wong, Wu & Chen (2014) examined whether phonological information is obligatorily activated in reading Chinese two-character compounds. The prime-target relationship was manipulated to probe the effects of word-form (i.e., character- or syllable-relatedness) and word-semantic relatedness on phonological (as indexed by an N250 ERP component) and semantic (as indexed by an N400 ERP component) processing. Significant and comparable facilitation effects in reaction time were observed in the Character-related and the Semantic-related conditions. ERP amplitudes (N250), relative to the control, were obtained in the Character-related condition in the time window of 150-250ms post target. In addition, attenuation in ERP amplitudes was found in the Semantic-related condition in the window of 250-500ms (N400). However, no significant results (neither behavioral nor ERP) were found in the Syllable-related condition. They proposed that phonological activation is not mandatory in reading Chinese two-character compounds. However, the present results are contrasting with Wu & Thierry's (2010) study, where participants had unconscious access to L1 sound form, but not L1 spelling. The contrasting results might be attributed to language experience. It should be one important factor modulating the accessibility of processing components. As is well established, the lexical-semantics interface is more susceptible to L1 attrition (Montrul, 2005). Wu & Thierry's (2010) participants studied in L2 English speaking country. They should have higher L2 proficiency. The relatively reduced L1 Chinese input might cause more vulnerable the linking between L2 English semantic representation and L1 Chinese word forms (sound/spelling representation). Thus, we tentatively propose that the bilingual semantic network, or at least the access to L1 word forms, is likely to be modified during the course of L1 attrition.

A related issue is whether the sound or spelling repetition effects on the subsequent word comprehension is similar to a semantic relationship. It is well established that N400 indexes semantic integration. For L1 Chinese explicit repetition, the N400 effect for sound repetition (sound repetition - semantically related) were not significantly different from the contrast between semantically unrelated and semantically related in the frontal lobes and left central lobe; the N400 effect for spelling repetition (spelling repetition vs. semantically related) did not differ from the semantic relationship in the left parietal lobe. These results indicate although unique brain areas are involved in spelling /sound repetition priming, the N400 effect is similar to the semantic related vs. unrelated relationship. Previous ERP studies have also reported a correlate of orthographic consistency and phonological priming within the N400 window (e.g., Pattamadilok et al., 2009; Perre & Ziegler, 2008; Thierry & Wu, 2007; Wu & Thierry, 2010). The relatively less sound priming effect reveals the role of L1 phonology representation during L2 comprehension is as minimal as they are in L1 word comprehension. Similarly, implicit access to L1 Chinese phonological representation is minimal. Accordingly, an N400 modulation due to orthographic or phonological overlap between primes and targets in the present study might reflect interactivity in the interface between L1 lexical (sound or spelling) representation and L2 meaning.

The third research question was devoted to whether the mechanism for L2 English implicit sound/spelling repetition was similar to L1 Chinese explicit access. For both

L1 explicit and L2 implicit, the behavioral results showed a main effect of experiment condition. Both L1 Chinese (explicit) and L2 English (implicit) spelling/sound repetition elicited attenuated N400 effects. The overall ANOVA failed to find a main effect of language. These results reflect a similar mechanism whether priming is explicit in L1 or implicit in L2 reading. However, participants made more response errors for Chinese word pairs that shared a radical compared with other conditions. English word pairs showed sound and spelling repetition has a facilitation effect, instead of the interference effect. Similar facilitation effects were found in previous studies on bilingual homographs (e.g., Brysbaert et al., 1999; Lemhofer & Dijkstra, 2004). For instance, bilinguals displayed decreased reaction time and error rate to words that sound the same in their two languages. Furthermore, Chinese radical /sound repetition (explicit) effects elicited more extended brain areas. The left parietal lobe was uniquely involved in sound repetition priming, whereas the spelling repetition activated additional areas such as the frontal lobes and the left central lobe (Fig. 18B). For L2 English tasks, both sound repetition and spelling repetition induced priming effects in the right central lobe; spelling repetition priming additionally involves the left central and the right parietal lobes (Fig. 19B). The distinct scalp topography (for details, see the "Results" section) as well as distinct behavioral responses reveals a significant variation between the L1 explicit and L2 implicit lexical access. This is partially attributed to the nature of the two languages (Chinese vs. English).

Thus, it could be that radical component repetition in Chinese could be activating a certain amount of "neighbors" including the lexical form (sound/spelling) of the target word. This could serve as a context for the subsequent target word integration, reducing the N400 like component compared to semantic unrelated pairs of words. The same could be happening with English prime-targets. A given prime in English would automatically activate its translation equivalent in Chinese. N400 would reflect the integration of prime and target at the interface between bilingual word representation and meaning. The availability of L1 word representation (sound or spelling) determines the magnitude of the N400 effect. Compared with the L1 explicit task, the less brain areas involved in the L2 implicit tasks reflects less availability of L1 representation for the subsequent L2 comprehension.

Various bilingual lexical models [e.g., Word Association Model, Hierarchical Model, the Revised Hierarchical Model, Bilingual Interactive Activation (BIA +) model] have accounted for the accessibility of bilingual word representation and meaning during L2 comprehension

(Dijkstra & van Heuven, 2002; Kroll & Stewart, 1994; Kroll, Michael, Tokowicz & Dufour, 2002; Sholl, Sankaranarayanan & Kroll, 1995). For example, according to the Revised Hierarchical model, the high L2 proficiency speakers have stronger links between L2 lexicon and concepts and rely less on the L1 translation equivalents. The low L2 proficiency speakers, on the other hand, rely on L1 translation equivalents more strongly and have weaker links from L2 lexicon to concepts. This theory is applicable to the present findings. In the present study, English reading level was positively correlated with the the N400 effect (i.e., the N400 amplitude in spelling repetition minus semantic related) evoked in the left frontal and central areas (Fig. 20). Since N400 is a negative going wave, the result indicates the higher L2 language proficiency, the less negative-going N400. In other words, participants with higher L2 proficiency will find it easier to access Chinese spelling in the Chinese explicit task. Conversely, the N400 effect in the right frontal is negatively correlated with English reading level. In the same vein, this means the higher English reading proficiency the speakers have, the larger N400 amplitude is induced in the L2 implicit spelling repetition task (Fig. 21). N400 effects index the difficulty in semantic integration (Kutas & Hillyard, 1984). The present results reveal that the high L2 proficiency speakers are less likely to access the the L1 spelling and they rely less on L1 translation equivalents.

13.5 Conclusion

To conclude, the present results replicate previous findings on unconscious and automatic access to L1 representations during L2 comprehension. On the process, different L1 components are not equally important. Phonological representation might be less likely to be accessed than orthographic representation. Additionally, L1 explicit lexical access might share a similar mechanism with L2 implicit lexical access to L1. These results contribute to the debate concerning the lexical access for bilinguals in twofold. First, the present study demonstrates bilinguals are not trying to deactivate L1 representations. Native-language activation operates in everyday second-language use from spelling to sound level. Second, L1 spelling representation seems to be easier to be accessed than sound representation. Nevertheless, further research is necessary to examine neurophysiological correlates of the changes due to higher L2 language proficiency and concurrent L1 attrition.

Chapter 14 An ERP Study on the semantic unification mechanism of Chinese native learners of English during L2 English reading comprehension

Abstract: In the present paper, EEG data were collected when Chinese native speakers of English process English homonyms in sentential contexts. An experimental design of context (consistent vs. inconsistent) * meaning frequency (dominant vs. subordinate)* reading level (skilled vs. less skilled) was adopted. The second language English (L2) readers were categorized into two groups, the less skilled readers ($N = 14$) and skilled readers ($N = 14$). Behavioral analysis showed skilled participants had higher accuracy on the sentence acceptability task. The overall ERP analysis showed a main effect of context type. Separate analysis on reading groups showed ERPs to dominant meanings of the homonyms for the skilled readers exhibited an increased N400 effects at the left central region, while ERPs to subordinate meanings of the homonyms exhibited an increased N400 effects at the right central region. The findings indicate that recruitment of brain areas in homonym processing is modulated by reading level.

Key words: meaning integration reading difficulty meaning analysis context integration second language

14.1 Introduction

Homonyms are word forms with multiple unrelated semantic meanings, which provide a good venue in examining ambiguity resolution in different contexts. Numerous psycholinguistic studies have indicated that context plays an important role in constraining inappropriate meanings for homonyms (e.g., Elston-Güttler & Friederici, 2005; Glucksberg et al., 1986; Tabossi, 1989). Monolingual literature on multiple meaning selections has raised several models concerning context effects on homonym processing.

The context-dependency model proposes that there is a strong interaction between top-down and bottom-up factors early or continuously in lexical access (McClelland, 1987; Simpson, 1994). Experimental evidence confirms that within a constraining context, readers have access to only the contextually relevant meaning of a homonym (Glucksberg et al., 1986). Alternatively, a feature-based version of context-dependency model claims that different types of sentential contexts constrain the activation of contextually inappropriate meanings to different degrees (Tabossi, 1989). Another view, the multiple access model (Seidenberg et al., 1982), proposes that contextual information does not contribute to homonym processing in earlier stages. Multiple meanings of a homonym are initially accessed, and constraining effects of sentence context on lexical selection are evident only at a later stage of processing (Swinney, 1979). A third approach is presented by the ordered access model (e.g., Duffy et al., 1988; Neill et al., 1988). In the ordered access model, initial activation is thought to be influenced not by context, but rather by relative frequency. Accordingly, dominant meaning of a homonym is always activated. Whereas, the subordinate meaning is activated only in constraining contexts and only the subordinate meaning can be suppressed by context (Tabossi & Zardon, 1993). Though vary in the time course of deactivation of contextually inappropriate information, a general consensus across different models is that dominant meanings of homonyms are usually mandatory regardless of contexts and contexts help activate contextually appropriate meanings of homonyms.

In the case of homonym processing by second language learners, evidence shows natives and non-natives differ in whether the subordinate meaning is activated and when the contextually irrelevant information is deactivated. For instance, Frenck-Mestre and Prince (1997) showed that advanced French learners of English exhibited significant priming of both dominant and subordinate meanings of ambiguous words at SOAs of 100 and 300ms. However, less proficient learners showed priming of only dominant meanings at both SOAs, despite a recognition task that showed that they indeed knew the subordinate meanings. Elston-Güttler and Friederici (2005) revealed the processing difference between native and non-natives was reflected in the later stage of deactivation. They found that in the early stage of homonym processing, dominant and subordinate meanings were activated for both native and non-native English readers regardless of context; and in the later stage, there was a decay of contextually irrelevant information for both groups. However, they speculated that non-natives appeared to be less effective than natives in the later deactivation of contextually irrelevant homonym meanings, as reflected by the persistent N400 effect at the 500ms SOA. Likely, a recent Event Related Potentials study examined balanced and unbalanced English homonym processing by high proficiency Chinese English as a Second language learners (Hu et al., 2011). They found a different processing mechanism for balanced and unbalanced homonyms. Related targets with the balanced or unbalanced dominant meanings elicited smaller N400 amplitude than unrelated ones but no such effect was found with unbalanced subordinate meaning. At 500ms stimulus-onset-asynchrony, only the dominant meaning of the unbalanced homonyms could be activated in inappropriate sentence context. Overall, the above findings suggest that for the second language learners, subordinate meanings are either less activated in integrating with appropriate contexts or inappropriate contexts.

The homonym processing difference between natives and non-natives should hinge on the nature of the subjects. Namely, less effective deactivation of inappropriate context or activation of subordinate meanings could possibly be attributed to the relatively low language proficiency (or reading skills in the case of reading tasks) by non-natives. As evidence shows, less skilled readers were less efficient in decoding and they increased their reliance on context when they integrated meanings and contextual information (e.g., Ben-Dror et al., 1991; Corkett & Parrila, 2008; Stanovich & West, 1983).

On the other, it is possible that less effective context deactivation and subordinate meaning activation for less-skilled readers might involve differential LH and RH contributions compared with skilled readers. A series priming studies by using divided visual field technique argue that the left hemisphere (LH) is more adept than the right hemisphere (RH) at utilizing sentence-level information to resolve lexical ambiguity, because LH interprets contextual information by using syntactic, Semantic and pragmatic information, while RH processes the semantic meaning via word-level (for a review, see Faust & Chiarello, 1998). The right hemisphere (RH) is more likely involved in the maintenance of meanings (for a review, see Grindrod & Baum, 2003). However, less-skilled reading involves brain malfunction and deficiency. Neuroimaging studies revealed that the left parietotemporal and occipitotemporal cortices of poor readers were underactivated in reading tasks; whereas, the neural signature of reading impairment was also marked by over-activation in the right parietotemporal regions during reading comprehension (e.g.,

Georgiewa et al., 2002; Shaywitz & Shaywitz, 2005; Simos et al., 2000; Meyler et al., 2007). They speculated that overactivation in the right hemisphere was a compensation for the left hemisphere deficiency. However, it is not yet known how less-skilled readers' brains respond during homonyms processing in sentential contexts.

Thus, the central aim of the present study was to examine reading-level related effect on the brain activation during homonym processing by second language learners. Event-related potentials (ERPs) provide an on-line measure with millisecond accuracy on a specific stimulus on the brain (Kutas & Hillyard, 1980; Osterhout & Holcomb, 1992). Thus, ERP technique is effective in tracking the multiple cognitive processes as they unfold in time. ERPs are labeled by their latency with respect to stimulus onset. The amplitudes of the ERP waveform relative to the baseline can be interpreted as the degree of engagement in a task. The positive and negative deflections (components) are found to be correlated with sensory, motor and cognitive processing (e.g., Kutas & Federmeier, 2000).

The ERP component relevant to the present study is the semantic processing component (N400). N400 is a negative deflection, occurring approximately 400ms after stimulus onset (Friederici, 2002). It is an index of difficulty in semantic integration (Hagoort, 2008) and the amplitude is larger when words semantically disassociate with each other (Rugg, 1984). N400 could be used to reflect the construction process of meaning constrained by context. When words appear in a congruous sentence context, they elicit smaller N400 than when they appear in an incongruous context (Kutas & Hillyard, 1980). Robinchon et al. (2002) showed when the ending word meanings were not consistent with the context, N400 latency was longer for the readers with reading difficulties. Interestingly, for the context consistent condition, only the readers with reading difficulties appeared N400. They proposed that the readers with reading difficulties had difficulty in integrating word meaning into the sentence context. Perfetti et al. (2008) also studied contextual effect related with N400 and found that readers with low proficiency had delayed processing in word recognition and meaning integration.

This study addressed two questions: ① whether reading level modulated the selection of homonym meanings in sentential contexts? ② if so, how was such a modulation effect evident on the right and left hemisphere of the brain? To explore these issues, an experiment design of 2 (reading level: skilled vs. less skilled) *2 (meaning frequency: dominant vs. subordinate) × 2 (context: consistent vs. inconsistent) was adopted. Electrophysiological data were collected when adult English learners made sentence acceptability judgment.

It was expected that the overall N400 amplitude for the consistent context is smaller than that of the inconsistent context (N400 effect). Regarding the reading-level related effect, for the less skilled readers, the N400 latency should be delayed. Because the left hemisphere is adept in message level information, it was expected that less skilled readers are deficient in left hemisphere function, and thus less sensitive in context information. The N400 effect in their left hemisphere should be more reduced than skilled readers. N400 effect in the right brain would be more obvious for the less skilled readers, since right hemisphere is more sensitive to word-level information while less skilled readers are deficient in word decoding.

14.2 Methods

14.2.1 Participants

Participants were 28 healthy adults (24 women and 4 men), average age 20.63 years (*SD* = 0.88). All individuals reported Chinese as their native language (L1) and English as the second language (L2). They were exposed to L2 English with a history of for an average of 8.00 years (*SD* = 3.02). Participants all had normal or corrected-to-normal vision and reported no history of neurological or psychiatric disorders. All participants were right-handed. They got compensation for their participation.

Table 27 Demographic information and bilingual skills of the two groups

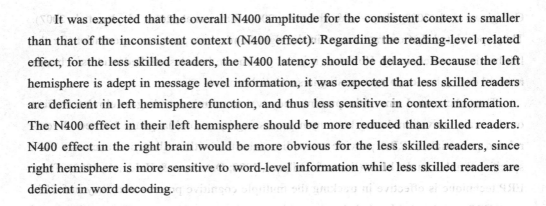

	Skilled readers		Less-skilled readers		
	M	***SD***	***M***	***SD***	***F (p)***
Age	20.33	0.49	20.07	0.997	0.68 (0.42)
Chinese listening	8.92	1.44	9.75	1.55	0.08(0.78)
Chinese oral	8.58	1.31	8.68	1.23	0.04(0.85)
Chinese reading	8.50	1.45	8.61	1.24	0.04(0.84)
Chinese writing	8.08	1.62	8.75	1.42	0.31(0.58)
English exposure year	8.42	3.09	7.64	3.03	0.41(0.53)
English listening	15.43	3.08	15.14	1.79	0.09(0.77)
English reading	25.00	2.69	17.86	2.67	50.00 (0.001)

Following Lorusso et al. (2004), participants in the present study were classified into less skilled readers and skilled readers according to their English reading and listening comprehension scores. The reading and listening test materials were adopted from National Standard English Tests of Level 4 in China. The less skilled readers were 1 *SD* lower than the grade mean in reading comprehension test while they were matched with the skilled reading on listening comprehension test. Based on grade average, 14 individuals were less skilled readers ($M = 17.86$, $SD = 2.67$). Another 14 were skilled readers ($M = 25.00$, $SD = 2.69$), whose reading scores were 1 *SD* higher than the grade mean. All participants were required to finish a demographic questionnaire before the experiment. The two groups were controlled on their age and English exposure years. According to the 10-point scale ratings on their native language Chinese skills, such as reading, writing, speaking and listening, the skilled and less skilled English readers were matched on their native Chinese language skills (see Table 27).

14.2.2 Materials

Unbalanced homonyms: Unbalanced homonyms are homonyms with one meaning more dominant than the other. The 30 unbalanced English homonyms were adopted from the materials by Elston-Guttler and Friederici (2005). The present study selected mixed-category homonyms, having noun and verb meanings. Their study demonstrated that for native English speakers RT and ERP data showed a similar time-course of processing for both same- and mixed-category homonyms. The frequencies of the dominant meaning and subordinate meanings of the homonym were double checked according to Corpus of Contemporary American English (COCA, http://corpus.byu.edu/coca/). There was significant difference in meaning frequency: for dominant meaning, $M = 34073.13$, $SD = 117\,991.59$; for subordinate meaning, 3 389.67, $SD = 4\,489.79$, $t\,(29) = 3.15$, $p = 0.004$.

Contexts: Two sets of contexts were generated respectively for the dominant and subordinate meanings of the 30 homonyms. Most of the contextual sentences were adapted from Elston-Guttler and Friederici (2005) with some alternations. These contexts biased to either dominant or subordinate meanings of the homonyms and thus provided necessary information to predict the critical meaning of the homonyms. The acceptability of the sentences was rated by 30 postgraduates of English majors on a 1 to 5-point scale. There was no significant difference on sentence acceptability between sentences with dominant meanings ($M = 3.88$, $SD = 0.58$) and sentences with subordinate meanings ($M = 3.78$, $SD = 0.61$), $t\,(29) = 1.39$, $p = 0.18$. All the critical words were located at the end of the sentences. Samples were shown in Table 28.

Table 28 Sample Stimuli

Sentence types	Examples
Dominant meaning, consistent	Wait for a moment. I'll be back in a ***tick***.
Dominant meaning, inconsistent	Wait for a moment. I'll be back in a ***brief***.
Subordinate meaning, consistent	Stop the clock. I don't want it to ***tick***.
Subordinate meaning, inconsistent	Stop the clock. I don't want it to ***plow***.

Note: Critical words in sentential contexts are shown in bold and italics.

The length of each sentence ranged from 6 words to 14 words, with an average of 11 words. To construct inconsistent contexts, another two sets of non-homonyms were generated to adapt the above-mentioned two sets of contexts, so that the contexts are controlled for consistent vs. inconsistent conditions. The non-homonyms were matched with the homonyms on word length (for dominant meaning with consistent context, $M = 4.8$, $SD = 1.16$; inconsistent context, $M = 4.63$, $SD = 1.35$; $t = 0.72, p = 0.48$. For subordinate meaning with consistent context, $M = 4.80$, $SD = 1.16$; inconsistent context, $M = 4.47$, $SD = 0.97$; $t = 1.62, p = 0.12$) and meaning frequency (for dominant meaning with consistent context, $M = 19\,083.37$, $SD = 28\,015.07$; inconsistent context, $M = 33\,586.90$, $SD = 118\,100.69$; $t = -0.67$, $p = 0.51$; for subordinate meaning with consistent context, $M = 2\,925.47$, $SD = 4\,129.34$; inconsistent context, $M = 2\,956.47$, $SD = 4\,143.25$; $t = -1.49, p = 0.15$).

14.2.3 Procedure

Participants were seated in a sound-attenuated approximately 1 meter from the computer monitor on which stimuli were presented. Sentences were presented segment by segment in black Times-Roman font on a white background. All segments were presented centrally, so that both left and right hemispheres could contribute normally to the formation of sentence-level representations that support context consistency effects. The sentences were presented in a random order determined by the computer program E-Prime, which also recorded the accuracy and reaction time and sent critical word onset information to the ERP acquisition software. During each trial, there was a " + " in the center of the screen as the focus point, which lasted for 300ms, then the experimental sentences would be presented word by word, with every word lasting for 500ms and intervals between words for 300ms. After the sentences were completely presented, a "?" would appear, which would last for 2s. The participants were required to make judgment on the acceptability of the sentences as soon as they saw the question mark by pressing "1" or "2" button of the computer. After the question mark, a blank window would appear for nearly 1s. When a response was made, another trial began. Two versions of materials were utilized to achieve counterbalance. The response buttons were counterbalanced across participants. Each participant had a short practice before the experiment. The experiment lasted for nearly one hour with 3 breaks.

14.2.4 Data Collection

All EEG data were collected by using Brain Vision Recorder software from Brain Production. Continuous EEG was recorded from 64 scalp sites by means of electrodes attached to an elastic cap. The 64 active electrodes (ActiCap, Brain Products GmbH, Munich) were according to standard international 10-20 system, referenced to bilateral mastoids and grounded to forehead. A vertical electro-oculogram (VEOG) was recorded from Ag/AgCl electrodes placed closely above and below the left eye in order to control for vertical eye movements. Horizontal eye movements were measured by a horizontal electro-oculogram (HEOG) recorded from Ag/AgCl electrodes that placed at the outer canthus of each eye. Allimpedances were kept below 5 kΩ during the experiment. EEG signals were bandpass filtered between 0.01 and 100Hz, and amplified and digitized at a rate of 500Hz using a BrainAmp amplifier (Brain Products GmbH, Munich). The bandpass during recording was 0.05-100Hz.

14.2.5 Data Analysis

The analyses were conducted on data from the 28 participants. The EEG data were processed off-line using Brain Vision Analyzer 2. They were re-referenced to the mean of the left and right mastoid, and filtered with a 0.1Hz high-pass filter to remove drifts and a 30Hz filter to eliminate line noise. Software of BP Company was used to eliminate the Ocular artifact reduction. The analysis epoch was from 200ms before the critical words to 800ms after the stimuli. A linear detrend was operated as well. The waveform of 200ms before the stimuli was used as the criteria of baseline correction. All the electrodes were used as the criteria of artifact rejection and the amplitudes higher than ±50μV were automatically eliminated with the rejection rate lower than 20%. All the EEG waveforms in the same condition were computed to get the average ERP waveform.

The mean amplitudes (average of non-rejected epochs from 0 to 800ms after the onset of the key words, calculated relative to a baseline from −200 to 0ms) of ERPs were measured for each participant. Statistical analysis involved repeated measures ANOVAs conducted on the mean amplitude of ERP waveforms measured in several specific time intervals as described in the next section. To have a relatively direct comparison with native English readers, five Regions of Interest (ROI) similar to the study on homonym processing (Elston-Güttler & Friederici, 2005) were included. Each Region of Interest was defined by a critical region of 3-4 scalp sites that were centro-parietal scalp regions typically associated with the N400 component. The five ROIs were defined in the analyses as follows: left central, FT7 FC3 T7 C3; right central, FT8 FC4 T8 C4; left posterior, CP5 P7 P3 O1; right posterior, CP6 P8 P4 O2; and the midline, Cz Pz POz. Significant main effects and interactions were followed up by simple one-way ANOVAs. For all analyses, original degrees of freedom were reported. A Greenhouse-Geisser correction for sphericity was applied to p-values when more than two levels of a factor were present. Any main effects not reported below were all non-significant (all $ps > 0.05$).

To frame the results theoretically, we report these critical data only: first, the main effect of condition factor Meaning Frequency; then main effects of other experimental factors (Reading Level and Context Consistency); then interactions that involve the three factors. Given that main effects of topographical factors (Region of Interest) are not of interest for the hypotheses posed, statistical analyses only report interactions of topographical factors with condition effects. Exact F and p-values (up to $p = 0.001$) are reported for significant critical data.

14.3 Results

14.3.1 Behavioral Accuracy

There was a predicted significant main effect of Meaning Frequency for both skilled readers [dominant meaning, $M = 0.70$, $SD = 0.12$; subordinate meaning, $M = 0.62$, $SD = 0.14$, $F(1, 27) = 4.83$, $p = 0.045$] and less skilled readers [dominant meaning, $M = 0.64$, $SD =$ 0.13 subordinate meaning, $M = 0.60$, $SD = 0.14$, $F(1, 27) = 7.33$, $p = 0.018$]. However, for the overall data, main effect oF Meaning Frequency was not significant [$F(1, 27) =$ 9.78, $p = 0.004$], although the dominant meaning showing fewer errors overall (67.41% correct, $SD = 12.57$) than the subordinate meaning (62.33% correct, $SD = 13.92$). The main effect of Context was not reliable [$F(1, 26) = 0.18$, $p = 0.68$]. The main effect of

Reading Group was not reliable [F (1, 26) = 0.90, p = 0.35]. The interaction of Reading Group and Meaning Frequency was also not significant [F (1, 26) = 0.57, p = 0.46]. But the interaction of Context and Meaning Frequency was significant [F (1, 26) = 7.93, p = 0.009]. Separate analysis on each reading group showed that there was no main effect on either Meaning Frequency or Context Consistency, or an interaction effect for skilled readers. In comparison, there was a reliable interaction between Meaning Frequency *Context Consistency (dominant meaning and consistent context, M = 0.64, SD = 0.13; dominant meaning and inconsistent context, M = 0.60, SD = 0.16; subordinate meaning and consistent context, M = 0.60, SD = 0.14; subordinate meaning and inconsistent context, M = 0.63, SD = 0.14; F (1, 14) = 4.88, p = 0.046. The behavioral results indicate that skilled and less skilled readers process homonyms a similar way. Besides, less skilled readers might be more conservative in rejecting subordinate meaning.

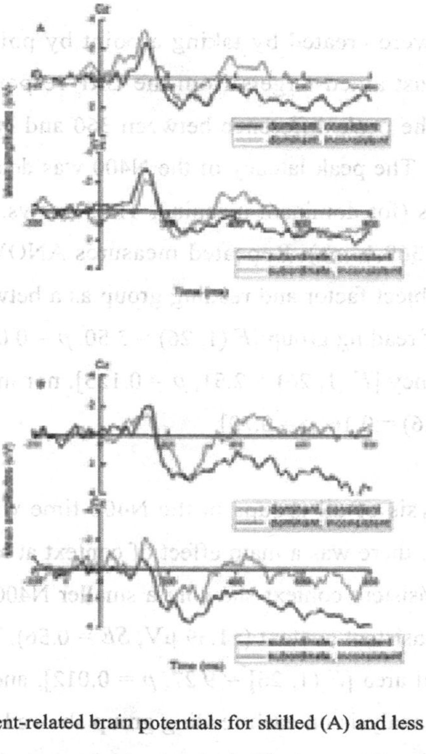

Figure 22 Grand average event-related brain potentials for skilled (A) and less skilled readers (B) during processing dominant and subordinate meanings

14.3.2 ERP analysis

Fig. 22 show grand average ERPs to sentence final targets at a representative sample of electrode sites. The overall morphology of the waveforms in all groups was relatively comparable. The theoretically relevant component is a negative-going wave at around 400ms (N400) with a relatively broad scalp distribution. The modulation of the N400 for consistent versus inconsistent contexts is visible across two meaning conditions (dominant vs. subordinate meanings) (see Fig. 22), though the onset of the N400 effect for skilled readers (Fig. 1A) is slightly earlier than for less skilled readers (Fig. 22B). Besides, skilled readers (Fig. 23, see color page 3) appear to be more effective than less-skilled readers (Fig. 24, see color page 4) in the later deactivation of contextually irrelevant homonym meanings, as reflected by the less N400 effect from 500 to 800 ms. Based on visual inspection, the N400 time window chosen for statistical analysis was 360-460 ms.

N400 latency

Difference waves were created by taking a point by point subtraction of the ERP response to strongly constrained targets from the ERP response to weakly constrained targets. The latency of the peak difference between 360 and 460ms was measured at the at all channels (58 sites). The peak latency of the N400 was delayed in less skilled readers relative to skilled readers (for dominant meaning, 414.57ms vs. 385.29ms; for subordinate meaning, 387.71ms vs. 369.14ms). Repeated measures ANOVA analysis with meaning frequency as a within-subject factor and reading group as a between subject factor showed a marginal main effect of reading group [F (1, 26) = 3.50, p = 0.07]. There was neither main effect of meaning frequency [F (1, 26) = 2.51, p = 0.125], nor meaning frequency* reading group interaction [F (1, 26) = 0.16, p = 0.70].

N400 amplitude

In the overall analysis of all groups in the N400 time window of 360-460ms after presentation of the target, there was a main effect of context at left central area [F (1, 26) = 7.28, p = 0.012] with consistent context showing a smaller N400 or higher amplitude (0.05 μV, SE = 0.56) than inconsistent context (−1.39 μV, SE = 0.56). The context effect was also significant at right central area [F (1, 26] = 9.27, p = 0.012], and midline area [F (1, 26) = 4.67, p = 0.04]. Separate analysis on each reading group showed that for less skilled readers (Fig. 24), the context main effect was reliable at the right central area [F (1, 13) = 6.85, p = 0.02], with consistent context showing a smaller N400 or higher amplitude (1.03μV, SE = 0.80) than inconsistent context (−0.89μV, SE = 0.92), while the context main effect at the left central area was only marginal [consistent context, 0.73μV, SE = 0.99, inconsistent context −1.00μV, $SE = 0.90$, $F(1, 13) = 3.45$, $p = 0.086$]. For skilled readers, the context effect was significant [$F(1, 13) = 4.94$, $p = 0.045$] at the left central area. No other effect was found.

To further assess meaning frequency effect for the two reading level groups, repeated measures ANOVAs with meaning frequency as a within-subject were performed on the two reading groups separately. For skilled readers, the dominant meaning (Fig. 23A) showed a reliable context effect at left central area [consistent context, $M = -0.68$, $SD = 2.14$; inconsistent context, $M = -2.21$, $SD = 2.15$; $F(1, 13) = 8.85$, $p = 0.01$], midline [consistent context, $M = 0.53$, $SD = 2.26$; inconsistent context, $M = -0.57$, $SD = 2.27$; $F(1, 13) = 6.99$, $p = 0.02$]; the context main effect was not reliable in the subordinate meaning processing (Fig. 23B). For less skilled readers, the dominant meaning (Fig. 24A) showed a marginal context effect at left central area [consistent context, $M = 1.02$, $SD = 3.52$; inconsistent context, $M = -1.14$, $SD = 1.89$; $F(1, 13) = 4.52$, $p = 0.053$]; subordinate meaning processing showed a reliable context effect at right central area [consistent context, $M = 0.74$, $SD = 3.40$; inconsistent context, $M = -1.55$, $SD = 5.11$; $F(1, 13) = 8.53$, $p = 0.01$] (Fig. 24B).

14.4 Discussion

In this experiment, we examined how reading level modulated Chinese-English bilinguals' behavioral and ERP responses to dominant and subordinate meanings of homonyms. We analyzed behavioral data and five brain regions of interest to examine the modulation effect on brain activation during homonym processing. Behavioral analysis showed skilled participants had higher accuracy on the sentence acceptability task. As predicted, the overall ERP analysis showed less skilled readers were delayed in N400 latency; and there was a main effect of context type. Interestingly, separate analyses on reading groups indicated recruitment of brain areas may be subjects specific. Skilled and less skilled readers have different neural response patterns during processing dominant vs. subordinate meanings of homonyms in different sentential contexts.

A somewhat surprising result of the present study was that ERPs to dominant meanings of the homonyms for the skilled readers exhibited an increased N400 effect in left central area, peaking around 360-460ms (Fig. 23A), whereas N400 effect over this region is attenuated for the less skilled readers(Fig. 24A). Since N400 effect indexes efforts in semantic integration, the results suggest skilled subjects, but not less-skilled subjects, show an effective differentiation between consistent and inconsistent contexts over the left central region. As is well established in behavioral studies (e.g., Ewers & Brownson, 1999; Kuhn & Stahl, 1998), proficient readers were more efficient in gaining unfamiliar word meanings from texts because they had a larger vocabulary size and they were more experienced in using context clues, as well as background information.

Comparatively, N400 effect for less skilled readers was less obvious than that for skilled readers over the left central area. The left hemisphere (LH) is supposed to the message level mechanism (Faust & Chiarello, 1998). Additionally, less-skilled readers have deficiency in meaning integrating into context (Goerss et al., 1999). Therefore, the left hemisphere was less sensitive to contextual information for the less skilled readers. It is likely that the deficit of word meaning analysis for less-skilled readers resulted in poorer context utilization. Reading level modulation effect on the left central region in the present study provides additional evidence for the claim that temporal region of the left hemisphere was closely related with language level (Frishkoff et al., 2009).

Another finding of interest was that less skilled readers showed a reliable N400 effect over the right central region during subordinate meaning processing (Fig. 24B). However, we found an absence of context consistency effects in right hemisphere for skilled readers (similar N400s for consistent and inconsistent during processing subordinate meanings for both subordinate meaning and dominant meaning processing). The message-blind right hemisphere model asserts that the right hemisphere is sensitive only to word-level context. As sentence final targets in the two contexts were controlled for their meaning frequency and word length, skilled readers exhibited an absence of N400 effect. Following the same logic, we could rule out the possibility that context inconsistency should devote to the N400 effect in right central region for less-skilled readers. Thus, one explanation for the presence of N400 effect over the right central region hinges on the meaning frequencies of homonyms. The subordinate meanings of homonyms are much more effortful for less skilled readers.

The central N400 component, which have previously been linked to learning and memory processes, also showed effects of lexicality (Frishkoff et al., 2009). The reading-level modulated N400 effect over the right hemisphere for the less-skilled readers could be explained by their poor lexical quality. The lexical access deficiency is more likely to aggravate the meaning integration, resulting in N400 effect. A recent study indicate right hemisphere is sensitive to both word and message (sentence) level information (Coulson et al., 2005; Frishkoff et al., 2009). The N400 effect in the right central area for the less skilled readers could be alternatively interpreted as a compensation for their deficiency in the left hemisphere.

14.5 Conclusion

An important result is that the recruitment of brain areas in semantic analysis during homonym processing is found to be modulated by reading level. The peak of the N400 latency was delayed in less skilled readers relative to skilled readers. ERPs to dominant meanings of the homonyms for the skilled readers exhibited an increased N400 effect in left central area. Less skilled readers showed a reliable N400 effect over the right central region during subordinate meaning processing. The results attach importance to assessing reading difficulty within a neurodevelopmental context. The parietotemporal region, particularly in the left hemisphere appears to be a locus of dysfunction in second language learners who are less-skilled in reading comprehension.

Part 4 Identification and Intervention for ESL Reading Difficulty

内容简介

这一部分共有三个研究，主要考察两个问题：①不同因素对阅读困难预测的准确性和有效性；②不同的教学干预怎样有效提高普通英语读者和阅读困难者的英语阅读成绩。研究中使用解码、认知和元认知三个关键的阅读加工过程对英语阅读困难进行预测和鉴别。同时，以影响阅读困难的重要语言和认知因素为着眼点，根据认知和元认知缺陷情况制定教学干预策略，使用追踪研究，对阅读困难者进行9个月的教学干预，并比较干预前后，阅读和相关语言和认知加工技能的变化。三个研究具体如下：

（1）研究1（第15章）题为“The predictive sensitivity and specifity of L2 English reading comprehension difficulty by code-breaking variables and language variables”（语码和语言变量对二语英语阅读理解困难鉴别的敏感性和准确率），以影响阅读困难的重要语言和认知因素为着眼点，尝试对汉语母语者的英语阅读困难者进行有效鉴别和预测。本研究探讨语码和语言变量对汉语母语背景下二语英语阅读理解困难预测的敏感性和准确性。研究中从我国英语专业学生中筛选出英语阅读理解困难组和控制组各15人，先对两组被试的语言（词汇、语法、语素）和语码变量（语音、解码和工作记忆）的差异进行方差分析，然后分别以语言变量和语码变量作为预测变量，以两个阅读水平组作为因变量做Logistic回归分析。结果发现，首先，阅读理解困难者在工作记忆、语法、词汇和语素意识都显著落后于控制组。其次，语码变量不能有效鉴别阅读困难者，鉴别准确率仅为66.7%；而语言变量（特别是语素意识）对英语阅读理解困难者鉴别正确率高达78.6%；语言和语码变量组合能提高阅读理解困难者鉴别率到85.7%。特别是，语素意识对控制组和阅读理解困难组的鉴别力分别是86.7%和78.6%。研究表明，相对于高水平的第二语言阅读者，语言变量能更有效鉴别阅读理解困难者；虽然语码变量对阅读理解困难的鉴别敏感性较低，但它在某种程度上有助于提高语言变量的鉴别力。二语英语阅读困难的鉴别可根据学习者的语言水平选择性地使用语言变量或者语码变量。

（2）研究2（第16章）题为“Reading metacognitive intervention: A preliminary study on EFL learners”（阅读元认知的教学干预：英语作为外语的学习者的初步研究），通过对照自然发展状态下和教学干预状态下的阅读元认知和阅读理解的变化。认知心理学和教育心理学表明阅读是一种复杂的心理活动。有效的阅读过程不仅是一种认知活动过程，更是一种对认知活动的监控过程。如何运用策略来提高阅读效率是很多研究者感兴趣的话题。元认知（metacognition）是由美国心理学家Flavell于20世纪70年代提出来的，是指认知主体对自己认知活动的监测和调控。许多理论及实证研究也已经表明元认知策略与英语阅读之间存在正相关。然而，中国传统的英语阅读教学重视语言知识的传授，忽视策略尤其是元认知策略及知识的传授与培养，因此学生缺乏阅读策略知识。而作为英语专业的学生，他们又必须花大量时间练习语言的基本技能，如听说读写，所以用来进行阅读元认知策略训练的时间就很少了，这也是导致学生自主阅读能力不足的原因之一。基于上述情况，本研究选取英语专业一、二年级的学生为实验对象，随机分成实验组和控制组，进行追踪研究，实验组同学接受最小程度元认知策略干预阅读训练。研究发现，二语学习者的阅读元认知意识以及阅读水平在自然状态下发展缓慢；两个年级实验组的阅读成绩及趋势表明最小程度的元认知策略干预有助于提高他们的阅读水平。研究也发现，元认知训练效果受语言水平的影响，训练效果和个体参与程度直接相关。

（3）研究3（第17章）题为“The relationship between bilingual morphological awareness and reading for Chinese EFL adult learners”（成人双语语素意识和阅读的关系），考察教学干预和汉英双语语素意识的发展的关系。语素意识是指对单词语素结构的认识以及对这种语素结构进行反应和操作的能力。它作为一种元语言意识，在词汇和阅读的发展过程中扮演着很重要的角色。不同书写系统中，语素意识作为单独变量在预测字词阅读与阅读理解水平方面发挥着非常重要的作用。前人研究发现，英语语素意识对英语的单词阅读和阅读理解有显著预测作用。而汉语语素意识对汉语阅读来说，更扮演关键角色。近年来，语素意识缺陷也被证实是解释汉语阅读困难的核心认知因素。汉语和英语作为两种不同的语言体系，二者语素意识和阅读的关系均可从派生语素、复合语素和屈折语素等方面分析，但语言各自的特异性又决定了对英语语素意识的研究主要是从派生词角度，而对汉语语素意识的研究侧重于复合词语素意识。然而，大多数研究都主要以拼音文字为对象，并且主要是从同一语言类型的角度对语素意识进行研究，而不同语言类型的跨语言跨文化研究还比较少。目前，在汉语母语背景下，对于第二语言为英语的成人，汉英双语语素意识与阅读水平关系的跨语言研究也相对较少。为了证实语素意识对汉英双语者阅读能力的作用，本研究以中国某大学一年级和二年级共140名学生为被试，采取了前测和后测的方法，实行了时间间隔9个月的教学干预和追踪研究。就语内研究来说，前后测研究均发现，英语语素意识与英语阅读水平相关显著，并发挥着重要的预测作用，且派生语素的贡献率高于复合语素；汉语的语素意识与汉语阅读水平亦呈现显著的相关性。从跨语言分析角度，前测中汉语复合词语素意识与英语字词阅读水平和阅读理解成绩均无贡献作用，但在后测结果中，却对二者均产生了显著贡献。实验表明，英汉语素意识对本语言阅读水平具有重要的影响和作用，并且在学生二语水平达到一定程度之后，母语语素水平向二语阅读发生了跨语言的迁移，汉语复合词语素对于二语阅读水平产生了重要的预测作用。研究说明，接受英语教育的成人学生，在第二语言学习的过程中，语素意识与阅读水平的关系不仅存在于本语言系统内部，还发生了跨语言的迁移现象，汉英语素意识对其第二语言阅读能力可发挥重要的影响作用。研究也说明，英语语素训练的有效性。

Chapter 15 The predictive sensitivity and specifity of L2 English reading comprehension difficulty by code-breaking variables and language variables

Abstract: The present study explores the predictive sensitivity and specifity of L2 English reading comprehension difficulty by code-breaking variables and language variables. A reading disability group (*N* =15) and a control group (*N* =15) were sampled from English majors in a domestic university. Sets of Logistic Regression with language variables (vocabulary, grammar, morphology) and code-breaking variables (phonological awareness, decoding and working memory) as predicators and the two groups as the dependent variable, examined the validity of identifying individuals with difficulty in reading comprehension. The results show that, first, the specifity rate for the control is higher than the reading disability group. Second, the code-breaking variables are not valid in screening individuals with reading disability, with specifity rate being 66.7%, while the language variables (especially, morphology awareness) has a specifity rate of 78.6% in identifying the reading disability group; besides, the combination of language and code-breaking variables increases the specifity rate to 85.7%. The results indicate L2 reading comprehension difficulty identification should select proper language variables or code-breaking variables according to the reader's language proficiency.

Key words: L2 English reading difficulty language variables code-breaking variables identification

15.1 Introduction

Reading difficulty influences learners' academic achievement and daily communication. From education perspective, early identification and intervention is very important. In the mother tongue reading difficulty diagnosis, early studies used the discrepancy between intelligence (IQ) to reading achievement. However, due to lack of validity, this diagnosis has believed to be neither necessary nor sufficient (Bradley, Danielson & Hallaban, 2002). In the latest 20 years, under the influence of cognitive psychology, skills research approach accounts have certain advantages for explaining the process of reading and reading disability (Koda, 2004). In this context, reading difficulty is defined from the gap between low reading achievement and core reading-related cognitive skills (刘云英 & 陶沙 , 2007). By this diagnosis method, screening of dyslexia is usually based on reading scores at the lowest 25% percentage or one standard deviation below average, and plus the gap between reading-related cognitive skills (薛锦 , 舒华 & 吴思娜 , 2009).

On the relationship between cognitive skills and reading, read variables can be divided into two broad categories: language variables and code-breaking variables. Language variables include vocabulary, syntax, and morpheme knowledge. Code-variables refer to the phonological processing skills, orthographic processing skills, rapid naming, working memory, and so on. Studies on mother-tongue have found that phonological processing skills, rapid naming, orthographic, morphological awareness and verbal working memory can effectively predict the reading achievements (Goswami, 2002; Ho et al., 2002). Dyslexics have defects in these cognitive skills. Therefore, the cognitive processing skills become effective indexes in the identification of dyslexia. However, different manifestations of linguistic features affect the discrimination of dyslexia. Thus, the effective predictors for dyslexia are different in different languages. For example, in the study of English as the native language, phonological processing skill is one of the core elements for English reading difficulties (van der Leij & Morfidi, 2006). In contrast, morphological awareness is the key to reading difficulties (Shu et al., 2006).

The findings in native languages have some implications for the reading difficulty in the second language. However, the characteristics of second language is further influenced by the reading ability in mother tongue, second language acquisition levels, socio-cultural background, bilingual development imbalances. Identification of reading difficulty in the second language is more challenging (Paradis, Genesee & Crago, 2010). Traditionally, there are three main methods for identification of second language reading difficulties (Lyon, Shaywitz & Shaywitz, 2003): teachers' rating, prediction from native language and prediction from the cognitive skills of the second language. These prediction methods are based the assumption that both languages for a bilingual should be similar in manifestation of reading difficulty (Knell, 2010; Wolf & Bowers, 1999). However, there were cases of dissociation between the two languages (Wang, Koda & Perfetti, 2003), leading to the fact that the most effective predictive variables for the second language will be influenced by language features and differences. Therefore, this study combines the most effective predictors in Chinese and English in identifying reading difficulties in the second/foreign language English.

The traditional second language learning research in China focuses on linguistic variables, suggesting that poor vocabulary and syntax analysis leading to difficulties in English reading comprehension(刘丹丹 , 2002). In recent years, several studies have concerned the relationship between second language reading and code variables. But such cognitive diagnostic study of second language reading difficulties are limited to primary school children (董燕 , 段建平 & 邵波 , 2004; 郭楠 , 杨晓慧 , 尹伊 & 陶沙 , 2009). Therefore, this study will examine both code and language variables in the context of the Chinese mother tongue in identifying English reading comprehension difficulties. Research questions of this study are: whether language variables (vocabulary size, morphemes, and syntax) can effectively identify foreign language English reading comprehension difficulties? Whether code-variable (decoding, working memory and phonological awareness) can effectively identify difficulties in English reading comprehension? Whether combination of language variables and code-variables can improve the accuracy of identification?

15.2 Research methods

15.2.1 Participants

Domestic English majors (first-year and second-year) on a total of 139 college students participated in this study (female $N = 122$ men, $N = 17$). According to the previous operation definitions (Shu et al., 2006), dyslexia screening is defined at reading scores below 1 *SD* of the average. Standardized reading comprehension tests [the Gates MacGinitie Reading Comprehension (Form 4, Level f)] were used. The 10.79% of the sample were discriminated as readers with reading difficulty, which was in line with the results of previous studies. The control group consisted 15 subjects, whose reading comprehension scores were above the average.

15.2.2 Measures

15.2.2.1 Reading tests

English word reading

A total of 106 words English words were included. Subjects were asked to read the words on the cards as much as possible. Repeated measurements to ensure a test-retest reliability. Repeated measurement of correlation coefficient is 0.48, and *p* were lower than 0.001, indicating a good reliability.

English reading comprehension

English reading comprehension tasks used standardized Gates MacGinitie Reading Comprehension (Form 4, Level F, 14 articles). There was a total of 48 questions. The students were required to finish reading in 30 minutes. Cronbach alpha was 0.70, indicating good reliability.

15.2.2.2 Code-variables

Decoding

This task was selected from Word Attack section in Woodcock, Test materials were 45 English words. Subjects were asked to read the words. Reliability Cronbach alpha = 0.77.

Phoneme deletion

There were 20 recorded English words. Participants were asked to listen to a sound (such as /toothbrush/), and make the sound by removing part of the sound (By removing /tooth/, that is /brush/). Cronbach alpha = 0.68.

Working memory

The task asked students to listen to some sentences, make some judgment on whether the sentences were true or false, and then repeat the last word of each sentence. Cronbach alpha = 0.86.

15.2.2.3 Language-variables

Morphological awareness

Subjects were asked to read and hear a sentence and write a suitable word to fill in the blank of the sentence. There were 31 sentences. Cronbach alpha = 0.70。

Vocabulary

Vocabulary subtest from Gates MacGinitie Vocabulary Test (Form 4, Level F) was adopted. Subjects were asked to complete a total of 65 questions within 25 minutes. Reliability Cronbach alpha = 0.82.

Syntactic awareness

According to Cain (2007), the syntactic awareness could be tested by measuring the awareness in word order, verb agreement, and the use of the word. Therefore, we used 36 sentences including the above three dimensions. Subjects were asked to determine whether the sentences were grammatically correct. Reliability Cronbach alpha = 0.58.

15.2.3 Procedures

Word reading, decoding, phonological awareness, working memory were individual measurement and were tested in about 30 minutes; reading comprehension, morphological awareness, vocabulary, syntax were collective tests in about 90 minutes. All were tested in the end of the second semester or the beginning of the first semester.

15.3 Results

15.3.1 Defining the experiment group and the control group

The control group and the experiment group selection were based on z-scores on reading comprehension. Those subjects were defined as the experiment group when they had less than one standard deviation below the average score. And the control group were subjects who had above average scores. Reading group and control groups consisted 15 subjects respectively. But because of missing data in the morpheme task, the number of the experiment group had only for 14 people in logistic regression analysis.

The following table shows that the experiment group lagged behind in word reading and reading comprehension when compared with the control group. The comparison in the language and code variables was present in the following table. The results showed the experiment group performed worse in working memory, syntax, vocabulary and morphological awareness.

Table 29 Comparison between the two reading groups

Variables	Group	*N*	*M*	*SD*	*F*	*p*
English word reading	Experiment group	15	74.47	7.99	4.77	0.04
	Control Group	15	80.80	7.88		
Reading comprehension	Experiment group	15	12.47	2.92	73.50	0.001
	Control Group	15	23.73	4.17		

Table 30 Language and code-variables between the two reading groups

Variables	Groups	*N*	*M*	*SD*	*F*	*p*
Phonological awareness	Experiment Group	15	11.93	3.39	1.64	0.21
	Control Group	15	13.47	3.16		
Decoding	Experiment Group	15	29.87	4.64	1.82	0.19
	Control Group	15	31.93	3.69		
Working memory	Experiment Group	15	16.00	2.04	5.19	0.03
	Control Group	15	19.00	4.68		
Syntax	Experiment Group	15	21.87	2.45	7.64	0.01
	Control Group	15	25.00	3.64		
Vocabulary	Experiment Group	15	15.33	6.13	4.60	0.04
	Control Group	15	21.00	8.19		
Morphological awareness	Experiment Group	14	10.36	4.55	21.95	0.001
	Control Group	15	17.13	3.16		

15.3.2 Sensitivity of variables in predicting reading difficulty

Table 31 Logistic regression analysis

Prediction Variables	**Likelihood**	**Freedom**	***p***
Model 1 (language variables)	21.40	3	0.000
Vocabulary			0.20
Syntax			0.74
Morphological Awareness			0.022
Model 2 (code variables)	35.83	3	0.12
Phonological awareness			0.61
Decoding			0.72
Working memory			0.09
Model 3 (language and code variables combined)	19.40	6	0.002
Vocabulary			0.69
Syntax			0.13
Morphological Awareness			0.035
Phonological awareness			0.54
Decoding			0.41
Working memory			0.26

Differential sensitivity (sensitivity) refers to whether the cognitive variable is able to distinguish between the experiment (reading difficulty) group and the control group. The present study used the Logistic Regression analysis (Enter method) to analyze the sensitivity and specifity of the language and the code variables. The following table showed the three models by Logistic regression analyses with excluding standard $p < 0.1$. When using the language variables (vocabulary, grammar, morpheme) as the predictor variables (Model 1), the logistic regression model was significant (−2logLLx2 = 21.40, $df = 3$, $p < 0.001$); When using the code variable as the predictor variables (Model 2), the logistic regression models were not significant (−2logLLx2 = 35.83, $df = 3$, $p = 0.12$). When using the combination of code and language variables as the predictor variables (Model 3), the logistic regression model was significant (−2logLLx2 = 19.40, $df = 6$, $p = 0.002$).

15.3.3 Accuracy in screening reading comprehension difficulties

The specifity of a test of reading difficulty depends on the accuracy of prediction. In general, the variables with good specificy should make a prediction with an accuracy of above 75% (Limbos & Geva, 2001). Accordingly, we calculated the accuracy: accuracy = the number correctly predicted /total number). Results showed that language variables (grammar, vocabulary, and morphemes) had an accuracy of 93.3% in predicting the control group and accuracy of 78.6% in predicting the experiment group (subjects with reading difficulties). Code-variables (voice, working memory, decode) has a predictive accuracy of 73.3% for the control group, and an accuracy of 66.7% for the experiment group. The the language and code variable combination (Model 3) had an accuracy of 93.3% for the control group and 85.7% for the experiment group.

15.4 Conclusion

Research results can be summarized as follows: first, the language and code-variables have predictive power in predicting reading comprehension difficulties. Second, code and variable combinations can increase the identification accuracy.

Chapter 16 Reading metacognitive intervention: A preliminary study on EFL learners

Abstract: Traditional English teaching in China is content-based and it has focused much attention on teaching language knowledge but neglecting teaching and cultivating strategies especially metacognitive strategies, which lead to students' lack of autonomous learning abilities. The present author conducted a longitudinal study on a minimal metacognitive intervention on Chinese native learners of English as a foreign language (EFL) and attempted to seek answers to the following question: Can EFL learners' reading metacognition and reading performance be enhanced by minimal metacognitive training? Participants were divided into control group and experimental group; the experimental groups learnt what metacognitive strategies were and how to apply them in the intensive English course. English reading comprehension test and metacognitive strategies questionnaire were measured. ANOVA analysis showed reading performance of the experimental group was better than the control group. The results indicate that metacognitive strategy intervention do enhance their reading performance. The effect of metacognitive strategy intervention is influenced by individual's language level and is directly related to the degree of individual's involvement.

Key words: metacognition metacognitive strategy English reading reading strategies

16.1 Introduction

Flavell (1976) first defined metacognition in his study on metamemory. Afterward, a large number of theoretical and empirical studies on the topic of metacognition have been carried out. Many researchers in China also contribute their studies to the classification of metacognition (Yang & Zhang, 2002; Liu, 2005; Li & Ni, 2007; Liu, 2009; Xue, 2011). When learners are equipped with metacognitive knowledge, they will understand their own thinking and learning process. Accordingly, they are more likely to oversee the choice and application of learning strategies, to plan how to proceed with a learning task, to monitor their own performance on an ongoing basis, to find solutions to problems encountered, and to evaluate themselves upon task completion (Zhang & Goh, 2006).

Reading is always regarded as the most important academic language skills for second language students, for reading provides the most efficient and important channel of language input. Reading has already become a lifelong skill which means that fostering reading skills should not only in the early years but also through life. Metacognitive strategies are significant in reading in that metacognitive strategies involve thinking about the reading process, planning before reading, monitoring while reading, knowing the time that reading breaks down and knowing the method to solve the problem, evaluating the reading process after the activity is completed.

Studies have shown that there is a positive relationship between metacognition strategy and reading proficiency (Anderson, 1991; Barnet, 1988; Garner, 1987; Carrell, 1998). According to Wenden (1987), good readers were flexible strategies users, while for the poor readers; they cannot differentiate effective strategies well from those that might be obstacles of their comprehension. What's more, they had deficiency in the application of metacognitive strategies to plan, to monitor, and to evaluate their understanding of reading materials. Base on the study of Pesseley et al. (1995), skilled readers applied comprehension monitoring which involves: how difficult the text is read, distinguish between familiar and new information in the text, check the test so as to see whether predictions about the text content are fulfilled, and evaluate the relevance of the text to reading goals. Different from skilled readers, the unskilled readers seldom used these metacognitive strategies. Javadi et al. (2010) investigated the relationship between metacognitive awareness of reading strategies and students' academic status. Metacognition Awareness Reading Strategies Inventory (MARSI) which was developed and validated by Mokhtari and Reichard (2002) was administrated among participants. Results revealed that advanced students used more complex cognitive and metacognitive strategies than lower level students. Moreover, a relationship between metacognitive awareness and academic achievement was found. Aghaie & Zhang (2012) conducted a study on effects of explicit instruction in cognitive and metacognitive reading strategies on Iranian EFL students' reading performance and strategy transfer. A contrast group and a treatment group were involved in this study and the treatment group was intervened. It showed that the treatment group achieved significantly better results than the contrast group after four months of strategy-based instruction in reading comprehension and strategy transfer. Furthermore, the results also showed that strategy instruction contributed to autonomous reading behaviors.

However, studies concerning metacognition in EFL reading for Chinese natives showed controversial results. For instance, Liu (2004) revealed that the Chinese students majoring in English used metacognitive strategies more or less in English reading and there was a positive relationship between the frequency of overall metacognitive strategy use and the results of English reading. However, Hu & Zhang's (2006) survey on non-English majors' use of metacognitive strategies found that they did not often use those strategies. Zhang (2005) showed that the English majors in China lack awareness of the importance of metacognitive strategy use, although she found that metacognitive strategies among which self-management strategy, selective attention strategy and planning strategy were closely related to the students' English achievement and that difference existed in the use of strategies of goal and plan, self-management and attention. Nevertheless, most studies in China affirmed the positive relation between metacognitive strategies use and English performance (e.g., Yuan & Xiao, 2006) and feasibility and validity of metacognitive training on different levels of EFL learners (e.g., Chen & Dai, 2007; Li & Ni, 2007; Pan, 2006; Xue, 2011; Yang & Zhang, 2002).

Overall, the above-mentioned studies on metacognition could be categorized into either free-develop model or direct-instruction model (Chen & Dai, 2007). According to the free-develop model, individuals can naturally learn metacognitive knowledge through exercise by themselves without direct instruction and cultivation from the teachers. The free-develop model pays little attention to metacognitive experience. Students are seldom taught when, where and how to use specific strategies so it is time-consuming and results in low efficiency in reading. In comparison, direct-instruction model acknowledges that individuals' metacognition cultivation needs direct instruction. Teachers have to provide clear and specific knowledge of metacognition. This model can help students master and apply metacognitive strategies more accurately which is especially suitable for younger students or poor students in reading. Most of the training in the above examples is related to the direct-instruction model. The direct-instruction model is efficient in improving students' reading metacognition because of its clear purpose, and the large amount of information delivered to the students.

As is well established, the traditional English teaching in China is content-based and focuses mostly on teaching language skills and knowledge but neglecting learning strategies especially metacognitive strategies, which lead to students' lack of autonomous learning abilities. For Chinese native learners of English as a foreign language in China, they usually follow the free-development model. Even though they have learned English reading for many years, they do not know exactly what strategies they should employ during the reading and when and how to use them (Hu & Zhang, 2006). Obviously, although they may have memorized a large numbers of English words, they desperately need instructions so as to become efficient readers.

Taking the current situation of Chinese native learners of English into consideration, the present study adopted a "minimal-intervention" model: the teachers gave direct instructions about metacognitive knowledge to the students and explained the definition, function, application of specific strategies during reading, which could give students a general and specific understanding about metacognitive strategy knowledge. Meanwhile, the present study urged students to rely on their own initiatives to practice these metacognitive knowledge and strategies in EFL reading. The present study tried to address the following question: whether EFL learners' reading metacognition and reading performance can be enhanced by the "minimal-intervention" model.

16.2 Research methods

16.2.1 Subjects

Participants were Grade 2 English majors from BISU. All the students have learned English as a second language for about 8 years. The participants were randomly divided into control group (N = 36) and experimental group (N = 44). The experimental groups learnt what metacognitive strategies were and how to apply them in the intensive English course.

16.2.2 Instruments

Reading Comprehension

The materials for reading comprehensions are shown in the following table.

Table 32 Test materials for pretest, mid–test and final test

Tests	Description
Pretest	English test for non-English majors about Level 4
Mid-test	reading sections selected from TOEFL 2001
Posttest	reading sections selected from TOEFL 2005

Questionnaire

The Metacognitive Awareness of Reading Strategies Inventory (MARSI) Sheorey & Mokhtari (2001) was adopted and used to investigate the students' overall state of metacognitive strategies use.

The questionnaire contained 28 items which were divided into three categories: metacognitive strategies (1-10 items), cognitive strategies (11-22 items) and support strategies (23-28 iterms). All the items were on a 5-point Likert Scale ranging from 1 "never", 2 "seldom", 3 "sometimes", 4 "often", to 5 "always". The higher the score was, the more frequently they used the strategy. The total score on this inventory could range from 30 to 60. Specific information is shown in Table 33.

Table 33 Structure and distribution of the MARSI

	Description
Metacognitive strategies	The strategies are those intentional, carefully planned techniques by which learners monitor or manage their reading. Such strategies include: having a purpose in mind, previewing the text as to its length and organization, or using typographical aids and tables and figures (10 items).
Cognitive strategies	They are the actions and procedures readers use while working directly with the text. These are localized, focused techniques used when problems develop in understanding textual information. Examples of cognitive strategies include: adjusting one's speed of reading when the material becomes difficult or easy, guessing the meaning of unknown words, and re-reading the text for improved comprehension (12 items).
Support strategies	They are basically support mechanisms intended to aid the reader in comprehending the text such as using a dictionary, taking notes, or underlining or highlighting the text (six items).

16.2.3 Procedures

Before the metacognitive strategy intervention, both the control group and the experimental group took part in the Metacognitive Awareness of Reading Strategies Inventory. The experimental group received the minimal intervention program, which lasted for two month from October 29th to December 20th. They were explicitly told the importance of the use of metacognitive strategies. Teachers just explained the knowledge about metacognitive knowledge and they did not spend much time on demonstrating and exercising how to use the strategies in class. During the intervention period, the teacher would ask the students whether they had any problems in the use of metacognitive strategies while reading and answered the questions. Meanwhile, the students were encouraged to ask any questions about metacognitive strategy use during reading. The experimental group students were asked to do some reading by themselves according to the stage learning materials distributed to them which included three stages.

At first stage, the student got a general understanding about the following two points: ① the different performance between the good readers and low readers before reading, while reading and after reading. For example, the good readers would forecast the content of the article and had some metacognitive reading strategies in mind before reading while the low readers had not any plans and purpose for reading before the task begins. During reading, the good readers could concentrate on what they read and did not allow themselves to be distracted. They also analyzed the structure of the article, monitored their reading process and controlled their reading speed. On the contrary, the low readers read the passage directly without analyzing the structure of the passage and did not know what to do when meeting difficulties. After reading, the good readers summarized the main idea of the passage and verified the message of the article while the poor readers just stopped the reading activity and never evaluated their reading effects. ② The definition and examples about frequently used metacognitive strategies. This stage provided students with basic knowledge of metacognition. Such as setting purpose for reading, using text features, context clues and typographical aid, adjusting reading rate, rereading for better understanding and underling information in text and so on. In order to develop metacognitive strategies, one's metacognitive knowledge must be enriched.

At the second stage, there were examples about several frequently met questions, such as: the questions about the main idea of the passage, the questions of guessing the meaning of new words, the question of abstracting the specific information from the passage and inferring the meaning of the sentence according to the context. Each kind of question was followed with typical examples, correct answers and detailed explanations as well. The generalization of each kind of question would help students better distribute their attention.

At the third stage, the reinforced exercises were provided. The learners were encouraged to independently apply these strategies while doing the reading exercise after class. Meanwhile, the control group from the two Grades did not receive the intervention program but under the traditional teaching instruction.

After the intervention program, both the experimental groups from the two Grades were asked to take part in the post tests and answer the same questionnaire again.

16.3 Data analysis and discussion

The Cronbach Alpha coefficient calculated in this study was more than 0.65, indicating that the internal consistency of the questionnaire is reliable which can be seen in Table 34.

Table 34 MARSI reliability analysis

Dimensions	Item numbers	Cronbach's alpha
PREMETA	10	0.76
PRECOG	12	0.79
PRESUP	6	0.68
POSTMETA	10	0.79
POSTCOG	12	0.76
POSTSUP	6	0.65

Notes: META = metacognitive; COG = cognitive strategies; SUP = the support strategies.

Table 35 showed that there was no significant difference on the three dimensions of metacognitive strategies use between interventional class and control class, $F(1, 78) = 0.01$, $p = 0.91$ in metacognitive strategy use; $F(1, 78) = 0.22$, $p = 0.64$ in cognitive strategy use and $F(1, 78) = 0.09$, $p = 0.677$ in support strategy use.

It was not difficult to find that the mean of the interventional class increased from 0.19 in pretest to 0.30 in mid-test but decreased to 0.19 in the posttest. In contrast, the mean of the control class decreased from −0.11 in pretest to −0.23 in mid-test but increased to −0.04 in posttest (Table 36).

The reasons might be as follows: the awareness of metacognitive strategy use of the interventional class increased as the intervention begins, so the participants consciously used the strategies while reading. It was understandable that everyone was interested in new things and especially students who had the motivation of improving their reading performance even for the students who were poor in English reading. Whereas, as time went on, their self-control decreased without teachers' regulation. They might be lazier to practice the strategy use in reading so their reading performance decreased again. Yet whether these were reasonable or not, it needed further research and investigation. Even if the reading patterns of interventional class increased first and decreased later, it was found that the mean score of interventional class was higher than that of control class. From this perspective, it further verified the result that the intervention program did enhance their reading performance.

Table 35　ANOVAs results for the control and the interventional groups

		N	*M*	*SD*	Min	Max	*F*	Sig
POSTMeta	Control class	36	3.56	0.46	2.80	4.40	0.01	0.91
	Interventional class	44	3.55	0.57	2.60	4.80		
POSTCog	Control class	36	3.60	0.52	2.50	4.67	0.22	0.64
	Interventional class	44	3.55	0.48	2.58	4.50		
POSTSup	Control class	36	3.33	0.63	2.33	5.00	0.09	0.77
	Interventional class	44	3.37	0.63	1.83	4.50		
Total		80	3.35	0.63	1.83	5.00		

Notes: Meta = metacognitive strategy; Cog = cognitive strategy use; Sup = supportive strategy.

To further prove whether metacognitive strategy was effective on students' reading metacognition and reading performance, the present study further compared the difference between pretest and posttest for the interventional classes.

Table 36　Reading performance comparison between two groups

		N	*M*	*SD*	Min	Max	*F*	Sig
Pretest	Control class	57	-0.11	1.03	-3.71	1.41	2.87	0.09
	Interventional class	51	0.19	0.96	-1.35	1.80		
Midtest	Control class	58	-0.23	1.22	-4.54	1.12	7.83	0.01
	Interventional class	51	0.30	0.62	-0.92	1.44		
Posttest	Control class	58	-0.04	1.04	-5.60	1.16	2.04	0.16
	Interventional class	51	0.19	0.97	-1.40	1.34		

Table 37 Metacognitive strategy use pre– and post the intervention

	M	*SD*	*N*
PREMETA	3.21	0.61	41
PRECOG	3.55	0.53	41
PRESUP	3.12	0.63	41
POSTMeta	3.55	0.59	41
POSTCog	3.54	0.50	41
POSTsup	3.36	0.64	41

Notes: META = metacognitive strategy; COG = cognitive strategy; SUP = support strategy.

The ANOVA analysis found that the interventional main effects was significant, $F(1, 40) = 5.99, p = 0.019$. In other words, the interventional group improved a lot after the intervention. There were main effect of level, $F(2, 80) = 8.88, p < 0.001$ and the significant effect of intervention * level interaction $F(2, 80) = 7.70, p < 0.001$, indicating that improvement on the three dimensions of metacognitive strategies was different.

16.4 Discussion

FroM the result oF ANOVAs analysis between the control group and the interventional group, it can be found that there is no significant difference on the three dimensions of metacognitive strategies use between interventional and control groups. Nevertheless, the reading patterns of interventional class increase first but decrease later with the $M = 0.19$ in the pretest, $M = 0.30$ in the midtest and $M = 0.19$ in the posttest. On the contrary, the reading scores of control group decrease first but increase later with the $M = -0.11$ in the pretest, $M = -0.04$ in the midtest and $M = -0.23$ in the posttest.

The interventional classes are further tested so as to finding out whether metacognitive strategy is effective on students' reading metacognition and reading performance. The intervention main effect is significant, $F(1, 40) = 5.99, p = 0.019$. Moreover, there is a main effect of level, $F(2, 80) = 8.88, p < 0.001$ and significant effect of intervention * level interaction $F(2, 80) = 7.70, p < 0.001$, demonstrating that improvement on the three dimension of metacognitive strategy is different.

For analyzing the results, some points have to be mentioned: First, the internalization of metacognitive strategies use needs a period of time (Chen & Dai, 2007) and this study lasts for about two month, therefore, the frequency of the strategies use on the metacognitive strategies may not so obvious.

Second, the minimal metacognitive strategy intervention conducted in this study, on one hand, needs the teacher's detailed explanations of metacognition and guidance in the course of students' reading practice; on the other hand, it relies more on students' self-control on reading practice. As what is learnt or practiced in class is far from enough, students should be good at managing their language learning outside class with sufficient authentic reading materials.

A study conducted by Zhang (2004) suggested that the efficiency of EFL teaching was largely determined by students' learning attitude and method. In this experiment, two models "Metacognitive Strategy Training in Class" and "Signing Learner Contract with the Learner after Class" were used, and the results showed that the method of signing learner contract with the learners not only developed learners' autonomous learning habit, but also improve learners' listening, reading and writing abilities; development of learners' autonomy is helpful in improving learners' learning achievement. "Signing Learner Contract with the Learner after Class" is not used in this study, which, at some extent, explained the reason why there is no statistically significance between interventional group and control group on the tree dimensions of metacognitive strategies use.

Third, though there is no statistically significance between interventional group and control group on the three dimensions of metacognitive strategies use, the reading performance of the interventional classes is much better than the control classes after the intervention. And the reading patterns do suggest that the interventional classes have improved their reading performance. The minimal metacognitive strategy intervention provides the participants clear and detailed knowledge of metacognition and the followed materials can directly offer participants metacognitive experience which is vital in reading comprehension.

By taking the teachers feedbacks into consideration, the intervention results were closely related to the time and quality of intervention. If the teachers reminded the students more, their consciousness of using strategies would be strengthened during reading and their self-regulation could also be improved. On the other, the participants should be self regulated so they practiced more.

16.5 Conclusions and implications

There were differences between weak and strong university students in their metacognitive knowledge and metacognitive strategies awareness. The patterns of reading performance of the interventional group indicate that metacognitive strategy intervention does enhance their reading performance. The findings reinforce and enrich the existing theories that metacognitive strategies have positive effects on EFL reading (O' Malley et al., 1985; Anderson, 1991; Palinscar & Brown, 1989; Gourgey, 1999; Chamot, 2005; Greenfell & Macaro, 2007; Zhang, 2008; Aghaie & Zhang, 2012). Result of the study demonstrated that metacognitive knowledge and metacognitive strategies awareness affected students' academic achievement.

It was mentioned that as English majors, they have to spend a lot of time on practicing the basic skills such as speaking, writing, reading, and listening and attending many lessons, so limited time and efforts are left for strategy training in class, leaving students to practice by themselves after class. The minimal-intervention could be a potential training model that fits into English teaching curriculum. To sum up, the present study inspires in some way for the future study on the relationship between metacognitive strategy and English reading. It is believed that this field can be consolidated and enriched in the future and more and more theoretical and empirical studies on metacognitive theory can be conducted to apply metacognition to the learning and teaching of English reading.

One related note is that a number of factors including students interests, motivation, their English proficiency and teachers' knowledge about metacognitive can influence the results of the experiment. Thus, it is suggested that teachers should be equipped with metacognitive strategy. Meanwhile, developing students' ability of autonomous learning is the most important factor in metacognitive strategy use while reading. It highlights their ability of independent and autonomous learning, which is supposed to be the ultimate goal.

Chapter 17 The relationship between bilingual morphological awareness and reading for Chinese EFL adult learners[1]

Abstract: The present research aimed to explore the developmental relationship between bilingual morphological awareness and reading for Chinese natives learning English as a Foreign language (EFL learners). A pre- and post-tests were conducted with an interval of 9 months. Bilingual morphological measures (English derivational morphology, English compounding, Chinese homographic morpheme identification, Chinese compound words) and literacy measures (Chinese character reading and reading comprehension, English word identification and reading comprehension) were administered on 139 participants. The results confirmed the intra-language correlations between morphological awareness and reading. The study also demonstrated that the contribution of English derivational awareness to English reading was higher than that of English compound awareness. Chinese compound morphology was found to contribute increasing variances to English reading in post-test. The results indicate the relationship between bilingual reading and morphological awareness was subjected to the similarity between the two languages in terms of the level of morphological complexity as well as language proficiency.

Key words: Chinese-English bilinguals morphological awareness development

17.1 Introduction

Morphology is an organizational level of language that deals with the smallest units than can be associated with meaning and grammatical function, namely morphemes.

---

[1] The content and data of this paper was published in "Reading and Writing", 2016 (in Press).

Morphological awareness (MA) is the ability to reflect upon and manipulate morphemes, the smallest phonological unit that carries meaning, and to use word formation rules to construct and understand morphologically complex words (Kuo & Anderson, 2006). It means perceiving a word's morphological structure and being able to manage this structure (Carlisle, 1995; Carlisle & Stone, 2003). This includes the accessibility of morphemes, reflecting an individual's ability to apply morphemic knowledge in identifying and creating more complex forms of words and in adapting the new structure to the given language (Perfetti, 1985).

A large body of research has consistently demonstrated that morphological awareness plays a very essential role in promoting word reading, and directly or indirectly contributes to reading comprehension in alphabetic languages such as English and French (e.g., Carlisle, 2000; Deacon & Kirby, 2004), in non-Latin based languages such as Hebrew and Arabic (e.g., Schiff & Calif, 2007; Saiegh-Hadadd & Geva, 2008), and in logographic languages like Chinese (e.g., Ku & Anderson, 2003; McBride-Chang, Cho, Liu, Wagner, Shu, Zhou et al., 2005; McBride-Chang, Cheung, Chow, Chow & Choi, 2006; Shu, McBride-Chang, Wu & Liu, 2006). However, most of previous studies were conducted on monolinguals, with only a small number of studies on the bilingual children. The cross-linguistic studies on the relationship between morphological awareness and reading have rather scarcely focused upon bilinguals of distant languages like Chinese and English. The current study was aimed at exploring the developmental relationship between bilingual morphological awareness and reading for Chinese adults who learn English as a foreign language.

17.1.1 English vs. Chinese morphology and measurement of morphological awareness

English and Chinese are two typologically-distant languages (Koda & Reddy, 2008). English belongs to an alphabetic language, in which phonological units to morphemes might be easily confounded, and written units carry morphological as well as phonological information. The three major types of English morphology are inflection, derivation and compounding (Kuo & Anderson, 2006). English is comparatively rich in inflectional and derivational morphology. Both inflected and derived words are formed through an amalgamation of a root and an affix(es). The difference between the two morphologies lies in that inflected words are formed by adding an inflectional affix to a root, such as -s (plural) or -ed (past tense) (e.g., *fly-flies, explain-explained*), which indicates both semantic and syntactic information of gender, case, tense, etc., whereas derived words are formed by adding a derivational affix, such as -er (agentive) or -ly (adverb) (e.g., *friend-friendly, discuss-discussion*), that changes the meaning and often the grammatical category of the root to which the affix is attached. Specifically, derived forms often involve phonological or/and orthographic changes (e.g., *decide and decision*), and adding a derivational affix to a base word usually leads to change of the meaning, and sometimes the grammatical category, of the base form. In addition, derivation is also constrained by the grammatical category of a base word. English compound words are formed through different form-class combinations and largely observe the right-headedness principle (e.g., *wet-cold, short-sighted*). The right component of a compound is usually the head, and syntactic head and semantic head often converge (Plag, 2003).

Measurement of morphological awareness should cater to morphological structures of the language in question, and serve the appropriate stage of language development. Kieffer and Lesaux (2008) identified English morphological awareness as a conscious awareness of word structure and semantic-functional meanings and thus the measurement of English morphological awareness should take into consideration the root, structure, base form, and suffixes representing inflectional and derivational processes. Previous research indicates that children's knowledge of inflectional morphology typically becomes well developed upon entering elementary school, since English inflectional affixes are small in number, and largely regular structurally, with no or very limited phonological or orthographic shift (e.g., jumps, jumping, and jumped) (Berko, 1958). In contrast, research on derivational awareness has shown that children before attending Grade 4 in elementary school didn't master the ability to recognize and manipulate derivation rules (Mann et al., 2000) due to the relatively large number of derivational affixes in English and the nature of derivational process. Like deviational awareness, tasks that tap complex compounding skills, such as discriminating meanings of roots in compounds and inferring meanings of unknown compounds, could still be difficult to English-speaking fourth and sixth graders (Ku & Anderson, 2003). In the present study, even though the adult participants were second language learners, they had well developed in inflectional morphology. Thus, English morphological awareness was operationalized into measuring English derivational morphology and compounding words.

By contrast, Chinese is generally considered to be a logographic, morpho-syllabic language. The most commonly used Chinese characters amount to about 7 000, but there are only 1 300 syllables for them In most cases one Chinese character corresponds to one morpheme and to one syllable, and the pronunciation and meaning of a regular Chinese character comes from its morphemes. Due to the large abundance of polyphonic words in Chinese, it becomes the greatest difficulty to match Chinese character and its syllable for Chinese learners. Thus, in the field of educational psychology, homophonic morphemes (e.g., "非" and "飞") and homographic morphemes (e.g., "生" in "生气" and "生菜") are partitioned. Additionally, one striking feature of Chinese is Chinese characters generally have no inflectional markings to indicate tense, gender, case etc. Due to such characteristics, the classification of Chinese morphemes is relatively complex and flexible. For example, according to the number of syllables, Chinese morphemes can be divided into monosyllabic morpheme (e.g., "天" /tian/, "人" /ren/) and polysyllabic morpheme (e.g., "琵琶" /pipa/, "乒乓" /pingpang/). In terms of word-formation capacity, they can be classified into free (e.g., "好" /hao/, "来" /lai/), half-free (e.g., "民" /min/, "视" /shi/) and non-free one (e.g., "者" /zhe/, "第" /di/). Another striking feature of Chinese is the compound words, which occupy a large proportion in Chinese morphology. Noticeably, in Chinese, on average, a single Chinese morpheme appears in about 17 compound words (Yin, 1984; Yuan & Huang, 1998). The number of Chinese words formed through compounding amounts to more than 75%. Over 65% of the words used in Modern Chinese are two-morpheme disyllabic compounds, and about 10% are three-morphemic compounds (Sun, Sun, Huang, Li & Xing, 1996).

The unique phonological, syntactic and orthographic systems in Chinese add new content to the conceptualization of Chinese morphological awareness. According to Li and Anderson (2002), morphological awareness in Chinese was composed by three parts: the first is phonetic radical and semantic radical awareness, referring to the deep understanding of Chinese character structures; the second is awareness of inner structure of word; the third is the ability to identify homophonic and homographic morphemes. In the viewpoint of Zhang et al., morphological awareness involves two types: the awareness of judging the validity of words and understanding the lexical structure; and the ability to split a whole word into morphemes and further interpret the meaning of single morpheme as well as morpheme combination (Zhang & Koda, 2014).

Previous studies on Chinese compound awareness are largely from two aspects. One was the ability to identify the head morpheme. According to Chen et al. (2009), the head morpheme can manifest the category of a compound word. Generally, whether in English and Chinese, the last morpheme always serves as the head of a compound noun. If children have acquired awareness of the head morpheme, they can extract the meaning of compound nouns which contain a familiar head. For instance, a child knowing the right-headedness of nouns can understand that "茶杯" (teacup) is some kind of "cup". This awareness may be particularly essential in Chinese because the same head morpheme often appears in substantial number of words. Nagy et al. (2003) reported that a morphological construct including a compound morphology task that required participants to identify the head morpheme of a compound noun, and several other morphological awareness tasks, was significantly correlated with oral vocabulary in second grade at-risk readers and fourth grade at-risk writers. Another aspect of compound awareness evaluated in previous research was the ability to form a new compound word by combining familiar morphemes (Chen et al., 2009). It was argued that forming a new compound word to represent a certain meaning may require a deeper understanding of both compound structure and morpheme meaning. Research on this aspect of compound awareness has been conducted among Hong Kong children (McBride-Chang et al., 2005, 2006). In these studies, children were required to answer questions such as, "If we see the sun rising in the morning, we call that a "sunrise". What should we call the phenomenon of the moon rising?" The correct answer to this question is "moonrise". This task was illustrated to predict unique variance in Chinese word recognition for kindergarteners and second graders (e.g., McBride-Chang et al., 2005).

In present research, Chinese compound awareness was operationalized into measuring the ability in identifying Chinese homographic morphemes and compound word meaning judgment.

17.1.2 Morphological awareness in bilingual reading

The relationship between bilingual morphological awareness and reading is subjected to the distance between the two language systems in terms of morphological representation. Those studies on morphological cross-linguistic transfer have indicated that morphological features influence the transfer direction of morphological skills.

One theory assumes that where the two languages morphological systems are similar in their level of complexity (like English and French), bidirectional cross-linguistic transfer of morphological awareness skills takes place. For instance, Deacon et al. (2009) measured the effect of morphological awareness on reading in two languages with deep orthography: English and French. They finally found a bidirectional cross-language transfer of morphological skills between the two languages. Namely, English morphological awareness was an important predictor of word reading in French, and morphological skills in French language contributed to word reading in English.

Another theory proposes it should be easier to transfer morphological kills from deep morphological systems like Arabic, Hebrew, Spanish, Finnish and Korean to transparent morphological systems, like English, but not vice versa. This is because transparent orthographies usually relate to a deep and complex morphological system, whereas deep orthographies accompany a transparent and simple morphological system. Previous findings have indicated that morphological awareness in orthographically shallow native languages significantly contributed to reading skills in English L2, but not the other way around. For instance, Schiff and Calif (2007) observed transfer effects of derivational awareness on word reading from Hebrew to English in Israeli children who learned English as a second language (L2). Result indicates that for Israeli fifth graders, a Hebrew morphological awareness task can predict the performance on a parallel English morphological awareness task and the performance on English word reading. In another study, Saiegh-Hadadd and Geva (2008) investigated the transfer of morphological awareness among Canadian-Arabic children. The researchers found that Arabic morphological awareness as measured by two derivational tasks predicted English word reading accuracy and fluency, but English morphological awareness was not related to Arabic word reading. Likewise, Ramirez, Chen, X., Geva, E. & Kiefer (2010) investigated within and cross-language effects of morphological awareness on word reading among Spanish-English bilingual children. The results illustrated that after controlling for other reading related variables, Spanish morphological awareness explained unique variance to Spanish word reading. English morphological awareness also predicted unique variance in English word reading. Cross-language influence of morphological awareness was found from Spanish to English, but not from English to Spanish.

In the case of Chinese-English bilinguals, the similarity in morphological rules between Chinese and English offers the possibility of the cross-linguistic transfer of morphological awareness between English and Chinese. Wang et al. (2006) evaluated both English compound awareness and English derivational awareness in children from Grade 1 to Grade 5. They detected that only English compound morphology predicted significant unique variance in Chinese reading comprehension. Owing to the rare occurrence of derivational morphology in Chinese, it was unlikely that English derivational awareness would facilitate Chinese vocabulary and reading, over and above Chinese compound awareness. Wang et al. (2009) further examined the contribution of phonology, orthography and morphology in Chinese-English biliteracy acquisition, and further illustrated that English compound awareness was related to Chinese word reading in Grade 1. Thus, it seems that the direction of contribution of morphological awareness, at least to the reading outcomes, is influenced by the morphological structure of children's first and second language.

Zhang et al. (2010) examined Chinese learners of English as second language (ESL) children in Grade 5 and offered a brief intervention among them on either Chinese or English compound structures. The result showed that children who received the Chinese intervention outperformed the control group on an English morphological awareness task. In comparison, among children who received the English intervention, only those with high English proficiency performed better than control group on a Chinese morphological awareness task. The findings indicate there should be a transfer of morphological skills from Chinese to English

Pasquarella et al. (2011) investigated the transfer of morphological awareness between English and Chinese and observed a bidirectional relationship between English compound awareness and Chinese vocabulary among 137 Chinese-English bilingual children in Canada. The study revealed that English compound awareness was a significant predictor of Chinese reading comprehension. Another enlightened idea from the study is that in the process of transfer between languages, what is transferred is abstract metalinguistic understanding rather than the concrete lexical knowledge. This study illustrated that the transfer of morphological awareness was largely influenced by the morphological structure of languages, and the transfer of compounding is more obvious due to the common characteristics of both Chinese and English. However, this research only observed unidirectional transfer from English compound awareness to Chinese reading comprehension, but not from Chinese compound awareness to English reading comprehension.

Zhang and Koda (2012) conducted a research about the intra- and inter-lingual relationships between L1 and L2 morphological awareness and reading acquisition. It was demonstrated that the transferring effect of derivational awareness was not observed from the research. Chinese compound awareness uniquely predicted the variance of English reading comprehension. However, this cross-language effect was not shown in the direction from English compound awareness to Chinese reading ability. Nonetheless, this might shed light on the idea that the effect of compounding in Chinese is more important than other types of morphology in explaining bilingual reading.

In sum, previous research findings indicated that morphological awareness predicts reading measures within the L1 and L2; morphological awareness can exert cross-language impact on reading between English and other alphabetic languages; the complexity of morphological features of two languages plays a vital role in determining the ultimate transfer direction. However, the research on cross-language contribution of morphological awareness to reading is still rather inadequate in China. It is also noticeable that a large portion of former research concentrates on children subjects. Research on the relationship between bilingual morphological awareness and reading for adult learners is rather limited and controversial, due to the different education context and language proficiency. For EFL adult learners in the context of Chinese as native language, the transfer effects of morphological awareness on reading development will still need to be further investigated.

17.1.3 The present study

Bilinguals can acquire their second language during the period of infancy, childhood, or adulthood whether simultaneous with or successive to their L1 acquisition. Adult subjects differ from children subjects in the process of first and second language acquisition as a result of biological readiness that is stimulated by exposure to language. Generally speaking, adults are supposed show superiority in manipulating cognitive skills during the process of L2 learning. Adults have more highly established cognitive skills, which enable them more skillful to employ learning strategies, more capable of understanding some abstract and logically related knowledge points requiring analytical ability, thus much easier to master a second language. Adults can also be differentiated from children in terms of L1 experience. Children could be learning L2 while they are developing their oral proficiency in both L1 and L2. L1 is usually well developed for adults. It is generally believed that the growing experience of L1 may have positive or negative effect on L2 learning (Harley, 1986).

The contribution of morphological awareness to bilingual reading is easily influenced by their L1 knowledge and L2 experience. Adult subjects might be better at applying L1 morphological awareness to L2 reading. Adults are easier to understand the meaning of L2 language. Besides, adults and children are also different in the aspect of lexical exposure. In the early stage of foreign language learning, the majority of the words that children are exposed to are monomorphemic. While morphologically complex words do appear, their number is very small (Nagy & Anderson, 1984). The restricted input in L2 would constrain the development of children's L2 morphological competence. By contrast, adults with a larger vocabulary size, have been exposed to more morphologically complex words, contributing to the acquisition of morphological rules in L2. Therefore, adults are supposed to be more adept at utilizing morphological awareness to assist bilingual reading.

Thus, the major purpose of present study was to investigate the developmental relationship between adult bilinguals' morphological awareness and reading from both intra- and inter-language perspectives. The present research sought to answer three questions: ① how different aspects of morphological awareness (derivational vs. compounding vs. homophone) contributed to intra-language reading; ② what was the direction of cross language contribution of morphological awareness to reading in the second language; ③ whether there was a developmental change in the intra- and cross-language relationship between bilingual morphological awareness and reading (word identification and reading comprehension).

Generally, three hypothesis would be raised: First, due to different composition and structure between Chinese and English morphology, it was expected that different aspects of morphological awareness play different roles in reading in their specific languages. Second, even though Chinese and English morphological systems are similar in some morphological rules such as compounding, Chinese is relatively deeper and more complex in morphological systems than English. And specifically, in the case of Chinese native adult learners of English, the participants were advanced in Chinese. Thus, the transfer between morphological skills was expected to be rather unidirectional from Chinese to English. Third, longitudinally, the relationship between bilingual morphological awareness and reading was expected to change over time due to the dynamic interaction between language proficiency and cognitive skills.

17.2 Method

17.2.1 Participants

139 subjects who were English majors from a university in China participated in the experiment. They were 80 freshmen and 60 sophomores whose ages ranged from 19 to 21 years. All individuals were Chinese native speakers who have learned English as a foreign

language for about 8 years. Testing took place at the end of a semester in May and June.

17.2.2 Measures

The experiment contains individual tests and group tests. The individual test measured students' English and Chinese word reading, and the group test examined students' bilingual morphological awareness and bilingual reading comprehension respectively.

English word reading

Participants' English word reading ability was assessed by using the Woodcock Reading Mastery Test-Revised Subtest (WRMT-R: Woodcock, 1987). This test required participants to identify 106 English words without time limit. The text was discontinued if the child read six consecutive words incorrectly. The raw score was the total number of words read correctly (Conbach alpha = 0.83).

English reading comprehension

For testing English reading comprehension, the Gates MacGinitie Reading Comprehension (Form 4, Level F) were adopted with fourteen passages in total for both the first-year students and the second-year students for answering the question. Each passage had several questions with five -answer multiple choices and there were 48 questions in total with a full score of 48. The students were asked to finish this part within 30 minutes and the total scores they got were regarded as the index of their reading performance (Conbach alpha = 0.87).

English morphological awareness

English morphological awareness was tested by adopting self-designed materials, including English derivational words and compound words production tasks.

For English derivational awareness task, they were presented with a root word and a sentence with a word missing, and were required to produce a derived form of the root word to complete the sentence, with a total score of 31(Conbach alpha = 0.73).

For English compound morphological awareness task, they were asked to create a novel compound after reading a sentence describing something unfamiliar, with a total score of 15 (Conbach alpha = 0.55).

Chinese character reading

Chinese word reading task was self-designed materials, and required participants to read 240 Chinese characters. The preliminary experiment indicated the differentiation degree of this task was appropriate (Conbach alpha = 0.76).

Chinese reading comprehension

The materials for Chinese comprehension were the translated version of the Gates MacGinitie Reading Comprehension (Conbach alpha = 0.72).

Chinese morphological awareness

Chinese morphological awareness was also tested by adopting self-designed materials, including a homographic morpheme identification task and a compound production task.

For Chinese homographic morpheme identification task, the participants were required to choose a word containing the same morpheme in the given target word. The test contained 40 items (Conbach alpha = 0.90).

For Chinese compound vocabulary, they were asked to choose one from the five options that was closest to the target word in meaning. The total score was 80 (Conbach alpha = 0.77).

17.2.3 Procedures

To give a more accurate picture of the changes in language performance over time, the current study utilized a pretest, post-test design. There was a 9-month period between the two testing times. There were two testing administrations: an individual assessment and a group assessment.

All of the individual tests took place in a large conference room in the university. The individual assessment was done on a one-to-one basis, and the subtests, such as English word identification and Chinese character reading were administered. Five postgraduate research assistants were participated as examiners to collect the data. They were all English majors and were highly proficient bilinguals. The individual tests took about 10 minutes.

The group assessment tasks, including the Chinese and English written reading comprehension, English morphological awareness, and Chinese morphological awareness were administered in the classroom by their course teachers. The group tests took approximately 1.5 hours to complete, and thus was administered in two sections.

17.3 Results

To evaluate the development of bilingual morphological awareness and bilingual reading, paired Sample Test was applied to examine the differences on the scores of all the tasks between pre-test and post-test. The following table summarized the means and standard deviations for all the measures in both pretest and posttest.

Significant differences were observed on English word reading $t(138) = 2.25, p < 0.05$, English reading comprehension $t(138) = 3.48, p < 0.05$, English derivational awareness $t(138) = 4.49, p < 0.01$ and Chinese compound awareness $t(138) = 6.82, p < 0.01$. Apparently, scores on English word reading, English reading comprehension, English derivational awareness were significant higher in pre-test than those in post-test. The result indicated that after 9-month English immersion learning, participants achieved a significant progress on their overall English proficiency, except English compound awareness $t(138) = -0.45, p > 0.05$. Comparatively, their Chinese proficiency was relatively stable, except that the scores of Chinese compound awareness were significantly improved.

Table 38 Descriptive statistics and comparison between pre– and post–tests

	Pre-test		Post-test		*t*	*p*
Variables	*M*	*SD*	*M*	*SD*		
EWR	77.92	8.48	82.22	7.91	2.15	0.03*
ERC	22.52	6.67	27.04	8.07	3.48	0.01**
EDM	14.19	4.39	17.82	3.92	4.49	0.00**
ECM	3.83	1.92	3.75	1.92	-0.45	0.65
CCR	223.85	12.97	221.05	13.04	0.66	0.51
CRC	37.29	4.57	37..33	5.56	-1.71	0.09
CHM	35.49	5.64	36.52	3.59	-0.73	0.47
CCV	51.52	5.54	68.06	5.33	6.82	0.00**

Notes: EWR = English word reading; ERC = English reading comprehension; EDM = English derivational awareness; ECM = English compound awareness; CCR = Chinese character reading; CRC = Chinese reading comprehension; CHM = Chinese homographic morpheme identification; CCV = Chinese compound vocabulary. *$p < 0.05$, **$p < 0.01$.

17.3.1 Correlation between morphological awareness and bilingual reading

In order to explore the correlation between morphological awareness and reading in English and Chinese respectively, Pearson correlation analysis was adopted. The following table presented correlations between English morphological awareness and English reading in both tests.

It revealed that in pretest, students' English derivational awareness was strongly associated with English word reading, $r = 0.40$, $p < 0.01$ and with English reading comprehension $r = 0.41$, $p < 0.01$. Nevertheless, English compound awareness only presents significant correlations with English word reading $r = 0.20$, $p < 0.01$, but not with English reading comprehension. By contrast, in posttest, the data shows that derivational awareness was not only significantly correlated with word reading ($r = 0.34$, $p < 0.01$) but also with reading comprehension ($r = 0.41$, $p < 0.01$). And it was worth noting that English compound awareness at this time was observed to be closely associated with both word reading ($r = 0.39$, $p < 0.01$) and with reading comprehension ($r = 0.39$, $p < 0.01$).

Table 39 Correlations between English morphological awareness and reading in pre– and post–tests

	Pretest		Posttest	
	EDM	ECM	EDM	ECM
EWR	0.40**	0.20*	0.34**	0.26**
ERC	0.41**	0.16	0.41**	0.39**

Notes: EWR = English word reading; ERC = English reading comprehension; EDM = English derivational morphology; ECM = English compound morphology. $*p < 0.05$, $**p < 0.01$.

The results above indicate that morphological awareness is significantly related with reading proficiency in English for Chinese EFL adult students. The correlation coefficients of English derivational awareness with the two reading outcomes are much higher than compound awareness in both two test times. With the improvement of English overall proficiency after 9-month English learning, the association between English compound awareness and reading were strengthened.

Table 40 Correlations between Chinese morphological awareness and reading in pre– and post–tests

	Pre-test		Post-test	
	CHM	CCV	CHM	CCV
CCR	0.06	0.17	0.45**	0.54**
CRC	0.25**	0.31**	0.51**	0 50**

Notes: CCR = Chinese character reading; CRC = Chinese reading comprehension; CHM = Chinese homographic morpheme identification; CCV = Chinese compound vocabulary. $*p < 0.05$, $**p < 0.01$.

Correlations between Chinese morphological awareness and Chinese reading in both tests were shown in the above table. The data demonstrated that both Chinese morpheme awareness and Chinese compound vocabulary have strong association with Chinese reading comprehension in pretest, the coefficients being $r = 0.25$, $p < 0.01$ and $r = 0.31$, $p < 0.01$ separately. However, neither of them is correlated with Chinese word reading significantly. Compared with this result, in posttest, the date reveals that both Chinese morpheme awareness and compound awareness were more significantly correlated with Chinese reading comprehension, $r = 0.51$, $p < 0.01$ and $r = 0.51$, $p < 0.01$. Noticeably, significant correlative relation was also observed between the two awareness tasks and Chinese word reading, $r = 0.45$, $p < 0.01$ and $r = 0.54$, $p < 0.01$.

This finding illustrated that in Chinese, strong association exists between morphological awareness and reading performance. In addition, the correlation coefficient in post-test was significantly higher in contrast to that in pre-test after a nine-month English "immersion" learning.

17.3.2 The contribution of bilingual morphological awareness to English reading

The Linear regression analysis was then carried out to investigate the intra-language contribution of morphological awareness to reading, and further explored whether morphological awareness would exert cross-language influence on reading for EFL adult learners. In the linear regression analysis, measures of bilingual morphological awareness were the predicators, and English word and reading comprehension as the dependent, respectively.

Table 41 Regression analysis on English word reading in pre– and post–tests

	Predictor	*B*	*SE*	Beta	*t*	*p*
Pretest	EDM	0.73	0.19	0.37	3.95	0.00**
	ECM	0.81	0.41	0.19	1.96	0.05*
	CHM	0.15	0.19	0.08	0.82	0.41
	CCV	-0.32	0.22	-0.13	-1.43	0.16

Continued

	Predictor	*B*	*SE*	Beta	*t*	*p*
Posttest	EDM	0.81	0.18	0.38	4.40	0.00**
	ECM	1.20	0.38	0.28	3.15	0.00**
	CHM	0.18	0.23	0.08	0.79	0.43
	CCV	-0.45	0.16	-0.28	-2.85	0.01**

Notes: EDM = English derivational morphology; ECM = English compound morphology; CHM = Chinese homographic morpheme identification; CCV = Chinese compound vocabulary.*$p < 0.05$, **$p < 0.01$.

According to the results in the above table, the regression model was significant, $R^2 = 0.23$, $F(4,134) = 7.09$, $p < 0.01$. The data revealed that in pretest, only English derivational awareness and English compound awareness can significantly predict English word reading, with $B = 0.73$, $t = 3.95$, $p < 0.01$ and $B = 0.81$, $t = 1.96$, $p = 0.05$ separately, whereas Chinese morpheme awareness didn't contribute to English word reading. The regression model in corresponding post-test was also significant, $R^2 = 0.25$, $F(4, 134) = 8.90$, $p < 0.01$. In addition that both English derivational awareness ($B = 0.81$, $t = 4.40$, $p < 0.01$) and compound awareness were significant contributors to English word reading ($B = 1.20$, $t = 3.15$, $p < 0.01$), it was worthy to note that Chinese compound awareness was also found to play a significant role in predicting English word reading ($B = -0.45$, $t = -2.85$, $p = 0.01$), which was not observed in n pretest. Obviously, with the improvement of overall English proficiency and Chinese compound awareness after nine-month English "immersion" learning, cross-language transfer effects of Chinese compound awareness on English word reading took place.

As displayed in Table 42, the regression model was significant, $R^2 = 0.14$, $F(4, 134) = 3.91$, $p < 0.01$in pre-test. Apparently, in pretest, only English derivational morphological awareness plays a significant predictive role in English reading comprehension ($B = 0.41$, $t = 2.99$, $p < 0.01$). English compound awareness and Chinese morphological awareness can't explain the performance of students' English reading comprehension. Meanwhile, the regression model was also very significant, $R^2 = 0.32$, $F(4, 134) = 11.84$, $p < 0.01$. The data demonstrated that except Chinese morpheme awareness, English derivational awareness ($B = 0.60$, $t = 3.54$, $p < 0.01$), English compound awareness ($B = 1.29$, $t = 3.71$, $p < 0.01$) and Chinese compound vocabulary

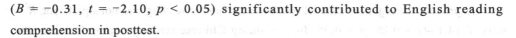

($B = -0.31$, $t = -2.10$, $p < 0.05$) significantly contributed to English reading comprehension in posttest.

Table 42 Regression analysis on English reading comprehension in pre- and post-tests

	Predictors	*B*	*SE*	Beta	*t*	*p*
Pre-test	EDM	0.41	0.14	0.29	2.99	0.00*
	ECM	0.51	0.30	0.17	1.69	0.09
	CHM	−0.03	0.14	−0.02	−0.24	0.81
	CCV	0.08	0.17	0.04	0.47	0.64
Post-test	EDM	0.60	0.17	0.30	3.54	0.00**
	ECM	1.29	0.35	0.32	3.71	0.00**
	CHM	0.29	0.20	0.02	0.15	0.88
	CCV	0.33	0.14	0.25	2.39	0.02**

Notes: EDM = English derivational morphology; ECM = English compound morphology; CHM = Chinese homographic morpheme identification; CCV = Chinese compound vocabulary. $*p < 0.05$, $**p < 0.01$.

17.3.3 The contribution of bilingual morphological awareness to Chinese reading

Similar regression analysis was performed to investigate whether Chinese and English morphological awareness can explain Chinese character reading and reading comprehension.

Table 43 Regression analysis on Chinese reading in post-test

Dependent variables	Predictors	*B*	*SE*	Beta	*t*	*p*
Chinese character reading	EDM	0.52	0.27	0.16	1.92	0.06
	ECM	0.76	0.55	0.12	1.37	0.17
	CHM	0.48	0.34	0.13	1.41	0.16
	CCV	0.96	0.23	0.39	4.13	0.00**
Chinese reading comprehension	EDM	−0.02	0.11	−0.02	−0.21	0.83
	ECM	0.24	0.24	0.09	1.02	0.31
	CHM	0.47	0.14	0.3	3.23	0.00**
	CCV	0.35	0.1	0.33	3.53	0.00**

Notes: EDM = English derivational morphology; ECM = English compound morphology; CHM = Chinese homographic morpheme identification; CCV = Chinese compound vocabulary. $*p < 0.05$, $**p < 0.01$.

In pre-test, the regression model on Chinese character reading was not significant, $R^2 = 0.01$, $F(4,134) = 0.28$, $p > 0.05$. In explaining Chinese reading comprehension, the regression model was not significant in pretest, $R^2 = 0.01$, $F(4, 134) = 0.28$, $p > 0.05$. The results indicate that both English and Chinese morphological awareness did not contribute to Chinese character reading and reading comprehension in the pretest.

In explaining Chinese character reading in posttest (as shown in the above table), however, the model was significant, $R^2 = 0.33$, $F(4,134) = 12.89$, $p < 0.01$. Among the four variables, only Chinese compound was a significant predictor for Chinese character reading, $B = 0.96$, $t = 4.13$, $p < 0.01$. Similarly, in explaining Chinese reading comprehension in posttest, the regression model was significant, $R^2 = 0.33$, $F(4, 134) = 13.09$, $p < 0.01$. It revealed that both Chinese morpheme awareness and Chinese compound vocabulary can predict Chinese reading comprehension, $B = 0.47$, $t = 3.23$, $p < 0.01$ and $B = 0.35$, $t = 3.53$, $p < 0.01$.

17.4 General discussion

The present study investigated the developmental relationship between bilingual morphological awareness and reading for Chinese EFL adult learners. The first research question was devoted to the intra-language contribution of morphological awareness to bilingual reading. The correlation and regression analysis demonstrated clear evidence that English morphological awareness was significantly related to English reading. Specifically, compared with compound awareness, derivational awareness can explain unique variance for English reading comprehension. Chinese morphological awareness (especially Chinese compound vocabulary) predicted unique variance for Chinese reading. The relationship between morphological awareness and reading among Chinese ESL adult learners in present study generally confirms the prediction. The results are also in consistency with relevant studies focusing on monolingual speakers.

It was revealed that the correlation coefficients between morphological awareness and reading in Chinese were relatively higher than those in English. English belongs to alphabetic language system, in which phonological units and morphemes might not be clearly distinguished. The contribution of morphological awareness to reading might be shared with phonological awareness. By contrast, in Chinese, which is considered as a morpho-syllabic language, in most cases one Chinese character corresponds to one morpheme and to one syllable, and the pronunciation and meaning of a regular Chinese character comes from its morphemes. Due to these features, morphological awareness is claimed to be more significant in Chinese reading development.

The second research question addressed to the direction of cross-language transfer. In the present study, Chinese compound vocabulary showed no significant contribution to English word reading and reading comprehension in pretest, whereas in posttest, Chinese compound awareness predicted significant variance to the outcomes of both English reading tasks (ie., word reading and reading comprehension). Our present finding is somewhat similar with Wang et al. (2006). Their research provided evidence for the cross-language transfer of English compound awareness to Chinese reading comprehension among bilingual children. However, it was undeniable that Wang et al.'s (2006) research had several limitations. First, neither Chinese compound awareness nor Chinese character reading were measured when examining the cross-language effect of English compound awareness, which might have inflated the transfer effect observed in the study. Another concern was that English and Chinese compound awareness tasks were not correlated, making the transfer effect difficult to understand (see comments in Pasquarella, Chen, Lam, Luo & Ramirez, 2011). However, the finding in the present study is not consistent with findings on children sample in Pasquarella et al. (2011). That study investigated the aspects and directions of the transfer of morphological awareness between English and Chinese among 137 Chinese-English bilingual children in Canada. The research only observed unidirectional effect from English compound awareness to Chinese reading comprehension.

For one thing, the transfer of compounding is more obvious due to the common characteristics of both Chinese and English. Namely, the aspect of morphological awareness (derivational or compound) that transfers is determined by the morphological structure of English and Chinese. Another point to be noted is that the transfer effect of Chinese homographic morpheme awareness was not observed. Since Chinese morpheme awareness task largely measured participants' homophonic morphemes, which is a Chinese-specific morphological structure, there is slim chance for it to contribute to English reading development. Overall, the above findings indicate that the transfer of morphological awareness is largely influenced by the level of similarity in morphological structure between languages.

For another, the controversial findings between the above studies should be attributed to differences in two factors: age (adults sample vs. children sample) and dominant language (Chinese vs. English). The current study only observed unidirectional contribution of Chinese compound awareness to English reading, but not cross-linguistic contribution of English morphological awareness to Chinese reading. The present results provide evidence for the assumtion on the direction of transfer in that cross-language morphological awareness transfer is influenced by relative proficiency of L1 and L2 (Deacon et al., 2007; Zhang et al., 2010). Transfer is not a two-way free highway, and it may be more likely to occur from the strong to the weak language, than vice versa (Saiegh-Hadded & Geva, 2010). For Chinese adults who started learning English as a foreign language at a later age, it is certain that their L1 proficiency is strongly higher than L2 proficiency, which determined the ultimate transfer direction.

The cause of such transferability was summarized in Saiegh-Hadded and Geva (2010). According to this research, three complex conditions under which transfer between languages would occur. One is concerned the features of the learners, such as their linguistic proficiency and the possibility of some proficiency threshold. The second determining condition is the structure specific features of the linguistic and orthographic structure of the languages involved. The third condition for the occurrence of transfer was contextual or instructional features such as explicit teaching, and amount of exposure. The present results well fit in the above first two conditions.

The third research question focused on the long-term effect on the relationship between bilingual morphological awareness and reading. One interesting finding was that the correlations between two aspects of morphological awareness were larger in the post-test for both Chinese reading and English reading. Another interesting finding was that after nine-month English learning, the intra-language contribution of morphological awareness to reading was significantly increased. Specifically, with the improvement of overall English proficiency and Chinese compound awareness, English compound awareness started to serve as a predictor for for reading comprehension. Moreover, the cross-language contribution of Chinese compound awareness to English word reading and reading comprehension took place only after nine-month English language learning. According to the statistic data, participants' overall Chinese reading were relatively stable, while their English proficiency had improved.

Theoretically, the Linguistic Threshold Hypothesis (Cummins, 1976) claims that the certain proficiency level is necessary for them to have a positive effect on their cognitive development and academic attainment. This assumption shed some light on the study of cross-linguistic transfer of morphological awareness. In this sense, only when L2 language proficiency reaches a certain level (linguistic threshold) can native language reading ability be transferred into second language reading. Before nine-month English "immersion" education, participants' native morphological awareness contributed no significant variance to their L2 reading proficiency. This explains why English morphological awareness is the only predictor for English reading during this stage. After attaining progress on their English overall proficiency through 9-month English learning, participants became more skilled in taking advantage of their knowledge and skills developed in L1 to help improve their L2 reading. Thus, the relationship between their native cognitive reading skills and second language reading proficiency has been strengthened. Thus, it is conceivable that second language proficiency might provide essential condition for such transferability. Nevertheless, the specific conditions under which transferability of morphological awareness can occur are still needed to be further examined.

In summary, through the analysis on the intra- and inter-language contribution of morphological awareness to reading, the results revealed: first, morphological awareness, as one of reading related cognitive skills, was significantly correlated with bilingual reading development; second, the contribution of Chinese compound morphology to L2 reading increased with the improvement of second language proficiency; third, the transfer between bilingual reading and morphological awareness was subjected to both native language proficiency and the similarity between the two languages in the level of morphological complexity.

17.5 Conclusions and implications

Very limited research has so far been conducted in this field on Chinese-English adult bilinguals with morphological awareness as a construct of central interest. The present study testified the development of bilingual morphological awareness and its relationship with reading from a longitudinal perspective. The present results confirmed the intra-language contribution of morphological awareness to reading. In addition, the unidirectional transfer of morphological awareness on reading was observed from Chinese to English but not from English to Chinese. Despite controversy, the present results reveal that the reciprocal relationship in bilingual reading and morphological awareness might be dependent on the language background (c.f. dominant language environment) as well as the literacy level.

The present findings expand our understanding of cross-language transfer of metalinguistic awareness.

The following implications can be obtained from the current research. At a theoretical level, it is hoped that this research would shed some light on the transfer study in the field of second language reading acquisition and the exploration of reading disability in bilinguals. On one hand, the present research discovered that during the process of L2 reading development, L1 morphological knowledge can be triggered automatically when students' overall English proficiency reached a certain threshold, which provides empirical evidence for Linguistic Threshold Hypothesis proposed. On pedagogical aspects, the most important implication is on the field of foreign language teaching. Current EFL teaching methods are inclined to center on the teaching of vocabulary and grammar. The results of this study highlight the importance of bilingual morphological awareness in L2 reading acquisition. If students could realize the similarity in morphological structures between English and Chinese, and learn the skills of triggering the L1 morphological awareness intentionally, the facilitating effects of transfer could be more beneficial. For language teachers, they can assist these learners with recognizing and manipulating new words by promoting their Chinese and English morphological awareness. It is suggested that they should take up teaching bilingual morphological awareness in the classroom as part of explicit language instruction by adopting some instructional strategies that can be adjusted to suit groups of different L2 reading proficiency.

The present study certainly had some limitations to be addressed for future research. First, the current research only explored the relationship between reading development and morphological awareness, without taking other reading related factors such as phonological awareness, orthographic awareness, word memory and oral proficiency into consideration. Second, the measurements of L1 and L2 morphological awareness in the current study were designed in terms of the general features of English and Chinese, so whether other specific aspects of morphological awareness (like conversional or blending) would contribute to transfer facilitation still needs to be investigated. Therefore, it is worthwhile for future researches to expand research scope on other cognitive factors for the sake of providing broader understanding of morphological awareness and reading problems in second language acquisition.

Acknowledgements

This work was supported by a grant from National Social Science Foundation of China (16BYY077). The author would like to express her heartfelt thanks to the five postgraduate students of Beijing International Studies University, namely, ZHANG Jie（张洁）, ZHENG Xiaoyan（郑晓燕）, JIANG Xiaoming（蒋小明）, PEI Xuna（裴旭娜）, and LI Ting（李婷）, for their contribution in data collection for those experiments reported in this book. Without their diligent work, this work is impossible. The author is also grateful for colleagues and participants for their support and participation in those experiments.

References

Abutalebi, J.,Brambati,S.M.,Annoni, J.M,Moro, A.,Cappa, S.F.,Perani, D. (2007).The neural cost of the auditory perception of language switches: an event-related functional magnetic resonance imaging study in bilinguals. *The Journal of Neuroscience*, 27 (50):13762-13769.

Aghaie, R. & Zhang, L. J. (2012). Effects of explicit instruction in cognitive and metacognitive reading strategies on Iranian EFL students' reading performance and strategy transfer. *Instr Sci*, 40, 1063-1081.

Altenberg, E.P. & Cairns, H.S. (1983). The effects of phonotactic constraints on lexical processing in bilingual and monolingual subjects. *Journal of Verbal Learning and Verbal Behavior*, 22, 174-188. doi: 10.1016/S0022-5371(83)90134-2.

Anderson, N. J. (1991). Individual differences in strategy use in second language reading and testing. *The Modern Language Journal*, 75(4), 460-472.

August, D. & Shanahan, T. (2006). *Developing literacy in second-language learners. Report of the National Literacy Panel on language-minority children and youth*. Mahwah, NJ: Lawrence Erlbaum Associates.

Baddeley, A. D. & Hitch, G. (1974). Working memory. *Recent Advances in Learning and Motivation*, 8: 47-89.

Baddley, A.D. (2003). Working Memory and Language: An Overview. *Journal of Communication Disorders*, 36:189-208.

Barnett, M. A. (1988). Reading through context: how real and perceived strategy use affects L2 comprehension. *The Modern Language Journal*, 72, 150-161.

Barsalou, L.W. (1999). Perceptual symbol systems. *Behavioral and Brain Sciences*, 22:577-609; discussion 610-560.

Bear, D. R. & Invernezzi, M. Templeton, S. & Johnston, F. *Words their way: Word study for phonics, vocabulary, and spelling instruction*. Columbus, OH: Merill/Macmillan, 2000.

Belke, E., Brysbaert, M., Meyer, A. S. & Ghyselinck, M. (2005). Age of acquisition effects in picture naming: evidence for a lexical-semantic competition hypothesis. Cognition, 96, B45-B54.

Ben-Dror, I., Pollatsek, A., Scarpati, S. (1991) Word identification in isolation and in context by college dyslexic students. *Brain and Language*, 40: 471-490.

Berko, J. (1958). The child's learning of English morphology. Word, 14, 150-177.

Booth, M. R. & Macwhinney, B. (1990). Development difference in visual and auditory processing of Complex Sentences. *Child Development*, 71: 981-1003.

Boroditsky, L. (2000). Metaphoric structuring: understanding time through spatial metaphors. *Cognition*, 75(1):1-28

Boroditsky, L. (2001). Does language shape thought? English and Mandarin speakers' conceptions of time. *Cognitive Psychology*, 43:1-22

Bradley, R., Danielson, L. & Hallaban, D. (2002). *Identification of learning disabilities: Research to practice*. Mahwah NJ : Erlbaum.

Breznitz, Z., Oren, R. & Shaul, S. Brain activity of regular and dyslexic readers while reading Hebrew as compared to English sentences. *Reading and Writing*, 2005,17(7-8):707-737.

Brysbaert, M., van Dyck, G. & van de Poel, M. (1999) Visual word recognition in bilinguals: evidence from masked phonological priming. *J Exp Psychol Hum Percept Perform*, 25:137-148.

Brysbaert, M., van Wijnendaele, I. & De Deyne, S. (2000). Age-of-acquisition of words is a significant variable in semantic tasks. *Acta Psychologica Sinica*, 104, 215-226.

Cain, K. (2007). Syntactic awareness and reading ability: Is there any evidence for a special relationship? *Applied Psycholinguistics*, 28(4): 679-694.

Carlisle, J. F. & Stone, C. (2003). The effects of morphological structure on children's reading of derived words. In E. Assink& D. Santa (Eds.), *Reading complex words: cross-language studies*. Dordrecht, The Netherlands: Kluwer, 27-52.

Carlisle, J. F. (1995). Morphological awareness and early reading achievement. In L. B. Feldman (Ed.), *Morphological aspects of language processing*. Hillsdale, New Jersey: Erlbaum, 189-209.

Carlisle, J. F. (2000).Awareness of the structure and meaning of morphologically complex words: Impact on reading. *Reading and Writing: An Interdisciplinary Journal*, 12, 169-190.

Carlo, M.S. et al. (2004). Closing the gap: Addressing the vocabulary needs of English-language learners in bilingual and mainstream classrooms. *Reading Research Quarterly*, (39): 188-215.

Carrell, P. L. (1989). Metacognitive awareness and second language reading. *The Modern Language Journal*, 73(2), 121-134.

Carrell, P. L. (1998). Can reading strategies be successfully taught? *TESOL Quarterly*, 59, 107-135.

Carrell, P., Pharis, B. & Liberto, J. (1989). Metacognitive strategy training for ESL reading. *TESOL Quarterly*, 23(4), 647-678.

Carver, R. P. (2000). *The causes of high and low reading achievement*. Mahwah, NJ: Lawrence Erlbaum Associates, 2000.

Casasanto, D. & Boroditsky, L. (2003). Do we think about time in terms of space? In: Alterman R, Kirsh D (eds.) *Proceedings of the 25th Annual Meeting of the Cognitive Science Society*. Lawrence Erlbaum Associates, Inc., Mahwah, NJ, pp 216-221

Casasanto, D. & Boroditsky, L. (2008). Time in the mind: using space to think about time. *Cognition*,106: 579-593.

Chamot, A. U. (2005). Language learning strategy instruction: current issues and research. *Annual Review of Applied Linguistics*, 25, 112-130.

Chan, D., Ho, S. & Tsang, S., et al. (2002). Behavioral characteristics of Chinese dyslexic children, The use of the teachers' behavior checklist in Hong Kong. *Annals of Dyslexia*, 53: 300-323.

Chee, M.W.,Caplan, D.,Soon, C.S.,Sriram, N.,Tan, E.W.,Thiel, T.,& Weekes, B. (1999). Processing of visually presented sentences in Mandarin and English studied with fMRI, *Neuron*, 23(1):127-137.

Chen, B. G., Zhou, H. X., Dunlap, S. & Perfetti, C. A. (2007). Age of acquisition effects in reading Chinese: evidence in favour of the arbitrary mapping hypothesis. *British Journal of Psychology*, 98(3), 499-516. doi: 10.1348/000712606X165484.

Chen, L., et al. (2007). ERP signatures of subject-verb agreement in L2 learning. *Bilingualism: Language and Cognition*, 10:161-174.

Chen, L., Shu, H., Liu, Y., Zhao, J., Li, P. (2007). ERP signatures of subject-verb agreement in L2 learning, *Bilingualism: Language and Cognition*, 10:161-174.

Chen, X., Hao, M., Geva, E., Zhu, J. &Shu, H. (2009).The role of compound awareness in Chinese children's vocabulary acquisition and character reading. *Reading and Writing:*

An Interdisciplinary Journal, 22, 615-631.

Chen, Xiangyang & Dai, Ji. (2007). An experimental study on the effects of metacognition reading strategy training for junior high school students. *Psychological Science*, 30(5), 1099-1103. [胡向阳，戴吉，2007，初中生元认知阅读策略训练效应的实验研究。心理科学，30（5）：1009-1103。]

Chiappe, P., Siegel, L. S. & Wade-Woolley, L. (2002). Linguistic diversity and the development of reading skills: A longitudinal study. *Scientific Study of Reading*, 6(4): 369-400.

Chow, B. W. Y., McBride-Chang, C. & Burgess, S. (2005). Phonological processing skills and early reading abilities in Hong Kong Chinese kindergarteners to read English as a Second language. *Journal of Educational Psychology*, 97(1):81-87.

Chung, K. K. & Ho, C. S. (2010). Second language learning difficulties in Chinese children with dyslexia: what are the reading-related cognitive skills that contribute to English and Chinese word reading? *Journal of Learning Disabilities*, 3(3):195-211.

Corkett, J.K. & Parrila, R. (2008) Use of context in the word recognition process by adults with a significant history of reading difficulties. *Annals of Dyslexia*, 58: 139-161.

Coulson, S., Federmeier, K.D., van Petten, C. & Kutas, M. (2005). Right hemisphere sensitivity to word- and sentence-level context: evidence from event-related brain potentials. *J Exp Psychol Learn Mem Cogn*, 31(1): 129-147. doi: 10.1037/0278-7393.31.1.129.

Crinion, J., Turner, R., Grogan, A. et al., (2006). Language control in the bilingual brain. *Science Magazine*, 312 (5779):1537-1540.

Cui, Y. et al. (1996). The predictive inference in reading comprehension. *Acta Psychologica Sinica*, (3): 238-244.

Cummins, J. (1976). The influence of bilingualism on cognitive growth: A synthesis of research findings and explanatory hypotheses. *Working Papers on Bilingualism*, 9, 1-43.

Daneman, M. & Carpenter, P. (1980). Individual differences in working memory and reading. *Journal of Verbal Learning and Verbal Behavior*, 19:450-466.

Daneman, M. & Merikle, P. M. (1996). Working memory and language comprehension: A meta-analysis. *Psychonomic Bulletin and Review*, 3:422-433.

De Groot, A. M. B., Delmaar, P. & Lupker, S. (2000). The processing of interlexical homographs in translation recognition and lexical decision: Support for non-selective access to bilingual memory. *The Quarterly journal of experimental psychology*, 53(2): 397-428.

Deacon, S. H. & Kirby, J. R. (2004). Morphological awareness: Just “more phonological”? The roles of morphological and phonological awareness in reading development. *Applied Psycholinguistics*, 25: 223-238.

Deacon, S. H., Wade-Woolley, L. & Kirby, J. (2007). Crossover: The role of morphological awareness in French immersion children’s reading. *Developmental Psychology*, 43 (3): 732.

Deacon, S. H., Wade-Woolley, L. & Kirby, J. R. (2009). Flexibility in young second-language learners: Examining the language specificity of orthographic processing. *Journal of Research in Reading*, 32: 215-229.

Dehn, M. J. (2008). *Working Memory and Academic Learning: Assessment and Intervention*. Hoboken, New Jersey: John Wiley & Sons, Inc.,73.

Dijkstra,T. & van Heuven, W.J.B. (2002). The architecture of the bilingual word recognition system: From identification to decision. *Bilingualism: Language and Cognition*, 5: 175-197. doi: 10.1017/S1366728902003012.

Doctor, E.A. & Klein,D. (1992).A model of bilingual word recognition and dyslexia- its use in assessment diagnosis and remediation. *International Journal of Psychology*, 27(3-4): 392.

Dowens, M. G., et al. (2011). Gender and number processing in Chinese learners of Spanish- Evidence from Event Related Potentials. *Neuropsychologia*, 49:1651-1659.

Duffy, S.A., Morris, R.K. & Rayner, K. (1988). Lexical ambiguity and fixation times in reading. *Journal of Memory and Language*, 27: 429-446.

Elston, G.K.E., Gunter, T.C. & Kotz, S.A. (2005). Zooming into L2: global language context and adjustment affect processing of interlingual homographs in sentences. *Cognitive Brain Research*, 25(1):57-70.

Elston-Güttler, K.E. & Friederici, A.D. (2005) .Native and L2 processing of homonyms in sentential context. *Journal of Memory and Language*, 52(2): 256-283. doi: 10.1016/j.jml.2004.11.002.

Everatt. J., et al., (2002). Dyslexia assessment of the bi-scriptal reader. *Topics in Language Disorders*, 22:32-45.

Ewers, C.A., Brownson, S.M. (1999). Kindergartners’ vocabulary acquisition as a function of active vs. passive storybook reading, prior vocabulary, and working memory. *Journal of Reading Psychology*, 20: 11-20.

Faust, M. & Chiarello, C. (1998). Sentence context and lexical ambiguity resolution by the two hemispheres. *Neuropsychologia*, 36(9): 827-835.

Federmeier, K. D. & Kutas, M. (2005). Aging in context: age-related changes in context use during language comprehension. *Psychophysiology*, 42(2), 133-141. doi: 10.1111/j.1469-8986.2005.00274.x.

Flavell, J. H. (1976). Metacognitive aspect of problem solving. In L. B. Resnick (Ed.), *The Nature of Intelligence* (pp. 231-235). New Jersey: Lawrence Erlbaum Assosiates.

Fletcher, J. M., Foorman, B. R., Boudousquie, A., Barnes, M. A., Schatschneider, C. & Francis, D. J. (2002). Assessment of Reading and Learning Disabilities A Research-Based Intervention-Oriented Approach. *Journal of School Psychology* 40(1): 27-63.

Franceschina, F. (2005). *Fossilized second language grammars: The acquisition of grammatical gender*. Amsterdam: Benjamins.

Francis, Norbert. (2008). Modularity in bilingualism as an opportunity for cross-discipline discussion. In J. Cummins & N. Hornberger (Eds.), *Encyclopedia of language and education: Bilingual education, Volume* 5(pp. 105-116). New York: Springer.

Francis, Norbert. (2010). A componential approach for bilingual reading and comparative writing system research: The role of phonology in Chinese writing as a test case. *Language Learning*, 60(4): 683-711.

Frenck-Mestre, C. & Prince, P. (1997). Second language autonomy. *Journal of Memory and Language*, 37(4): 481-501.

Friederici, A.D. (2002). Towards a neural basis of auditory sentence processing. *Trends in Cognitive Sciences*, 6 (2), 78-84. doi:10.1016/S1364-6613(00)01839-8.

Frishkoff, G.A., Perfetti, C.A. & Westbury, C. (2009). ERP measures of partial semantic knowledge: left temporal indices of skill differences and lexical quality. *Biol Psychol*, 80(1): 130-147. doi: 10.1016/j.biopsycho.2008.04.017.

Gallese, V. & Lakoff, G. (2005). The brain's concepts: the role of the sensory-motor system in conceptual knowledge. *Cogn Neuropsychol*, 22:455-479.

Gao, W., Wei, J., Peng, X., Xing, W. and Luo, Y. (2002). Brain dynamic mechanisms on the visual attention scale with Chinese characters cues. *Chin Sci Bull*, 47 (19): 1644-1649.

Garner, R. (1987). *Metacognition and reading comprehension*. NJ: Ablex Publishing.

Georgiewa, P., Rzanny, R., Gaser, C., et al. (2002). Phonological processing in dyslexic children: a study combining functional imaging and event related potentials. *Neuroscience Letters*, 318(1): 5-8.

Geva, E. (1998). *Learning to read in a second language (L2) — Does L2 oral proficiency matter?* Paper presented at the annual meeting of the Society for the Scientific Studies of Reading, San Diego, CA.

Glucksberg, S., Kreuz, F.J. & Rho, S.H. (1986). Context can constrain lexical access: Implications for models of language comprehension. *Journal of Experimental Psychology: Learning, Memory, and Cognition*, 12: 323-335.

Goerss, B., Beck, I. & McKeown, M. (1999) Increasing remedial students' ability to derive word meaning from context. *Reading Psychology*, 20: 151-175.

Golestani, N., Alario, F., Meriaux, S. Le Bihan, D., Dehaene, S.& Pallie, C. (2006). Syntax production in bilinguals. *Neuropsychologia*,44:1029-1040.

Goswami, U., et al. (2005). The effects of spelling consistency on phonological awareness, a comparison of English and German. *Journal of Experimental Child Psychology*, 92: 345-365.

Goswami, U. (2002). Phonology, reading development, and dyslexia. A cross-linguistic perspective. *Annals of Dyslexia*, 2: 141-163.

Goswami, Usha. (2003). Why theories about developmental dyslexia require developmental designs. *TRENDS in Cognitive Sciences*, 7(12): v534-541.

Gourgey, A. F. (1999). Teaching reading from a metacognitive perspective: theory and classroom experience. *Journal of College Reading and Learning*, 30(1), 85-93.

Graves, M.F. (2006). *The vocabulary book: Learning and instruction*. New York: Teachers College Press.

Greenfell, M. & Macaro, E. (2007). Claims and critiques. In A. D. Cohen & E. Macaro (eds.), *Language learner strategies: Thirty years of research and practice* (pp. 9-28). Oxford: Oxford University Press.

Greenhouse, S. W. & Geisser, S. (1959). On methods in the analysis of profile data. *Psychometrika*, 24: 95-112.

Grindrod CM, Baum SR. (2003). Sensitivity to local sentence context information in lexical ambiguity resolution: Evidence from left- and right-hemisphere-damaged individuals. *Brain and Language*, 85: 503-523.

Guo, J. et al. (2009). ERP evidence for different strategies employed by native speakers and L2 learners in sentence processing. *Journal of Neurolinguistics*, 22:123-134.

Guo, T., Misra, M., Tam, J.W. & Kroll, J.F. (2012). On the time course of accessing meaning in a second language: An electrophysiological and behavioral investigation of translation recognition. *Journal of Experimental Psychology: Learning, Memory, and Cognition,* 38(5), 1165-1186. doi: 10.1037/a0028076.

Hagoort, P. (2008). The fractionation of spoken language understanding by measuring electrical and magnetic brain signals. *Philosophical Transactions of Royal Society* B, 363 (1493), 1055-1069. doi:10.1098/rstb.2007.2159.

Hahne, A. & Friederici, A. D. (2001). Processing a second language: Late learners' comprehension mechanisms as revealed by event-related brain potentials. *Bilingualism: Language and Cognition*, 4:123-141.

Hahne, A. (2001). What's Different in Second-Language Processing? Evidence from Event-Related Brain Potentials. *Journal of Psycholinguistic Research*, 30: 251-266.

Hahne, A., Friederici, A.D. (2002). Differential task effects on semantic and syntactic processes as revealed by ERPs. *Cognitive Brain Research*,13: 339-356.

Hargrove, L. & Poteet, J.A. (1984). *Assessment in special education*. Englewood Cliffs, New Jersey: Prentice-Hall, Inc.

Harley B. (1986). *Age in second language acquisition*. Clevedon: Multilingual Matters.

Haspelmath, M. (1997). *From space to time: temporal adverbials in the world languages*. Newcastle, UK: Lincom Europa.

Hernandez, A. E. & Li, P. (2007). Age of acquisition: its neuronal and computational mechanisms. *Psychological Bulletin*, 133(4), 638-650. doi: 10.1037/0033-2909.133.4.638

Hernandez, A. E., Hofmann, J. & Kotz, S. A. (2007). Age of acquisition modulates neuronal activity for both regular and irregular syntactic functions. *Neuroimage*, 36(3), 912-923.

Ho, C. S., et al., (2004). Cognitive profiling and preliminary subtyping in Chinese developmental dyslexia. *Cognition*, 2004, 91: 43-75.

Ho, C. S. & Fong, K. M. (2005). Do Chinese dyslexic children have difficulties learning English as a second language? *Journal of Psycholinguistic Research*, 34 (6): 603- 618.

Ho, C. S. & Lai, D. N. (1999). Naming-speed deficits and phonological memory deficits in Chinese developmental dyslexia. *Learning and Individual Differences*, 11:173-186.

Ho, C. S. et al., (2002). The cognitive profile and multiple-deficit hypothesis in Chinese developmental dyslexia. *Developmental Psychology*, 38(4): 543-553.

Ho, C. S., Chan, D. W., Tsang, S. & Lee, S. (2002). The cognitive profile and multiple-deficit hypothesis in Chinese developmental dyslexia. *Developmental Psychology* 38(4): 543-553.

Ho, C. S., et al., (2004). Cognitive profiling and preliminary subtyping in Chinese developmental dyslexia. *Cognition*, 91: 43-75.

Holm,A. & Dodd, B. (1996). The effect of first written language on the acquisition of English literacy. *Cognition*, 59(2):119-147.

Hopper, P.J. & Traugott, E.C. (2003). *Grammaticalization* (2nd ed.). Cambridge: Cambridge University Press

Hu, J., Zhang, W., Zhao, C., Ma, W., Lai, Y. & Yao, D. (2005). Non-native Homonym Processing: an ERP Measurement. *International Journal of Bioelectromagnetism*, 13(4): 207-211.

Hu, Yang. & Zhang, Weimin. (2006). A survey of non-English majors' use of metacognitive strategies at the tertiary level. Foreign Language Education, 27(3), 59-62. [胡阳，张为民，2006，大学英语学习者使用元认知策略的能力。外语教学，27（3）：59-62。]

Hu,C.H. & Catts, H.W.(1993). Phonological recoding as a universal process? *Reading and Writing*, 5(3): 325-337.

Jared, D., Cormier, P., Levy, B. A. & Wade-Woolley, L. (2011). Early predictors of biliteracy development in children in French Immersion: A four-year longitudinal study. *Journal of Educational Psychology*, 103(1): 119-139.

Javadi, M., Keyvanara, M., Yaghoobbi, M., Hassanzade, A. & Ebadi, Z. (2010). The relationship between metacognitive awareness of reading strategies and students' academic status in Isfahan University of Medical Sciences. *Iranian Medical Science Journal*, 3(10): 246-254.

Jing, Shijie. (2003). The relationship between middle school students' reading comprehension and working memory. *Journal of Ningbo University*, (4): 26-29.

Just, M. A. & Carpenter, P. A. (1992). A capacity theory of comprehension: individual differences in working memory. *Psychological Review*, 99:122-149.

Just, M. A., Carpenter, P. A. & Keller, T. (1996). Working memory: new frontiers of evidence. *Psychological Review*, 103: 773-775.

Kaan, E., Harris, A., Gibson, E. & Holcomb, P. (2000). The P600 as an index of syntactic integration difficulty. *Language and Cognitive Processes*,15(2): 159-201.

Kemmerer, D. (2005). The spatial and temporal meanings of English prepositions can be independently impaired. *Neuropsychologia*, 43:797-806.

Kiefer, M., Sim, E.J., Herrnberger, B., Grothe, J. & Hoenig, K. (2008). The sound of concepts: four markers for a link between auditory and conceptual brain systems. *J Neurosci*, 28:12224-12230.

Kieffer, M. J. & Lesaux, N. K. (2008). The role of derivational morphological awareness in the reading comprehension of Spanish-speaking English language learners. *Reading and Writing: An Interdisciplinary Journal*, 21, 783-804.

Kieffer, M.J. & Lesaux, N.K. (2007). Breaking Down Words to Build Meaning: Morphology, Vocabulary, and Reading Comprehension in the Urban Classroom. *The Reading Teacher*, (2):134-144.

Kim, K.H.,Relkin, N.R.,Lee, K.M.,&Hirsch,J. (1997). Distinct cortical areas associated with native and second languages. *Nature*,388(6638): 171-174.

Kim, K.K. ,Byun, E., Lee, S.K., Gaillard, W.D., Xu, B. Theodore ,W.H. (2011). Verbal working memory of Korean-English bilinguals: An fMRI study. *Journal of Neurolinguistics*, 24, 1-13.

King, J. & Just, M. A. (1991). Individual differences in syntactic processing: the role of working memory. *Journal of Memory and Language*, 30:580-602.

Kintch, W. & Dijk, T. A. (1978). Toward a model of text comprehension and production. *Psychological Review*, 85: 363- 394.

Klein, D., Moka, K., Chen, J.-K. & Watkins, K. E. (2014). Age of language learning shapes brain structure: A cortical thickness study of bilingual and monolingual individuals. *Brain & Language*, 131, 20-24. doi: 10.1016/j.bandl.2013.05.014.

Klein, D., Milner, B., Zatorre, R. J., Meyer, E.,& Evans, A.C.(1995).The neural substrates underlying word generation: a bilingual functional-imaging study. Proc Natl Acad Sci U S A,92 (7): 2899-2903.

Knell, E., Qiang, H., Miao, P., Chi, Y., Siegel, L.S., Zhao, L. & Zhao, W. (2007). Early English immersion and literacy in Xi'an, China. *Modern Language Journal*, 91:395-417.

Knell, E.S. (2010). *A longitudinal study of early English immersion and literacy in Xi'an*, China. Doctoral Dissertation, the University of Utah.

Koda, K. & Reddy, P. (2008). Cross-linguistic transfer in second language reading. *Language Teaching*, 41(04) , 497-508.

Koda, K. (2004). *Insights into second language reading: A cross-linguistic approach*. NY: Cambridge University Press.

Koda, K. (2007). Reading and language learning: Crosslinguistic constraints on second language reading development. *Language Learning*, 57, 1-44.

Kong, L., Zhang, B., Zhang, J.X. and Kang, C. (2012). P200 can be modulated by orthography alone in reading Chinese words. *Neuroscience Letters*, 529(2):161-165.

Kotz, S. A. (2009). A critical review of ERP and fMRI evidence on L2 syntactic processing. *Brain and Language*, 109: 68-74.

Kroll, J. F. & Stewart, E. (1994). Category interference in translation and picture naming: Evidence for asymmetric connections between bilingual memory representations. *Journal of Memory and Language*, 33, 149-174.

Kroll, J. F., Bogulski, C. A., McClain, R. (2012). Psycholinguistic perspectives on second language learning and bilingualism: The course and consequence of cross-language competition. *Linguistic Approaches to Bilingualism*, 2 (1):1-24.

Kroll, J. F., van Hell, J.G., Tokowicz, N. & Green, D.W. (2010). The Revised Hierarchical Model: A critical review and assessment. *Biling (Camb Engl)*, 13(3): 373-381. doi: 10.1017/S136672891000009X.

Kroll, J.F.,Tokowicz, N. & Dufour, R. (2002). The development of lexical fluency in a second language. *Second Language Research*, 18(2):137.

Ku, Y. & Anderson, R. C. (2003). Development of morphological awareness in Chinese and English. *Reading and Writing: An Interdisciplinary Journal*,16: 399-422.

Ku, Y. M. & Anderson, R. C. (2001). Chinese Children's Incidental Learning of Word Meanings. *Contemp Educ Psychol*, 26(2): 249-266. doi: 10.1006/ceps.2000.1060.

Kuhn MR, Stahl S (1998) Teaching children to learn word meanings from context: A synthesis and some questions. *Journal of Literacy Research* 30: 119-138.

Kuo, L. & Anderson, R. C. (2006). Morphological awareness and learning to read: Across-language perspective. *Educational Psychologist*, 41 (3): 161-180.

Kutas M, Federmeier K (2000) Electrophysiology reveals semantic memory use in language comprehension. *Trends in Cognitive Sciences*, 4 (12): 463-470.

Kutas M, Hillyard SA (1980) Reading senseless sentences: brain potentials reflect semantic incongruity. *Science*, 207: 203-205.

Kutas, M. & Federmeier, K. (2000). Electrophysiology reveals semantic memory use in language comprehension. *Trends in Cognitive Sciences*, 4 (12): 463-470.

Kutas, M. & Hillyard, S.A. (1980) Reading senseless sentences: brain potentials reflect semantic incongruity. *Science*, 207: 203-205

Kutas, M. & Hillyard, S. A. (1984). Brain potentials during reading reflect word expectancy and semantic association. *Nature*: 307, 161-163.

Lakoff, G. & Johnson, M. (1999). *Philosophy in the flesh*. Chicago: University of Chicago Press.

Leij, A. & E. Morfidi. 2006.Core deficits and variable differences in dutch poor readers learning English. *Journal of Learning Disabilities*, 39(1): 74-91.

Lemhofer, K. & Dijkstra, T. (2004) Recognizing cognates and interlingual homographs: effects of code similarity in language specific and generalized lexical decision. *Mem Cogn*, 32, 533-550.

Li, Hong. (2003). Effects of vocabulary knowledge in second language semantic extraction. *Modern Foreign Language*, (4): 385-393.

Li, Jun & Ni, Hangying. (2007). An interventional research on metacognitive strategies of non-English majors. *Foreign Language World*, (2), 49-53.[李俊，倪杭英，2007，非英语专业学生元认知策略的介入性研究。外语界，（2）：49-53。]

Li, P., et al. (2004). Neural representations of nouns and verbs in Chinese: An fMRI study. *NeuroImage*, 21:1533-1541.

Li, Y. & Kang, J. S. (Eds.). (1993). *Analysis of phonetics of the ideophonetic characters in Modern Chinese*. Shanghai: Shanghai Education Publisher (in Chinese).

Limbos, M. M. & Geva, E. (2001). Accuracy of teacher assessments of second-language students at risk for reading disability. *Journal of Learning Disabilities*, 34: 136-151.

Liu, Huijun. (2004). The relationship between metacognitive strategies and English reading. *Foreign Languages and Their Teaching*, (12), 24-26. [刘慧君，2004，元认知策略与英语阅读的关系 [J]。外语与外语教学，（12）：24-26。]

Liu, Y., Perfetti, C.A. & Hart, L. (2003). ERP evidence for the time course of graphic, phonological, and semantic information in Chinese meaning and pronunciation decisions. Journal of Experimental Psychology. *Learning, Memory, and Cognition,* 29(6):1231-1247

Liu, Y., Perfetti, C.A. & Hart, L. (2003). ERP evidence for the time course of graphic, phonological, and semantic information in Chinese meaning and pronunciation decisions. *Journal of Experimental Psychology: Learning, Memory and Cognition*, 29(6), 1231-1247.

Liu, Y.C. & Perfetti, A. (2003). The time course of brain activity in reading English and Chinese: An ERP study of Chinese bilinguals. *Human Brain Mapping*, 18:167-175.

Liu, Ying. (2009). A study of effectiveness on EFL reading metacognitive strategy training.

Foreign Languages and Their Teaching, (10), 38-41. [刘莺，2009，大学英语阅读低分者元认知策略培训的有效性研究。外语与外语教学，（10）：38-41。]

Lorusso, M.L., Facoetti, A., Pesenti, S., et al. (2004) Wider recognition in peripheral vision common to different subtypes of dyslexia. *Vision Research*, 44: 2431-2424.

Lossifova, R. & Marmolejo-Ramos, F. (2012). Spatial and temporal deixis. The role of age and vision in the ontogeny of a child's spatial and temporal cognition. *Journal of Speech and Language Pathology*, 2(2): 75-98.

Luck, S.J., Vogel, E.K. & Shapiro, K.L. (1996). Word meanings can be accessed but not reported during the attentional blink. *Nature*, 383, 616-618.

Lundberg, I. (2002). The child's route into reading and what can go wrong. *Dyslexia*, 8: 1-13.

Lyon , G. R. (1995). Toward a definition of dyslexia. *Annals of dyslexia*, 45:3 - 27.

Lyon, G. R., Shaywitz, S. E. & Shaywitz, B. A. (2003). Defining dyslexia, comorbidity, teachers's knowledge of language and reading: A definition of dyslexia. *Annals of Dyslexia*, 3(1): 1-14.

Lyon G R. Toward a definition of dyslexia. *Annals of Dyslexia*, 1995,45:3-27.

Lyon, G. R., Shaywitz, S. E. & Shaywitz, B. A. (2003). Defining dyslexia, comorbidity, teachers's knowledge of language and reading: A definition of dyslexia. *Annals of Dyslexia*, 3(1): 1-14.

Lyytinen, H., et al. (2006). Trajectories of Reading Development: A Follow-up From Birth to School Age of Children with and without Risk for Dyslexia. *Merrill-Palmer Quarterly*, 52(3): 514-547

Manis, F. R., Seidenberg, M.S., Doi, L. M., McBride-Chang, C. & Petersen, A. (1996). On the bases of two subtypes of development dyslexia. *Cognition*, 58,157-195.

Mann, V. A. &Wimmer, H. (2002). Phoneme awareness and pathways into literacy: a comparison of German and American children. *Reading and Writing*, 15, 653-682.

Marian, V. & Spivey, M. 2003. Competing activation in bilingual language processing: Within- and between-language competition. *Bilingualism: Language and Cognition*, 6 (2): 97-115.

Marian, V., Spivey, M. & Hirsch, J. (2003). Shared and separate systems in bilingual language processing: converging evidence from eye tracking and brain imaging. *Brain and Language*, 86, 70-82.

Mayberry, R. I., Chen, J.-K., Witcher, P. & Klein, D. (2011). Age of acquisition effects on the functional organization of language in the adult brain. *Brain & Language*, 119, 16-29. doi: 10.1016/j.bandl.2011.05.007.

McBride-Chang, C., Cheung, B.W. -Y. Chow, C.S.-L. Chow.& Choi, L. (2006). Metalinguistic skills and vocabulary knowledge in Chinese (L1) and English (L2). *Reading and Writing*, 19, 695-716.

McBride-Chang, C., Cho, J. R., Liu, H. Y., Wagner, R. K., Shu, H.& Zhou, A. (2005). Changing models across cultures: Associations of phonological awareness and morphological structure awareness with vocabulary and word recognition in Second Graders from Beijing, Hong Kong, Korea, and the United States. *Journal of Experimental Child Psychology*, 92, 140-160.

McClelland, J.L. (1987). The case for interactionism in language processing. In M. Coltheart (ed), Attention to Performance XII: *The Psychology of Reading* (pp 3-36). Mahwah, NJ, Lawrence Erlbaum.

Mclaughlin, J. D., et al. (2010). Brain potentials reveal discrete stages of L2 grammatical learning. *Language Learning*, 60: 123-150.

McLaughlin, J., Osterhout, L. & Kim, A. (2004). Neural correlates of second-language word learning: minimal instruction produces rapid change. *Nature Neuroscience*, 7(7): 703-704.

Meyler, A., Keller, T.A., Cherkassky, V.L., Lee, Donghoon, Hoeft, Fumiko, Whitfield-Gabrieli, S., Gabrieli, D.D.E & Just, M.A. (2007). Brain activation during sentence comprehension among good and poor readers. *Cerebral Cortex*, 17: 2780-2787. Doi:10.1093/cercor/bhm006.

Miller-Guron, L. & Lundberg, L. (2000). Dyslexia and second language reading: a second bite at the apple. *Reading and Writing*, (12): 41-61.

Mokhtari, K. & Reichard, C. (2002). Assessing students' metacognitive strategy awareness of reading strategies. *Journal of Educational Psychology*, 94: 249-259.

Montrul, S. (2005). Second language acquisition and first language loss in adult early bilinguals: exploring some differences and similarities. *Second Language Research*, 21(3): 199-249. doi:10.1191/0267658305sr247oa.

Montrul, S. (2005). Second language acquisition and first language loss in adult early bilinguals: exploring some differences and similarities. *Second Language Research*, 21(3): 199-249. doi:10.1191/0267658305sr247oa.

Moreno, E.M., Rodriguez-Fornells, A. & Laine, M. (2008). Event-related potentials (ERPs) in the study of bilingual language processing. *Journal of Neurolinguistics*,

21(6): 477-508.

Mueller, J. L. (2005). Electrophysiological correlates of second language processing. *Second Language Research*, 21(2):152-174.

Mueller, J.L., Hahne, A., Fujii, Y. & Friederici, A.D. (2005). Native and Nonnative Speakers' Processing of a Miniature Version of Japanese as Revealed by ERPs. *Journal of Cognitive Neuroscience*, 17(8):1229-1244.

Naglieri, J.A. (1985). *Matrix Analogies Test - Expanded Form*. San Antonio, TX: The Psychological Corporation.

Nagy, W.E. & Anderson, R.C. (1984). How many words in printed school English? *Reading Research*, 19: 304-330.

Nagy, W.E., Berninger, V.W. & R.D. Abbott. (2006). Contributions of morphology beyond phonology to literacy outcomes of upper elementary and middle-school students. *Journal of Educational Psychology*, (98):134-147.

Nagy, W. E., Berninger, V., Abbott, R., Vaughan, K. &Vermeulen, K. (2003). Relationship of morphology and other language skills to literacy skills in at-risk Second-Grade readers and at-risk Fourth-Grade writers. *Journal of Educational Psychology*, 4: 730-742.

Nam, K., Shin, Y., Lee, Y., Hwang, Y., Lee, J. & Skrypiczajko, G. (1999). Orthographic and phonological processing in foreign language word recognition. *Korean Journal of Experimental and Cognitive Psychology*, 11, 107-130.

Neill WT, Hilliard DV, Cooper EA (1988). The detection of lexical ambiguity: Evidence for context-sensitive parallel access. *Journal of Memory and Language*, 27(3): 279-287.

Niu, Y.N., Wei, J.H. & Luo, Y.J. (2008). Early ERP effects on the scaling of spatial attention in visual search. *Prog Nat Sci*, 18:381-386.

Nosarti, C.,Mechelli, A.,Green, D.W. & Price, C.J. (2010). The impact of second language learning on semantic and nonsemantic first language reading. *Cerebral Cortex*, 20(2):315-327.

O'Donnell, B.F., Swearer, J.M., Smith, L.T., Hokama, H. & McCarley, R.W. (1997). A topographic study of ERPs elicited by visual feature discrimination. *Brain Topogr*, 10:133-143.

O'Malley, J. M., Chamot, A. U., Stewner Manzanares, G., Hupper, L. & Russo, R. (1985). Learning strategies used by beginning and intermediate ESL students. *Language learning*, 35, 24-46.

Onton, J. & Makeig, S. (2006). Information-based modeling of event related brain dynamics. *Progress in Brain Research*, 159, 99-120. doi:10.1016/S0079-6123(06)59007-7.

Oren, R. & Brenznitz, Z. (2005). Reading processes in L1 and L2 among dyslexic as compared to regular bilingual readers: behavioral and electrophysiological evidence. *Journal of Neurolinguistics*, 18: 127-151.

Osterhout, L. & Holcomb, P.J. (1992). Event-related brain potentials elicited by syntactic anomaly. *J Mem Lang*, 31:785-806.

Osterhout, L. & Mobley, L. (1995). Event-related brain potentials elicited by failure to agree. *Journal of Memory and Language*, 34:739-773.

Osterhout, L. & Nicol, J. (1999). On the distinctiveness, independence, and time course of the brain responses to syntactic and semantic anomalies. *Language and Cognitive Processes*, 14:283-317.

Palinscar, A.S. & Brown, A. L. (1989). Instruction for self-regulated reading. In L. B. Resnich & L. E. Klopfer (eds.), *Toward the Thinking Curriculum: Current Cognitive Research*. Alexandaria, VA: Association for Supervision and Curriculum Develop Yearbook.

Pan, Liping. (2006), An experimental study of the teachability of ESL reading metacognitive strategy in ESL reading Class. *Foreign Language Education*, 27 (1): 49-54. [潘黎萍，2006，元认知策略在二语课堂阅读中的可教性实验研究。外语教学，27（1）：49-54。]

Paradis, J., Genesee, F. & Crago, M. (2010). *Dual Language Development and Disorders: A Handbook on Bilingualism and Second Language Learning* (2nd ed.). Baltimore: Paul H. Brookes.

Pasquarella, A., Chen, X., Lam, K., Luo, Y. C. & Ramirez, G. (2011). Cross-language transfer of morphological awareness in Chinese-English bilinguals. *Journal of Research in Reading*,34: 23-42.

Pattamadilok, C., Perre, L., Dufau, S. & Ziegler, J.C. (2009). On-line orthographic influences on spoken language in a semantic task. *Journal of Cognitive Neuroscience*, 21: 169-179. doi:10.1162/jocn.2009.21014.

Perani, D. &Abutalebi, J. (2005). The neural basis of first and second language processing. *Current Opinion in Neurobiology*,15(2)：202-206.

Perfetti C, Yang CL, Schmalhofer F. (2008). Comprehension skill and word-to-text integration processes. *Applied Cognitive Psychology*, 22(3): 303-318.

Perfetti, C. A. (1985). *Reading ability*. New York: Oxford University Press.

Perfetti, C. A., et al. (2007). Reading in two writing systems: Accommodation and assimilation of the brain's reading network. *Bilingualism: Language and Cognition*, 10:131-146.

Perre, L. & Ziegler, J.C. (2008). On-line activation of orthography in spoken word recognition. *Brain Research*, 1188: 132-138. doi:10.1016/j.brainres.2007.10.084.

Plag, I. (2003). *Word-formation in English*. Cambridge: Cambridge University Press.

Presseldy, M. & Afflerbach, P. (1995). *Verbal Protocols of Reading*. New Jersey: Lawrence Erlbaum.

Pulvermuller, F., Hauk, O., Nikulin, V.V. & Ilmoniemi, R.J. (2005) .Functional links between motor and language systems. *Eur J Neurosci*, 21:793-797.

Quirk, R., Greenbaum, S., Leech, G. & Svartvik, J. (1972). *A grammar of contemporary English*. Frome and London: Longman Group Ltd.

Radford, A. (1988). *Transformational Grammar*. Cambridge: Cambridge University Press.

Ramirez, G., Chen, X., Geva, E. & Kiefer, H. (2010). Morphological awareness in Spanish-Speaking English language learners: Within and cross-Language effects on word reading. *Reading and Writing*, 23: 337-358.

Rayner, K. & Frazier, L. (1989). Selection mechanisms in reading lexically ambiguous words. *Journal of Experimental Psychology: Learning, Memory, and Cognition*, 15(5): 779.

Robinchon, F., Besson, M. & Habib, M. (2002). An electrophysiology study of dyslexic and control adults in a sentence reading task. *Biological Psychology*, 59: 22-53.

Rossi, S., et al. (2006). The impact of proficiency on syntactic second-language processing of German and Italian: Evidence from event-related potentials. *Journal of Cognitive Neuroscience*, 18: 2030-2048.

Rugg, M.D. (1984) Event-related potentials in phonological matching tasks. *Brain Lang*, 23: 225-240.

Rugg, M.D. (1984). Event-related potentials in phonological matching tasks. *Brain Lang*, 23:225-240.

Russo, F.D., Aprile, T., Spitoni, G. & Spinelli, D. (2008). Impaired visual processing of contralesional stimuli in neglect patients: a visual-evoked potential study. *Brain*, 131 (3): 842-854.

Sabourin, L. (2003). *Grammatical gender and second language processing: an ERP study*,

Unpublished doctoral dissertation, University of Groningen.

Saiegh-Haddad, E. &Geva, E. (2008). Morphological awareness, phonological awareness, and reading in English-Arabic bilingual children. *Reading and Writing*, 21: 481-504.

Saiegh-Hadded, E. & Geva, E. (2010). Acquiring reading in two languages: an introduction to the special issue. *Read Writ*, 23: 263-267.

Sakai, Kuniyoshi L. (2005). Language Acquisition and Brain Development. *Science* 310(4): 815-819.

Sawyer, D. J., Wade, J. & Kim, J. (1999). Spelling errors as a Window on variations in phonological deficits among students with dyslexia. *Annals of Dyslexia*, 49:137-160.

Scarborough, D. L., Gerard, L. & Cortese, C. (1984). Independence of lexical access in bilingual word recognition. *Journal of Verbal Learning and Verbal Behavior*, 23 (1): 84-99.

Schiff, R. & Calif, S. (2007). Role of phonological and morphological awareness in L2 oral word reading. *Language Learning*, 2: 271-298.

Schiff-Myers, N. B. (1992). Considering arrested language development and language loss in the assessment of second language learners. *Language, Speech and Hearing Services in Schools*, 23: 28-33.

Schmidt R. (1992). Psychological mechanisms underlying second language fluency. *SSLA*, (14):357-357.

Schwartz, A.I. & Kroll, J.F. (2006). Bilingual lexical activation in sentence context. *Journal of Memory and Language*, 55, 197-212. doi:10.1016/j.jml.2006.03.004.

Seidenberg, M.S., Tanenhaus, M.K., Leiman, J.M. & Bienkowski, M. (1982). Automatic access of the meanings of ambiguous words in context: Some limitations of knowledge-based processing. *Cognitive psychology*, 14(4): 489-537.

Seigneuric, E., Ehrlich, M. F. & Oakhill, J. V. & Yuill, N. M. (2000). Working Memory resources and children's reading comprehension. *Reading and Writing: An Interdisciplinary Journal*, 13:81-103.

Shaywitz, S.E. & Shaywitz, B.A. (2005). Dyslexia (specific reading disability). *Biol Psychiatry*, 57: 1301-1309.

Sholl. A., Sankaranarayanan, A. & Kroll, J.F. (1995). Transfer between picture naming and translation: A test of asymmetries in bilingual memory. *Psychological Science*, 6 (1): 45.

Shu H. et al. (2006). Understanding Chinese Developmental Dyslexia, Morphological Awareness as a Core Cognitive Construct. *Journal of Educational Psychology*, 98(1):122-133.

Shu, H., McBride-Chang, C., Wu S. & Liu, H. (2006). Understanding Chinese Developmental Dyslexia, Morphological Awareness as a Core Cognitive Construct. *Journal of Educational Psychology*, 98(1):122-133.

Shu, H., et al. (2006). Understanding Chinese Developmental Dyslexia, Morphological Awareness as a Core Cognitive Construct. *Journal of Educational Psychology*, 98(1):122-133.

Shu, H., McBride-Chang, C., Wu, S. & Liu, H. (2006). Understanding Chinese developmental dyslexia: Morphological awareness as a core cognitive construct. *Journal of Educational Psychology*, 98, 122-133.

Simos, P.G., Breier, J.I., Fletcher, J.M., Bergman, E. & Papanicolaou, A.C. (2000). Cerebral mechanisms involved in word reading in dyslexic children: a magnetic source imaging approach. *Cereb Cortex*, 10:809-816.

Simpson, G. B. (1994). Context and the processing of ambiguous words. In M. A. Gernsbacher (Ed.), *The Psycholinguistic Handbook* (pp. 359-374). New York:Academic Press.

Siok, W. T., et al., (2004) Biological abnormality of impaired reading is constrained by culture. *Nature*, 431:71-76.

Siok, W.T. & Fletcher, P. (2001).The role of phonological awareness and visual-orthographic skills in Chinese reading acquisition. *Developmental Psychology*, 37(6): 886-899.

Snowling, M. J., et al. (1997). A connectionist perspective on the development of reading skills in children. *Connectionism and Reading Skills*, 1(3): 88-90.

Song, Y., Peng, D.L., Li, X.L., Zhang, Y., Kang, J., Qu, Z. & Ding, Y. (2007) Neural correlates of short-term perceptual learning in orientation discrimination indexed by event-related potentials. *Chin Sci Bull*, 52:352-357.

Spalek, K., Hoshino, N., Wu, Y.J., Damian, M. & Thierry, G. (2014). Speaking two languages at once: Unconscious native word form access in second language production. *Cognition*, 133 (1), 226-231.

Spironelli, C. & Angrilli, A. (2009). Developmental aspects of automatic word processing: language lateralization of early ERP components in children, young adults and middle-aged subjects. *Biol Psychol*, 80(1), 35-45. doi: 10.1016/j.biopsycho.2008.01.012.

Stanovich, K. E. & West, R. F. (1983). On priming by a sentence context. *Journal of Experimental Psychology: General*, 112: 1-36.

Stevenson H W, et al. Reading disabilities: the case of Chinese, Japanese and English. *Child Development*, 1982, 53:1164-1181.

Steyvers, M. & Tenenbaum, J. B. (2005). The language scale structure of semantic networks: statistical analyses and a model of semantic growth. *Cognitive Science Society*, 29, 41-78.

Su, I-R. (2001). Transfer of sentence processing strategies: A comparison of L2 learners of Chinese and English. *Applied Psycholinguistics*, 22:83-112.

Sun, H. L., Sun, D. J., Huang, J. P., Li, D. J. & Xing, H. B. (1996). The description on the corpus system of modern Chinese studies. In Z. S. Luo& S. L. Yuan (Eds.), *Studies of Chinese and Chinese character in the computer era*. Beijing: Tsinghua University Publisher.

Sunderman, G. & Kroll, J.F. (2006). First language activation during second language lexical processing: An investigation of lexical form, meaning, and grammatical class. *Studies in Second Language Acquisition*, 28, 387-422. doi:10+10170S0272263106060177.

Swinney, D. A. (1979). Lexical access during sentence comprehension: (Re) consideration of context effects. *Journal of Verbal Learning and Verbal Behavior*, 18: 645-659.

Tabossi, P. & Zardon, F. (1993). Processing ambiguous words in context. *Journal of Memory and Language*, 32: 359-372.

Tabossi, P. (1989). What's in a context. In D.S. Gorgfein (Ed.), *Resolving Semantic Ambiguity* (pp. 25-39). New York: Spinger-Verlag.

Tan, L. H., Spinks, J. A., Feng, C.-M., Siok, W. T., Perfetti, C. A., Xiong, J., et al. (2003). Neural systems of second language reading are shaped by native language. *Human Brain Mapping*, 18, 158-166.

Tang, Y., Ma, L. D., Zhao, J., Weng, X., Zhang, W. & Hu, X. (2001). Automatic activation and attention regulation of phonological and semantic processes in reading of Chinese words. *NeuroImage*, 13(6).

Thierry, G & Wu, Y.J. (2007). Brain potentials reveal unconscious translation during foreign-language comprehension. *PNAS*, 104, 12530-12535. doi: 10.1073/ pnas. 0609927104.

Tlauka, M., Clark, C.R., Liu, P. & Conway, M. (2009). *Encoding modality and spatial memory retrieval. Brain Cogn*, 70:116-122.

Tokowicz, N. & MacWhinney, B. (2005). Measures of sensitivity to violations in second language grammar. *Studies in Second Language Acquisition*, 27 (2), 173-204. doi:10.1017/S0272263105050102.

Tokowicz, N. & MacWhinney, B. (2005). Measures of sensitivity to violations in second language grammar. *Studies in Second Language Acquisition*, 27:173-204.

Tokowicz, N. & Kroll, J.F. (2007). Number of meanings and concreteness consequences of ambiguity within and across languages. *Lang Cogn Process*, 22, 727-779. doi:10.1080/01690960601057068.

Torralbo, A., Santiago, J. & Lupianez, J. (2006). Flexible conceptual projection of time onto spatial frames of reference. *Cognitive Science*, 30:745-757.

Tyler, A. & Nagy, W.E. (1999). The acquisition of English derivational morphology. *Journal of Memory and Language*, (28): 649-667.

Ullman, M. T. (2001). The neural basis of lexicon and grammar in first and second language: The declarative/procedural model. *Bilingualism: Language and Cognition*. 4:105-122.

Vallesi, A., McIntosh, A.R., Stuss, D.T. (2011). How time modulates spatial responses. *CORTEX*, 47(2):148-156.

van Daal , V. &.van der Leji, A. (1999). Developmental dyslexia : related to specific or general deficits. *Annals of dyslexia*, 49: 71-104.

van der Leij, A & Morfidi, E. (2006). Core deficits and variable differences in Dutch poor readers learning English. *Journal of learning Disabilities*, 39: 74-90.

van Petten, C. & Luka, B. J. (2012). Prediction during language comprehension: Benefits, costs, and ERP components. *International Journal of Psychophysiology*, 83:176-190. doi: 10.1016/j.ijpsycho.2011.09.015.

Vellutino, F. R. , Fletcher., J. M., Snowling, M. J. & Scanlon, D. M. (2004). Specific reading disability (dyslexia) : what have we learned in the past four decades? *Journal of Child Psychology and Psychiatry*, 45 (1): 2-40.

Verhoeven, L. (2007). Early bilingualism, language transfer, and phonological awareness. *Applied Psycholinguistics*, 28(3): 425-439.

Wade-Wooley, L. 1999. First language influences on second language word reading: All roads lead to Rome. *Language Learning*. 49,447-471.

Walsh, V. (2003). A theory of magnitude: common cortical metrics of time, space, and quantity. *Trends in Cognitive Sciences*, 7:483-488.

Wang, M., Cheng, C. & Chen, S. (2006). Contribution of morphological awareness to Chinese-English biliteracy acquisition. *Journal of Educational Psychology*, 98: 542-553.

Wang, M., Cheng, C. & Chen, S-W. (2006). Contribution of morphological awareness to Chinese-English Biliteracy Acquisition. *Journal of Educational Psychology*, 3: 542-553.

Wang, M., Koda, K. & Perfetti, C. A. (2003). Alphabetic and non-alphabetic L1 effects in English semantic processing: A comparison of Korean and Chinese English L2 learners. *Cognition*, 87: 129-149.

Wang, M., Perfetti, C. A. & Liu, Y. (2005). Chinese-English biliteracy acquisition: cross-language and writing system transfer. *Cognition*, 97: 67-88.

Wartenburger, I., Heekeren, H. R., Abutalebi, J., Cappa, S. F., Villringer, A. & Peran, D. (2003). Early setting of grammatical processing in the bilingual brain. *Neuron*, 37: 159-170.

Waters, Caplan. (1996). The capacity theory of sentence comprehension: critique of Just and Carpenter. *Psychological Review*, 103:761-772.

Weber, K. & Lavric, A. (2008). Syntactic anomaly elicits a lexico-semantic (N400) ERP effect in the second language but not the first. *Psychophysiology*, 45: 920-925.

Weber-Fox, C.M & Neville, H.J. (1996). Maturational Constraints on Functional Specializations for Language Processing: ERP and Behavioral Evidence in Bilingual Speakers. *Journal of Cognitive Neuroscience*,8(3): 231-256.

Wenden, A. L. (1987). What do second-language learners know about their language learning? A second look at retrospective accounts. *Applied Linguistics*, 2, 186-201.

Wolf, M. & Bowers, P.G. (1999). The double-deficit hypothesis for the developmental dyslexias. *Journal of Educational Psychology*, 91: 415-438.

Wolf, M. & T. Katzir-Cohen. (2001). Reading fluency and its intervention. *Scientific Studies of Reading*, 5: 211-239.

Wolf, M., O'Rourke, A.G.,.Gidney, C., Lovett, M., Cirino, P. & Morris, R. (2002). The second deficit: An investigation of independence of phonological and naming-speed deficits in developmental dyslexia. *Reading and Writing: An Interdisciplinary Journa*l, 15:43-72.

Wong A.W., Wu, Y. & Chen, H.C. (2014). Limited role of phonology in reading Chinese two-character compounds: evidence from an ERP study. *Neuroscience*, 256: 342-351.

Wu, Y. J., Cristino, F., Leek, C. & Thierry, G. (2013). Non-selective lexical access in bilinguals is spontaneous and independent of input monitoring: Evidence from eye tracking. *Cognition*, 129 (2): 418-425.

Wu, Y.J. & Thierry, G.(2010). Chinese-English Bilinguals Reading English Hear Chinese. *The Journal of Neuroscience*, 30(22): 7646-7651.

Wu, Y.J. & Thierry, G.(2012).Unconscious translation during incidental foreign language processing. *Neuroimage*, 59(4): 3468-3473.

Wydell, T.N. & Butterworth, B. (1999).A case study of an English-Japanese bilingual with monolingual dyslexia, *Cognition*, 70(3): 273-305.

Xue, G., Dong, Q., Jin, Z. & Chen, C. (2004).Mapping of verbal working memory in nonfluent Chinese-English bilinguals with functional MRI. NeuroImage, 22: 1-10. Breznitz, Z., Oren, R & Shaul, S. (2004). Brain activity of regular and dyslexic readers while reading Hebrew as compared to English sentences. *Reading and Writing*, 17(7-8): 707-737.

Xue, J., Shu, H., Li, H., Li, W. & Tian, X. (2013). The Stability of Literacy-Related Cognitive Contributions to Chinese Character Naming and Reading Fluency. *Journal of Psycholinguistic Research*, 42(5): 433-450.

Xue, J., Yang, J., Zhang, J., Qi, Z., Bai, C., Qiu, Y. (2013). An ERP study on Chinese natives' second language syntactic grammaticalization, *Neuroscience Letters*, 534: 258-263.

Xue, Jin. (2011). Interaction of EFL Proficiency and metacognitive experience on reading training: A Longitudinal Study. *Foreign Language World*, (2): 50-56.[薛锦，2011，阅读训练中英语水平和元认知体验的交互作用—来自追踪研究的证据。*外语界*，（2）：50-56。]

Yang, J. & Xue, J. (2011). Spatial metaphor processing during temporal sequencing comprehension. *Experimental Brain Research*, 213: 475-491.

Yang, Xiaohu & Zhang, Wenpeng. (2002). The correlation between metacognition and EFL reading comprehension of Chinese college students, *Foreign Language Teaching and Research*, (3): 213-218. [杨小虎 , 张文鹏，2002，元认知与中国大学生阅读理解相关研究。*外语教学与研究*，（3）：213-218。]

Yin, B. Y. (1984). Quantitative analysis of Chinese morpheme. *Chinese*, 5, 338-347.

You, W., Chen, B. & Dunlap, S. (2009). Frequency trajectory effects in Chinese character recognition: Evidence for the arbitrary mapping hypothesis. *Cognition*, 110: 39-50.

Yuan, C. F. & Huang, C. N. (1998). Chinese morphemes and compounds: A corpus study. *Applications of Languages and Writing Systems*, 3: 7-12.

Yuan, F. & Xiao, D. (2006), On the applications of cognitive and metacognitive strategies in

TEM4 and its relationships with test Scores. *Foreign Language and Their Teaching*, (3): 31-34. [袁凤识，肖德法，2006，元认知策略在 TEM4 中的运用及其与成绩的关系研究。*外语与外语教学*，（3）：31-34。]

Zevin, J. D. & Seidenberg, M. S. (2002). Age of acquisition effects in word reading and other tasks. *Journal of Memory and Language*, 47: 1-29.

Zhang, D. & Koda, K. (2012). Contribution of morphological awareness and lexical inferencing ability to L2 vocabulary knowledge and reading comprehension among advanced EFL learners: Testing direct and indirect effects. *Reading and Writing*, 25: 1195-1216.

Zhang, D. & Koda, K. (2014). Awareness of derivation and compounding in Chinese-English biliteracy acquisition. *International Journal of Bilingual Education and Bilingualism*,17: 55-73.

Zhang, D. & Goh, C. (2006). Strategy knowledge and perceived strategy use: Singaporean students' awareness of listening and speaking strategies. *Language Awareness*, 15: 199-299.

Zhang, J., Anderson, R. C., Li, H., Dong, Q., Yu, X. & Zhang, Y. (2010). Cross-language transfer of insights into the structure of compound words. *Reading and Writing: An Interdisciplinary Journal*, 23: 311-336.

Zhang, L. J. (2008). Constructivist pedagogy in strategic reading instruction: exploring pathways to learner development in the English as a second language (ESL) classroom. *Instructional Science*, 36: 89-116.

Zhang, X. (2005). A survey of English majors' use of metacognitive strategies. Journal of PLA University of Foreign Languages, (3): 59-62. [张萱，2005，基础阶段英语专业学生元认知策略调查。*解放军外国语学院学报*，（3）：59-62。]

Ziegler, J. C. & Goswami, U. (2005). Reading acquisition, developmental dyslexia, and skilled reading across languages: A psycholinguistic Grain Size Theory. *Psychological Bulletin*, 131: 3-29.

董燕，段建平 . (2004). 英语阅读障碍儿童词汇命名加工特征的研究 . *中国行为医学科学* ,13(5): 565-566.

董燕，段建平，邵波 . (2004). 英语阅读障碍与正常儿童在 Stroop 任务上的差异 . *中国临床康复* , 8(36): 8287-8289.

段士平 . (2008). 词汇学习策略对词汇能力的影响 —— 一项基于网络环境的词汇习得状况的实证研究 . *西安外国语大学学报* , (4): 77-80.

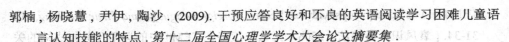

郭楠，杨晓慧，尹伊，陶沙．(2009). 干预应答良好和不良的英语阅读学习困难儿童语言认知技能的特点．*第十二届全国心理学学术大会论文摘要集*．

何胜昔，尹文刚，杨志伟．(2006). 发展性阅读障碍儿童视听觉整合的事件相关电位研究．*中国行为医学科学*，15(3)：242-244.

胡伟．(2012). 英语合成复合词构词：从词库论到分布形态学．*外语与外语教学*，(5): 53-58.

赖朝晖．(2006). 英语阅读困难与阅读成绩的关系，*基础英语教育*，8(3): 27-31.

李虹，舒华．(2009). 阅读障碍儿童的语言特异性认知缺陷．*心理科学* 32 (2)：301- 303.

李俊，倪杭英．(2007). 非英语专业学生元认知策略的介入性研究．*外语界*，(2): 49-53.

李荣宝，陈素梅，王幼琨，李光泽．(2011). 儿童语音经验对其语音意识发展的影响．*中国外语*，(1): 36-43.

李学建．(1984). 谈谈英语构词法中的“嵌合法”．*外语教学*，1984(1): 25-27.

林新事．(2008). 英文阅读困难与语音技能缺陷的相关性研究．*齐齐哈尔大学学报（哲学社会科学版）*，（6）：94-96.

刘丹丹．(2002). 中国英语学习者的阅读策略研究．*外语界*，(6)：13-18.

刘黎．(2002). 元认知和元认知策略及其对外语教学的启示．*陕西师范大学学报（哲学社会科学版）*，(6):300-302.

刘文理，刘翔平．(2006). 阅读发展相关的认知技能 汉语和英语的比较．*心理科学进展*，（14）：665-674.

刘云英，陶沙．(2007). 阅读困难诊断标准与模式的后智力成就差异趋势．*北京师范大学学报（社会科学版）*，5: 13-21.

买合甫来提 坎吉，刘翔平，王燕．(2010). 发展性阅读障碍的跨文字一致性和特异性，*中国特殊教育*，(23)：58-63.

孟俊一．(2006). 英语语素及语素变体的音位制约和形态制约研究．*贵州师范大学学报（社会科学版）*，(6):131-134.

孟祥芝，舒华．(1999). 西方发展性阅读障碍研究进展．*心理学动态*，(7): 14-19.

孟悦．(2004). 大学英语阅读策略训练的实验研究．*外语与外语教学*，(2)：24-27.

彭鹏，陶沙．(2009). 单词解码、英语语言理解和一般认知能力在汉语儿童英语阅读学习中的作用．*外语教学与研究*，41(1)：30-37.

陶沙．(2009). 儿童汉语和英语阅读不良的认知技能缺陷：跨语言的普遍性和语言间的特异性，*第十二届全国心理学学术大会论文摘要集*．

王文静．(2010). 阅读困难儿童语言认知缺陷的干预研究及发展趋势．*教育学报*，6（1）：77-81.

席旭琳 . (2009). 英语发展性阅读障碍研究概述 . *黑龙江高教研究* , 6:199-201.

薛锦，舒华，吴思娜 . (2009). 阅读障碍亚类型的理论框架和研究中的问题 . *中国心理卫生杂志* , (23)2: 112-116

闫嵘 , 霍健才 . (2013). 外语篇章阅读元理解监测能力的发展及其跨语言迁移效应 . *现代外语* , 2:158-165.

杨志伟 , 龚耀先和李雪荣 . (1998). 汉语阅读障碍的临床评定与分型研究 . *中国临床心理学杂志* , 6(3): 136-137.

姚喜明 , 梅晓宇 . (2003). 我国阅读理论研究的发展 , *山东外语教学* , (6）: 15-18.

张景 . (2012). 在英语阅读中培养学生的猜词能力 —— 基于构词法的猜词策略探讨 . *新西部 (理论版)*, (6):147-148.

张庆宗 , 刘晓燕 . (2009). 英语阅读自我效能感、阅读策略和阅读成绩关系的实证研究 . *教育研究与实验* , (1): 92-96.

赵微 , 荆伟 , 方俊明 . (2012). 阅读认知加工的跨语言研究 . *陕西师范大学学报 (哲学社会科学版)*, 41 : 71-76.

周晓林 , 孟祥芝. (2001). 中文发展性阅读障碍研究 . *应用心理学* , 7: 25-30.